THE IMAGE OF GOD IN THE

ANTIOCHENE TRADITION

THE IMAGE OF GOD
IN THE ANTIOCHENE
TRADITION

Frederick G. McLeod, S.J.

The Catholic University of America Press

Washington, D.C.

The paper used in this publication meets the minimum
requirements of American National Standards for
Information Science—Permanence of Paper for
Printed Library materials, ANSI z39.48–1984.
∞

Library of Congress Cataloging-in-Publication Data
McLeod, Frederick G.
      The image of God in the Antiochene tradition / Fredrick G.
McLeod.
            p.   cm.
      Includes bibliographical references and indexes.
      ISBN 0–8132–0930–7 (alk. paper)
            1. Image of God—History of doctrines—Early church, ca. 30 – 600.
2. Antiochian school. I. Title.
      BT702.M39   1998
      233'.5—dc21
      98–21262

To my Mother—
For the Precious Gifts
To Me
of Life, Vocation, Selfless Caring
and a Faith-Inspiring Death

CONTENTS

ACKNOWLEDGMENTS

THE PRESENT WORK is the culmination of a long investigation into the question of the meaning and theological significance of "image" within the Antiochene tradition. It began as an offshoot of my doctoral investigation into the teaching on salvation by Narsai, a fifth-century East Syrian theologian who first headed the School of Edessa and then later founded the famed School of Nisibis. I was so impressed by his understanding of image that it led first to the publication of a monograph[1] for the Gregorian University Press and then of an article for *Theological Studies*.[2] This prompted a later exploration to determine how much Narsai was dependent on Theodore of Mopsuestia and to the surprising discovery that Theodore held a view of "image" in sharp contrast with the other leading Antiochene theologians, at least with Diodore, Chrysostom, and Theodoret. This resulted in another article published in the Annual Publication of the College Theology Society that expanded upon my earlier works.[3] All these have laid a foundation upon which this present inquiry has been built.

I am especially grateful to all those who have written about "image," "Antioch," "Theodore of Mopsuestia," and the role of women in the early

1. Frederick G. McLeod, *The Soteriology of Narsai* (Rome: Pontificium Institutum Orientalium Studiorum, 1973).

2. Frederick G. McLeod, "Man as the Image of God: Its Meaning and Theological Significance in Narsai," *Theological Studies* 42 (Sept. 1981): 458–68.

3. Frederick G. McLeod, "The Antiochene Tradition Regarding the Role of the Body Within the 'Image of God,'" in *Broken and Whole: Essays on Religion and the Body*, ed. Maureen Tilley and Susan Ross, The Annual Publication of the College Theology Society 1993 (Lanham, Md.: UP of America, 1995), 23–53.

church. I have benefited in no small measure—to which my footnotes will amply attest—from their careful, thorough, and insightful scholarly research. I also want to thank all those at Saint Louis University and my Jesuit community who enabled me by their generous financial assistance and personal support to spend a year's sabbatical to bring this work to a successful conclusion in a book form. I am particularly indebted to the late Richard Smith, S.J., for his detailed and insightful commentary on this work and Fr. Daniel Costello, S.J., for helping me to translate difficult Greek and Latin passages in Theodore, as well as Fr. Anthony Daly, S.J., for letting me read his unpublished thesis on Nestorius, Fr. Sidney Griffith and Robin Darling Young for approving and encouraging the publication of my text, Kathleen McVey for her many detailed critical suggestions for improving this work, Kevin O'Connor for his research, and Bruce Cromwell, Charles Noel, John Bequette and Kyung-Soo Kim for the technical assistance that each in turn provided in preparing this text for publication, and finally David J. McGonagle, the Director of the Catholic University of America Press, who patiently brought this work to its completion, and Alexandra Schmidl, his editorial assistant, who found a host of corrections that escaped my attention and that of several others.

ABBREVIATIONS

CCSG   Corpus Christianorum, Series Graeca.

CSCO   Corpus Scriptorum Christianorum Orientalium.

EEC   *Encyclopedia of the Early Church.*

NEM   *Cyril of Jerusalem and Nemesius of Emesa*, ed. and trans. William Telfer.

NES   *The Bazaar of Heracleides*, ed. Godfrey Driver, trans. Leonard Hodgson.

NPNF   The Nicene and Post Nicene Fathers.

PET   "L'homme créé 'À l'image' de Dieu quelques fragments grecs inédits de Théodore de Mopsueste," ed. Françoise Petit.

PG   Patrologia Graeca.

PO   Patrologia Orientalis.

SC   Sources Chrétiennes.

TEP   *Theodori Episcopi Mopsuesteni in Epistolas B. Pauli Commentarii*, ed. H.B. Swete. 2 vols.

TFS   *Theodori Mopsuesteni Fragmenta Syriaca*, ed. Edward Sachau.

THC   *Les Homélies Catéchétiques de Théodore de Mopsueste*, trans. Raymond Tonneau with Robert Devreese.

TJA   *Commentarius In Evangelium Iohannis Apostoli*, trans. J.-M. Vosté.

TP   *Pauluskommentare aus der Griechiscen Kirche*, ed. Karl Staab.

WS 5   Woodbrooke Studies 5: *Commentary of Theodore of Mopsuestia on the Nicene Creed*, trans. A. Mingana.

WS 6   Woodbrooke Studies 6: *Commentary of Theodore of Mopsuestia on the Lord's Prayer and on the Sacraments of Baptism and the Eucharist.*

THE IMAGE OF GOD IN THE

ANTIOCHENE TRADITION

INTRODUCTION

E VER SINCE THE BEGINNING of Christianity, scripture scholars and theologians have struggled to plumb the true meaning of what the author of Genesis intended when he proclaimed that "God made man in his image; in the divine image he created him; male and female he created them" (1:27).[1] They have employed this simple statement as though it were a Hubble telescope enabling them to penetrate more deeply into the mysterious depths of how humans are related to God. While denying that a human being can image God in the same exact way a photograph captures the physical details of a person, they believed, nonetheless, that the Genesis passages on image, as well as several others scattered throughout both testaments, can expand our knowledge of who God is and what constitutes our human makeup and divinely appointed roles within the created cosmos.

Christian theologians have also been keenly aware that one's stance on image will have profound, ripple ramifications for other theological fields. For instance, it raises a christological issue as to how one is to interpret what the author of Colossians means when he proclaims that Christ is "the image of the invisible God, the firstborn of all creation" (1:15). The theme of image has also been used as a key to enter into such questions as how one can grow spiritually to become more like unto God and whether women are to be looked upon as equal or subordinate to men. The various

1. Except for passages translated from the works of Diodore, John Chrysostom, Theodore of Mopsuestia, and Nestorius, all citations from Scripture have been taken from *The New American Bible* (New York: Catholic Book Publishing Co., 1970).

interpretations the Fathers have proposed for the meaning of image exemplify too the hermeneutical principles that have guided their exegesis.

While theologians agree in general that one's understanding of image provides an opening for entering into the questions mentioned above, they disagree as to how specifically humans image God, where this "image" resides within the human person, and whether it should also apply to women. Like a person who creates new colored patterns in a kaleidoscope by rotating its lens, they manipulated out of the same scriptural passages on image many varied montages uniting all of these issues. Or to switch the metaphor, the multi-faceted opinions concerning image resemble a large glittering diamond that sparkles in new, fascinating ways when rotated to the light. Since an individual's perspective will determine what elements stand out, all angles have to be studied if one hopes to appreciate its full beauty. Thus, one can find that the spiritual approaches taken by the Alexandrian, Cappadocian, and Augustinian Fathers are nicely complemented by those of the leading Fathers from the famed School of Antioch. By contrasting their viewpoints, one is then in a good position to assess their strong as well as their vulnerable points, their insights as well as their blind spots, and their masteries of the material as well as the lacunae and flaws in their overall syntheses of how humans image God.

Our chief preoccupation is centered upon a detailed analysis of what Diodore of Tarsus, John Chrysostom, Theodore of Mopsuestia, Nestorius, and Theodoret taught regarding image.[2] Regrettably much of Diodore, Theodore, and Nestorius's writings have been destroyed by their theological adversaries. And those initially preserved by their East Syrian defenders have suffered the inevitable loss that every century inflicts upon almost all but a relatively few of its outstanding figures. However, more than enough selections from their writings and from the more extensive works of John Chrysostom and Theodoret are now at hand to know what the Antiochenes as a school maintained. Their fragmentary passages on "image" provide an entry into their thought in ways similar to how a DNA sample can testify to person's identity.

The theologians that will be discussed belong to what has been acknowledged as the "Golden Age" of the School of Antioch. They span a

---

2. Unfortunately, very little in the extant writings of other historically significant Antiochenes, such as Theophilus, Lucian, Eusebius of Emesa, and John of Antioch, provides a coherent, reflective view about the meaning of "image of God."

period of about a hundred years from the middle of the fourth to the middle of the fifth century c.e.[3] They were the ones who were involved in an intense rivalry with the other most famous exegetical and theological school of the patristic period, that of Alexandria. They were the inheritors of a centuries-long tradition that opposed the Alexandrians' allegorical method of interpreting the Scriptures and their readiness to assimilate allegorical views into their theological syntheses. These methodological quarrels later erupted into a full-blown crisis during the first half of the fifth century when Nestorius and Theodoret were forced to take part in an all-out bitter theological controversy over how to safeguard and express the personal unity of the divine and the human natures in Christ in a way that preserved the natural integrity of each.

The christological conflict between the schools was resolved for a time by the Pact of Union that Cyril of Alexandria and John of Antioch forged in 433. But within thirty years, for reasons that are not now clear, the School of Antioch disappeared from the scene. Its traditional defenses of a literal, historical method of exegesis and of Christ's human nature as the responsible source of his free human actions were assumed first by the School of Edessa under Ibas and Narsai and then sometime in the second part of the fifth century by the School that Narsai founded in Nisibis in the Persian Empire. During this period, Antioch became a battleground between two other antagonistic parties in a seesaw struggle for ecclesiastical control of the city. Those who defended the christological formula of faith enunciated at Chalcedon opposed those who belonged to the so-called Monophysite or Jacobite movement now known as the Syrian Orthodox Church. By the sixth century, not only had the former great glory of the School of Antioch receded into a distant memory but the School itself had become reviled as the one that had nurtured "the evils of Nestorianism."

3. For a history of Antioch in Late Antiquity, see Glanville Downey's monumental scholarly yet still highly readable work, *A History of Antioch in Syria from Seleucus to the Arab Conquest* (Princeton: Princeton UP, 1961) as well as the recent studies by J. H. W. G. Liebeschuetz, *Antioch: City and Imperial Administration in the Later Roman Empire* (Oxford: Clarendon, 1972) and D. S. Wallace-Hadrill, *Christian Antioch: A Study of Early Christian Thought in the East* (Cambridge: Cambridge UP, 1982); see also the extended articles on "Antioch" by Benjamin Drewery in *Theologische Realenzyklopädie*, ed. F. Shumann and M. Wolter (Berlin: de Gruyter, 1990), 3:107; Glanville Downey, in the *New Catholic Encyclopedia* (New York: McGraw-Hill, 1967), 1:623–26; and the *New Encyclopedia Britannica*, 15th ed. (Chicago: U. of Chicago, 1993).

Outline

This study follows a cyclical pattern. First it will examine the Antiochene Fathers' commitment to their literal, historical, and rational exegetical interpretation of the Scriptures, for all were biblical theologians hostile to, or at least very suspicious of, those employing allegories and philosophical insights as ways to enlarge their understanding of the Christian message. Despite their opposition to these approaches, they did, however, see a value in a speculative method, called *theoria*, as a means to explore the meaning of a type in relationship to its antitype or archetype. Their understanding of metaphysical terms and opinions was also subtly influenced by the meaning assigned to these terms by the cultural view that then prevailed at Antioch, yet, as will be seen, their understanding of these can be shown to have been primarily derived from Scripture.

The next downward spiral will bring us to the center of what this inquiry seeks to establish. To set the stage for this, there will first be a survey of what modern-day scholars believe the priestly redactor of Genesis and Paul actually intended regarding image. This will be followed by a summary of what Irenaeus held regarding the meaning of image; Irenaeus will provide a background against which the Antiochene thought can be assessed. Then the view elaborated by Theodore will be developed at length, for it is the most detailed and thought provoking. While Diodore, Chrysostom, and Theodoret associated image with the power or office they believed God entrusted to males that they might rule as His viceroys over the material world, Theodore understood the phrase "image of God" as primarily referring to the threefold revelatory, unitive, and cultic roles that Christ plays within God's plan for salvation.

In order to understand Theodore's views on how Christ fulfills his unitive function as God's image and how this relates to the meaning of Theodore's controversial term for the union—*prosōpon*—the present study will also be expanded to include a consideration of what he held regarding the union between Christ's divine and human natures. Because the question is complicated, the approach will require incremental steps. First, the major terms that the Fathers of the Councils of Nicea and Constantinople used to express their trinitarian and christological beliefs will be examined in order to determine what impact they might have had upon the extant writings of the Antiochene Fathers. Afterward, we will explore in detail how the Christian philosopher/theologian Nemesius elaborated his own lucid, classical synthesis of the Christian view of human nature out of what he encountered in Greek thought. Because Nemesius is believed to have lived in or close to Antioch in the late fourth century, his philosophical viewpoints, together with the theological outlook of Irenaeus, provide a matchless backdrop against which one can compare and contrast what is now known about the Antiochene anthropological outlook. This study will substantiate the view that the Antiochene Fathers derived their ideas about human nature not from any philosophical school but from the Christian Scriptures and the then-prevailing eclectic cultural outlook reflected in the conciliar creeds of Nicea and Constantinople I and the writings of Nemesius.

The next chapter will progress one step further. It will seek to determine how the Antiochenes understood the basic terms used to express the various elements of human nature and the different kinds of union that are possible for uniting the divine and human natures in Christ. This will help illuminate what Theodore and Nestorius intended when they described the union of two natures in Christ as one of "good pleasure in one *prosōpon*." After this has been established, the following chapter will explore what Theodore meant when he asserted that Christ functions as the image binding all creation to a totally transcendent Divinity. For since Theodore held that Christ is the one linking everyone in the cosmos to God, it is important to know the kind of "personal" union his humanity possesses with the Word.

The next step will be to consider the question of whether the Antiochenes also apply "image" to women. Since it is a heated issue today, it requires an expanded chapter. To situate the Antiochene viewpoint within its cultural context, we will first outline from other sources what appear to have been the latent attitudes in Late Antiquity towards the role of women within society and the church. Afterward, what each of the Fathers has to state about this issue will be considered. Diodore, Chrysostom, and Theodoret contend that women are to be considered subordinate to men, because Scripture has assigned image to males only. Chrysostom, in particular, spends a considerable amount of time spelling out exactly what a woman can and cannot do in public. The positions of Theodore and Nestorius regarding this issue can only be surmised. Nestorius states absolutely nothing about women in his surviving work, *The Bazaar of Heracleides*, and what Theodore held we now have to infer from what has survived of his vast theological output. While some passages of

Theodore affirm that women are subordinate to men, his overall thought on image, however, if logically pursued to its end, would seem to require that women have also been created as God's images.

This study will conclude with a summary of the findings on the Antiochene views on image. Since Theodore's thought on image is the most developed, insightful, systematized, and stimulating of all the Antiochenes, his position on image will be primarily stressed, along with the ramifications that his synthesis has for Christology, soteriology, eschatology, women's equality, and ecology. His point of view is especially rich in bringing out how image expresses human nature's most basic relationships to God, others, and the universe and, interestingly, how all these have been reincorporated in Christ.

Contemporary Value

As we explore how the Antiochenes have understood the phrase "image of God" through copious English translations of pertinent passages—some previously untranslated—we may find new insights. These not only serve to stimulate thought as to what the Scriptures mean when they refer to Adam and Christ as God's image, but also pinpoint the differences between those holding image as a spiritual "reality" residing in the highest reaches of the rational soul and those referring it to the whole human composite of soul and body. Theodore's interpretation, in particular, offers us a complex but stimulating explanation of image and an opportunity for obtaining further insights into what the School of Antioch taught regarding what Scripture and tradition revealed to be the true understanding of human nature, the personal union of natures in Christ, and this union's role in salavation. All this can be valuable for those who possess only a vague grasp of the school's controversial theological stance.[4]

---

4. The only recent scholarly work I am aware of that treats in an extended way the background and theological thought of the School of Antioch is by Wallace-Hadrill. It is a clear critical summary of the literature that deals with not only the Antiochene Fathers but also the East Syrian theologians who promoted their teaching. While there is overlap with what is being attempted in my chapters on the influences of exegesis and Greek philosophy upon the Antiochenes and their christological understanding, my present work does not so much repeat as it does complement Wallace-Hadrill's. He provides a much wider background to my specific focus on the Antiochene Fathers' views regarding the *imago Dei*.

The present inquiry also offers another point of contemporary interest. It delves into what was the foremost patristic attempt to elaborate a
"low" Christology. When the School of Antioch fell into disgrace in what
today would be stereotyped as an ideological clash between a "conservative right" and a "liberal left," or between the Antiochenes who wanted to
remain with whatever Scripture explicitly affirms and the Alexandrians
who applied philosophical insights to ferret out deeper truths contained
within Christian teaching, this had a profound impact upon the way
Christology was to be treated afterwards. The defeat of the Antiochenes'
emphasis upon Christ's humanity as the starting point for Christology led
inevitably to the ascendency of an Alexandrian emphasis upon a "high"
Christology as the approved way. The stress upon a "high" Christology remained—overall—firmly established within most of Christianity until the
rise of Rationalism.[5] The efforts that began with David Strauss to uncover
the historical Jesus within the Gospels inexorably forced a revision as
more Christians focused upon Jesus' humanity. Such an emphasis succeeded to such an extent that a "low" Christology today appears within
theological literature and in the popular outlook as the preferred way to
think of Christ. He is thought of as a brother rather than as the Lord of
the universe. So besides extending and deepening our awareness of the
kind of functional Christology that was present at Antioch at the beginning of the fifth century, the present study advances a paradigm for examining the advantages and pitfalls of a "low" Christology.

5. One noteworthy exception was the widespread devotion to the humanity of
Christ, which was abetted by Francis of Assisi in the High Middle Ages. See Ewert
Cousin, "The Humanity and the Passion of Christ," *Christian Spirituality: High Middle
Ages and Reformation*, ed. Jill Raitt (New York: Crossroad, 1987), 375–91.

1

THE ANTIOCHENE SCRIPTURAL METHOD

ESIDES BEING BOTH MONKS AND BISHOPS, all the principal exponents of the School of Antioch were, in differing degrees, biblical theologians. They were not wholly averse to using metaphysical terms and world-views current in the cultural milieu of their day, but they considered Scripture their source for answers to the meaning of their Christian lives and stayed as close as they could to Scripture's language and worldview. This is clear from an examination of all their extant works. For them, the Jewish and Christian Scriptures were the revealed, infallible word of God. All other disciplines of knowledge were dismissed as being inferior to what the Scriptures disclosed to them. Since the Scriptures were such a determining intellectual force in their lives, there is a need, first of all, to examine their exegetical method and how this approach was to condition their mindset and their specific interpretations regarding the "image of God."[1]

---

1. For relatively recent assessments of the principal role Scripture has played in the thinking of the Antiochenes, above all of Theodore, see Dimitri Zaharopoulos, *Theodore of Mopsuestia on the Bible: A Study of His Old Testament Exegesis* (New York: Paulist, 1989), 103–41; Rowan A. Greer, *Theodore of Mopsuestia: Exegete and Theologian* (Westminster: Faith, 1961), 86–111; and Karlfried Froehlich, trans. and ed., *Biblical Interpretation in the Early Church*, Sources of Early Christian Thought (Philadelphia: Fortress, 1984), 19–23.

A look at the history of Jewish exegesis in the first centuries of the present era will help to establish what, if any, influence Jewish exegesis might have exercised upon the Fathers' thought, for it was mainly from a Jewish womb that Christianity emerged. As Christianity grew into a new religion, it had to contend with a newly refashioned Judaism over how rightly to interpret the Jewish Scriptures, which they shared. A discussion of the general terms that characterize the Antiochene exegesis will follow this section. Then each of the Antiochene Fathers will be treated, with emphasis upon Theodore whose exegesis is the most advanced and by far the most commented upon by contemporary Scripture scholars.

Jewish Exegetical Influences

Coming out of a Jewish matrix, the first Christians were very familiar with the Jewish Scriptures and the conventional methods of interpreting them. The earliest Christian writers portrayed Jesus as the Messiah whose coming was foretold in a prophetic way within the Jewish Law, Prophets, and other sacred writings. They accepted these works not only as an integral part of their own heritage but as inspired revelation, even before they had established the canon of Christian Scriptures. So it comes as no surprise that their hermeneutical principles were initially influenced and even determined by Jewish thought.[2] The pertinent questions, however, are to what extent and for how long.

Contemporary rabbinic scholarship[3] has determined that there was a considerable fluidity of views among Jewish writers between roughly the fourth century B.C.E. and the sixth century C.E. over the content and the method for interpreting sacred writings. Beginning some time between the fourth and the second centuries before the Christian era, Jewish religious authorities evolved in their belief that God had revealed His mind and will in a detailed way in Scripture. By the time of Christ, they were

2. For a study tracing the formative influence of Rabbinic Judaism upon Christianity, see Alan F. Segal, *Rebecca's Children: Judaism and Christianity in the Roman World* (Cambridge: Harvard UP, 1986).

3. I am dependent upon the following works for my comments on early Jewish exegesis: the *Jewish Encyclopedia*, 12 vols., gen. ed. Isidore Singer (New York: Ktav, 1964); Jacob Neusner, ed., *Introduction to Rabbinic Literature*, Anchor Bible Reference Library (New York: Doubleday, 1994); and, for his brief insightful commentary, Froehlich, *Biblical Interpretation*, 1–8.

convinced that there was not a word or even a letter found in the Pentateuch, Prophets, and their other sacred books that ought to be looked upon as useless or merely superfluous. When they joined this outlook to their conviction that the Jewish people would not repossess their national identity until they lived in accordance with the Law that God had established for them, they insisted that every Jew had to be taught the meaning of Scripture. This, in turn, brought home to them the pressing need to work out in an authoritative way how they could apply this Law to wholly new situations. This led not merely to the development of an unwritten law of interpretation with its own exegetical methods and rules for defining how a conscientious Jew ought to act in a particular case not addressed by the Pentateuch, but also to the formation of a new class of religious scholars who were called scribes or lawyers.

By accepting this new way of establishing authoritative norms that could spell out how to live out their everyday lives in matters not covered by their Scriptures, religious leaders were freed from always having to show a direct, unimpeachable connection between a biblical text and their opinions. It opened a broad way for them to progress beyond having to interpret a text solely in a literal way, enabling them to develop a new method for interpreting their sacred writings. It was also responsible for the flowering of a number of opposing Jewish sects within the intertestamental period. The New Testament witnesses to three such groups. Besides the scribes there was a ruling party, called the Sadducees, that was composed of the Temple priests and the wealthy. This group rejected such doctrines as the resurrection and the existence of angels because these were not in the Law.[4] While the Pharisees believed in such doctrines, they too were noted for their strict observance of the written Law and for their insistence upon the legitimacy of their own oral interpretations of the Law. And as we are aware today, there also seems to have existed some sort of ascetical sect, most likely that of the Essenes, whose writings found at Qumran indicate that they were opposed to the priesthood at Jerusalem and construed the Jewish prophecies from an apocalyptic perspective.[5]

4. See Acts 23:6–8. Froehlich (3) notes that the Sadducees' insistence that scriptural authority be assigned only to the five books of Moses forced the rabbis to demonstrate from biblical texts the validity of their claims for their written and oral tradition.

5. Neusner, 6.

Philo's Allegorical Method

There also appeared in the first century of the Christian era another hermeneutical approach to the Jewish Scriptures. While the religious authorities in Palestine based their interpretations upon what the Law stated, others at Alexandria, the best known being Philo (c.20 B.C.E.–42 C.E.), sought to combine Platonic and Stoic allegorical principles[6] with Jewish midrash and to use this as a valid method for uncovering a deeper meaning within a text.[7] They could move in this direction because of the exegetical freedom that Jews then enjoyed in interpreting the Scriptures. It was a time too when the culture of the day encouraged an eclectic attitude toward both philosophy and religion. So when Philo attempted to combine reason with faith, he was showing himself to be a product of his own age.

What is interesting about Philo is his theory on how one could penetrate to the truth or truths hidden in an obscure biblical text by interpreting it allegorically. But in order to achieve this, he insisted that a person had to believe that God exists and that He has implanted hidden truths that can be found within an inspired Scripture.[8] One could succeed in this undertaking, Philo argued, provided that a person had first subdued his or her unruly passions. After the death of Philo and the destruction of the Temple at Jerusalem in 70, the Jews at Alexandria ceased using allegory as an exegetical tool in their interpretations of Scripture and subscribed to the principles that were being agreed upon in Palestine and Babylon.[9] The Christians at

6. For a comprehensive study of allegorical interpretation in the antique world, see Jean Pépin, *Mythe et Allégorie: Les origines grecques et les contestations judéo-chrétiennes*, 2d ed. (Paris: Études Augustiniennes, 1976), especially 215–516.

7. For a treatment of Philo's influence, see Zaharopoulos, 104–7; Greer, *Theodore* 89–91, and Froehlich, 5–8; and for a clear exposition of how Philo's attempt to combine Hebrew and Greek thought affected his understanding of "person," Graham J. Warne, *Hebrew Perspectives on the Human Person in the Hellenistic Era: Philo and Paul* (Lewiston, N.Y.: Mellen, 1995), 123–55.

8. See Froehlich (6–7) for an account of the legend that the elders who undertook separately to translate the Septuagint in isolation "emerged with the same choice of words and phrases 'as if a teacher was dictating to each of them invisibly'" (Philo, *The Life of Moses* II.37).

9. Henri Crouzel, "Philo," EEC 2:682–83; and Manlio Simonetti, "Patristic Exegesis," EEC 1:309–11. Froehlich (2) approves of D. Daube's ("Rabbinic Methods of Interpretation and Hellenistic Rhetoric," *Hebrew Union College Annual* [Cincinnati] 22 [1949]: 239–64) argument that the early rabbinic rules "reflect the logic and methods of Hel-

Alexandria, beginning with Clement (c.150–215) and continuing under his successor, Origen (+253), were the ones who then promoted Philo's allegorical methodology as the way to interpret the sacred Scriptures. They treated the Jewish Scriptures as a vast allegory where every scriptural detail in some way or other pointed mystically toward Christ. They added, however, an important caveat to Philo's criteria: obscure passages ought to be judged in light of the Christian apostolic tradition.[10]

Jewish Exegesis After 70

The Jewish exegesis of the intertestamental period underwent a radical change in the second half of the first century c.e. After the fall of Jerusalem, the Pharisees joined forces with the scribes to assume control over Jewish religious thought. The two espoused a way of life that proved more than adequate to deal with the faith crisis that the destruction of the Temple caused for Jewish cultic life and Jewish self-awareness as God's specially chosen people. They resisted attempts to establish the speculative Hellenistic Judaism promoted by Philo as a legitimate Jewish method of exegesis. Because of their efforts the belief was nurtured that God continually manifests His will in an oral as well as a written way, called Torah. Over the next several centuries, those who were then recognized as authoritative commentators of Torah slowly established both the content and the method of Judaism as it is known today.

From 70 to the Bar Kokhba insurrection (c. 132–135), various rabbinical authorities laid down the foundations of what has become known as the Mishnah. Their oral traditions were compiled in 200 c.e. into a single collection, composed of 63 treatises divided into six sections. This compilation too became subject to further reflection by the two main rabbinical schools at that time. Their redactions, in turn, became known as the Talmud of Palestine (or the Talmud of the Land of Israel) and the Talmud of Babylonia (known also as the Bavli).[11] Because

---

lenistic grammar and forensic rhetoric" and that the rabbi's techniques for finding deeper mysteries in the words of Scripture provide grounds for making "a case for rabbinical allegorism" (3–5). The exclusion of allegory from Jewish exegesis during the Christian era, therefore, needs to be nuanced.

10. See Zaharopoulos, 109.

11. The Bavli became the authoritative repository of what is now referred to as the Jewish "tradition."

of their labors, the Mishnah was accepted with the Scriptures as an authoritative source for God's revelation, despite the fact that it had little connection with Scripture. From the sixth century onward rabbinical literature can be characterized as a commentary on either Scripture or the Mishnah.[12]

The Mishnah and its commentaries (called Gemara) comprise the Talmud. Two methods of interpretation are normally employed here—the "literal" and the "practical." A "literal" aims at establishing the basic meaning of a text, including what is narrated in a metaphorical or figurative way. What is derived here is then used to determine how one ought to respond in a "practical" way to specific situations. The "practical" is subdivided into two further groupings: the *halakhah*, that body of Jewish law that deduces rules of conduct, and the *haggadah*, the non-legal part of the Talmud that derives conclusions and applications from Jewish lore. The *haggadah* often makes use of a type of imaginative writing, called a midrash, that seeks to comment upon and/or explain in a homiletic way what the literal states. By their study into all aspects of the Talmud, the rabbis were able on the basis of their consciences and their practical experience to develop new doctrines and practices not expressly mentioned in Scripture.

Two points regarding Jewish exegesis need to be emphasized here: first, the belief that one could compare words and ideas contained in different biblical passages, so as to determine the meaning implied in all the passages; and second, the use of paraphrases, called Targums, which were employed in Aramaic translations to alter the Hebrew or Greek text, so as to bring out a contemporary theological opinion that an exact translation would fail to do. While the Targums were later treated as irrelevant because they contain little material that can be considered authoritative, they have become subjects for contemporary studies[13] interested in finding out what Aramaic-speaking Jews held before the Talmud was definitively established around the sixth century.

12. Neusner (128) affirms this when he remarks: "So the entirety of rabbinic literature testifies to the unique standing of the Mishnah, acknowledging its special status, without parallel or peer, as the oral part of the Torah." For a discussion of the Jewish exegetical terms, see Greer, *Theodore*, 86–89.

13. For an article on the contemporary studies of the Targums, see Paul V. Mc-Cracken-Flesher, "The Targumim in the Context of Rabbinic Literature," in Neusner, 611–29.

16

The Antiochene Exegesis

While it is difficult to state what were the historical roots of the exegesis practised at the School of Antioch, it does reflect certain similarities with what had evolved in the conservative Jewish talmudic schools in Palestine and Babylon.[14] The Antiochene emphasis upon a literal, rational interpretation of a scriptural text and their rejection of the Alexandrian view that all Scripture has an allegorical meaning, but not necessarily a literal meaning, clearly resemble what was being promoted in rabbinical circles of that period. But as Chrysostom's eight homilies "Against the Jews" would seem to suggest when he inveighs against those attracted by Jewish ceremonies, any immediate and direct dependence upon Jewish exegesis must have taken place very much earlier in the Antiochene tradition than the fourth century.[15]

While one cannot state definitively when, why, and from what source the Antiochene method of exegesis developed as it did,[16] we can discern traces of its presence in the late second century work of Theophilus[17] and at the beginning of the fourth century also, so it seems, in the writings of Lucian and Methodius of Olympus. It can also be presumed to have been the method that Eusebius of Emesa taught Diodore when he studied

14. See Benjamin Drewery in *Theologische Realenzyklopädie*, ed. F. Shumann and M. Wolter (Berlin: de Gruyter, 1990), 3:107; and D. S. Wallace-Hadrill, *Christian Antioch: A Study of Early Christian Thought in the East* (Cambridge: Cambridge UP, 1982), 27–51.

15. Robert L. Wilken argues suasively in his *John Chrysostom and the Jews: Rhetoric and Reality in the Late Fourth Century* (Berkeley: U of California P, 1983) that a significant segment of the Jewish community was a well-educated, wealthy, influential, and religious force in Antioch in the late fourth and early fifth centuries. So while the Antiochenes were firmly established in their exegetical methodology at this time, they may have also been influenced by their exchanges, friendly as well as hostile, with the rabbis of their day.

16. For a suggestive study into the influence that the rhetorical training the Antiochenes received may have had upon their exegesis, see Frances Young, "The Rhetorical Schools and Their Influence on Patristic Exegesis," in *The Making of Orthodoxy: Essays in Honour of Henry Chadwick*, ed. Rowan Williams (Cambridge: Cambridge UP, 1989), 188–93.

17. For a convincing study into the Stoic influence upon Theophilus in at least one instance, see Kathleen McVey's article, "The Use of Stoic Cosmogony in Theophilus of Antioch's *Hexaemeron*," *Biblical Hermeneutics in Historical Perspective: Studies in Honor of Karlfried Froehlich on his Sixtieth Birthday*, ed. M. S. Burrows and P. Rorem (Grand Rapids, Mich.: Eerdmans, 1991), 32–58. She argues that when Theophilus described the generation of the Logos through Sophia, he must have used a Hellenistic Jewish source that had remained close to its Stoic roots.

under him[18] and can be established as the exegetical method of the theologians coming after Diodore. Yet one point needs to be highlighted at the start. While all the Antiochenes accepted the same hermeneutical principles, this did not prevent them from interpreting individual passages in their own manner. This is exemplified in the divergent way Theodore and, seemingly, Nestorius explain the phrase "image of God" in opposition to what Diodore, Chrysostom, and Theodoret have proposed. Their writings also seem to differ from Chrysostom's emphasis upon the Word's role within Christ's humanity.[19]

Besides the possibility that the Antiochene exegesis may have evolved out of some earlier Jewish inspiration, there is also some possibility that it may have been influenced by the Aristotelian methodological principles, for the later Antiochene Fathers sought to base their interpretations on well-reasoned arguments. They saw the necessity of maintaining an objective nexus between a spiritual and the literal meaning of a scriptural passage. As will shortly be seen, they believed that an allegorical interpretation severed this by introducing an imaginative explanation.[20] Since no text can be found that substantiates an Antiochene dependence upon Aristotle on this point, Rudolf Bultmann concludes that one cannot determine with any certainty the origin of the Antiochene exegesis. Bultmann suggests that it may have arisen out of the fact that Christianity is a historical religion that justifies its dogmatic and moral beliefs by appealing to a sacred, inspired work and is concerned with what has actually happened and will occur in the future within the history of salvation.[21] While the origin of the Antiochene exegesis seems to be due to more factors than this, Rowan A. Greer probably expresses the reality of the situation best when he admits, in general: "it is necessary to realize that in great measure that [Theodore's] exegesis was determined by Jewish ideas of the subject."[22]

18. Jerome, *The Lives of Illustrious Men*, ed. and trans. Ernest Cushing Richardson, NPNF, Second Series, ed. Philip Schaff and Henry Wace (1892; reprint, Peabody, Mass.: Hendrickson, 1994), 3:382. In this selection, Jerome relates in passing that Diodore followed Eusebius's interpretation, at least in his *Commentary on the Epistles*.

19. See Aloys Grillmeier, *Christ in Christian Tradition: From the Apostolic Age to Chalcedon (451)*, trans. John Bowden, 2d ed., vol. 1 (Atlanta: John Knox, 1975), 418–21.

20. Zaharopoulos, 110–11. See also Robert M. Grant, *The Letter and the Spirit* (New York: McMillan, 1957), 105.

21. Rudolf Bultmann, *Die Exegese des Theodore von Mopsuestia*, ed. H. Feld and K. Schelke (Stuttgart: W. Kohlhammer, 1984), 126.

22. Greer, *Theodore*, 86.

Greer firmly believes that, at least in the case of Theodore, the answer "must lie in the spirit with which Theodore approached Scripture. . . . because he had an understanding of the way of thinking implicit in the Bible."[23] This indicates that there must have existed among the Antiochenes a much deeper commitment to traditional Semitic thought than to a Greek love for speculation.

Fundamental Antiochene Principles

To situate the Antiochene position, it may be helpful to view it, first of all, in a broadly sketched way against an Alexandrian backdrop.[24] Origen, who stands out as the primary exponent for the Alexandrian method of exegesis, held for three kinds of exegesis. He likened these to his threefold division of human nature into body, soul, and spirit.[25] He compared—in an ascending level of importance—the literal to the human body, the moral to the psychic soul, and the mystical to the spirit. He looked upon the Bible as though it were indeed a sacrament, in which every detail possesses a spiritual meaning placed there by God's Spirit. While not denying the value of the literal meaning, he believed that one could also attain what he considered its deeper, transcendent meaning through the use of an allegorical interpretation, especially when the literal meaning was obscure, inappropriate, or unworthy of an infallibly inspired sacred document. A classic example would be the way the story of Martha and Mary

23. Greer, Theodore, 110.

24. In his analysis of the Alexandrian and Antiochene exegetical traditions, J. Guillet ("Les exégèses d'Alexandrie et d'Antioche. Conflit ou malentendue?" *Recherches de Science Religieuse*, April 1947: 297) has concluded that these traditions do not really contradict each other. He sees the differences more in what each has accented from its particular point of view, its attitudes, and its temperament, as well as a lack of clear formula (298). He suggests that the proper perspective for understanding a type is to evaluate the literal sense in light of all the dimensions of Scripture (302). For three more recent studies on the differences between the Alexandrian and Antiochene Schools of interpretation, see Rowan A. Greer, *The Captain of Our Salvation: A Study in the Patristic Exegesis of Hebrews* (Tübingen: Mohr, 1973); Robert M. Grant and David Tracy, *A Short History of the Interpretation of the Bible*, 2d ed. (Philadelphia: Fortress, 1984); and Manlio Simonetti, *Biblical Interpretation in the Early Church: An Historical Introduction to Patristic Exegesis*, trans. John A. Hughes, ed. A. Bergquist and M. Bockmuehl (Edinburgh: T&T Clark, 1994).

25. Origen expresses this in PG 11:364–66. For a summary of Origen's thought, see Greer, *Theodore*, 91–93; Zaharopoulos, 108–9; Wallace-Hadrill, 27–32; and Froehlich, 16–18.

has been allegorically interpreted as indicating that a contemplative vocation is much higher than an apostolically active life.[26] The Antiochenes would strongly object to such an interpretation on the grounds that it is not justified by a literal examination of the original text.

What surfaces as the most prominent feature of the Antiochene methodology is the way they have inverted Origen's comparison. They set their priority upon the establishment of the literal meaning of a text. The literal understanding of a text was not meant only for those who were unsophisticated and lacking a spiritual outlook; it ought to be the foundation on which all exegesis begins and rests securely. The Antiochenes believed that it was here that one was to seek out what God intended to reveal. Rather than prescinding from what the sacred writer actually meant when he wrote, an exegete had first of all to establish which text was the authentic one and then to be sensitive to what the individual words meant in their own context. With this kind of exegetical outlook, it is not surprising that the Antiochenes were strenuously opposed to what they judged to be the far-fetched, imaginative interpretations employed by those following an allegorical exegesis. They dismissed these as the substitution of one's own subjective intuition or musings for what the Spirit was actually inspiring a sacred writer to reveal.

Despite their insistence upon establishing the linguistic and historical significance of a scriptural text, the Antiochenes were open to the possibility that a text can contain a deeper spiritual message. The terms they used to express this are *theoria*, *typus*, and *anagogē*. They understood *theoria* as the mind's ability to discover a real fundamental relationship existing between two texts. It is to perceive within the historical elements of a text another higher or more sublime "reality" to which the present text points as being its own fulfillment.[27] While in the cultural and philosophical milieu of the time the term does have a technical meaning indicating a contemplation of the truth, it seems here to be a term that the Antiochenes employed to express the mind's ability to perceive a real relationship

26. See fragment 80 of Origen's Commentary on St. John in A. E. Brooke, ed., The Commentary of Origen on S. John's Gospel, 2 vols. (Cambridge: Cambridge UP, 1896), 2:296.

27. Greer (*Theodore*, 94) describes this well: "Typology not only preserves the two realities, but it sets those realities against an historical background. And by 'historical' is simply meant the view of life which sees things in terms of events moving towards a goal of some sort."

existing between a type and its archetype, a prophecy and its fulfillment, and Adam and Christ as the first and the second Adams. Its meaning among the Antiochenes is to be sought primarily from its use as a scriptural, exegetical tool.

The meaning of the term can be clearly seen from the way that the Antiochenes understood how a type—*typus*—can be said to be related to its archetype or model; that is, how a person, thing, action, or event actually foreshadows or anticipates something else.[28] For example, Adam is affirmed to be a true type representing Christ, the Exodus event as presaging the Jewish nation's return from the Babylonian captivity; and baptism and the eucharist as two sacramental types portending one's future life in heaven. But if there is no actual historical connection between two poles, the Antiochenes insisted upon calling this an allegory. The term *anagogē* fits in with this understanding in that it signifies a search for a spiritual meaning within a text.

The Antiochenes also admitted the presence of an accommodated sense of Scripture. As the term itself indicates, the accommodated sense refers to those situations where a person points out how his or her present situation can be said to be similar to or congruous with another situation with which it has no inherent connection. For instance, Theodore considered those passages where Jesus was said to be fulfilling an Old Testament prophecy as examples of an accommodated sense of Scripture. He held that such prophecies were not originally meant to be prophesying about Jesus. Yet they are, nevertheless, close enough that one can point out how appropriate they are to this new, later situation. Preachers often accommodate scriptural verses to a particular setting, such as the account of Jesus' conversation with Martha concerning her brother Lazarus's death being applied at a funeral Mass, especially when a brother is the deceased.

Diodore

While there exists ample material to pass critical judgments on Chrysostom, Theodore, and Theodoret's knowledge of Scripture, so few of Diodore's and Nestorius's writings have come down that we are limited in what we can say about their methods of exegesis. History, however,

---

28. For an explanation of how allegory represents 'left wing' typology, and the fulfilment of prophecy as 'right wing' typology, see Greer, *Theodore*, 94–95.

records that Diodore's own contemporaries esteemed him as one of the foremost exegetes of their day.[29] If one can judge by the exceptional breadth and depth of Chrysostom and Theodore's knowledge of Scripture, Diodore's reputation was truly well deserved. He was most likely the one responsible for instructing them in a literal, historical, and rational method of exegesis and possibly the one who had instilled in them a deep love for the Scriptures. Furthermore, if one can accept R. Leconte's speculations regarding the courses that were taught at Diodore's school, his students would have been well versed in the Pentateuch, the Psalms, the Prophets, the Gospels, and the Pauline epistles.[30]

Sources reveal that Diodore wrote a now lost treatise on *The Difference between Theory and Allegory*. Fortunately his *Commentary on the Psalms* was discovered at the beginning of this century.[31] Its introduction contains a valuable prologue in which he declares that *theoria* and *allegoria* differ from each other on the basis of *historia*, by which he meant not "history" as such but an author's real intent: "We do not object to *anagoge* [a search for a higher meaning][32] and a more lofty *theoria* [seeing the actual spiritual fulfillment of a text] . . . For *historia* [the author's actual meaning] does not exclude a more lofty *theoria*. Rather it is the basic substructure for higher insights. This alone must be held to, lest *theoria* be ever looked upon as subverting that upon which it is founded. For such would no longer be *theoria* but *allegoria*."[33]

29. The Emperor Theodosius I declared that Diodore's teaching set the standard for orthodoxy at that time. *Codex Theodosianus*, ed. C. H. Coster (Cambridge, Mass.: Medieval Academy of America) 16:1, 3.

30. R. Leconte, "L'Asceterium de Diodore," *Melanges bibliques rediges en l'honneur d'Andre Robert* (Paris: Bloud, 1957), 531–36.

31. *Diodori Tarsensis Commentarii in Psalmos*, CCSG 6, ed. Jean-Marie Olivier (Turnhout: Brepols, 1980). Olivier argues suasively in his preface (ciii-cviii) that the author is indeed Diodore and not Anastasius, the Metropolitan of Nicea.

32. The word *anagoge* literally means to refer one thing to another but connotes here, as the English word "anagogy" today signifies: the discovery of a spiritual or mystical meaning within a text. For a readable translation of Diodore's *Preface*, see Froehlich, 87–94 and, for a brief commentary, 21–22.

33. Olivier, xcii. I have translated the quotation from the Greek text, adding in brackets my understanding of the terms. Zaharopoulos (111) and Greer (*Theodore*, 93) translate the passage thus: "We do not forbid the higher interpretation and allegory, for the historical narrative does not exclude it, but is on the contrary the basis and substructure of loftier insights. . . . We must, however, be our guard against letting the *theoria* do away with the historical basis, for the result would then be, not *theoria*, but allegory."

In commenting upon this passage, Jean-Marie Olivier explains *theoria* as a speculative search to discover in the literal explanation of a text some connection linking it to another text: "It differs from what occurs in the allegorical exegesis [in that] the second object must maintain a connection with the first where it is simply not mentioned, so as to permit [one] to discover the second."[34] It is important to note that Diodore was using the term here in a way that differs notably from the ways that Nemesius understood it in the Aristotelian sense of the mind contemplating something simply for knowledge's sake,[35] that Christian spiritual writers were employing it to signify the mind and heart's prayerful quest to know God's will and God Himself experientially, or that exegetes at Alexandria used it to express the meaning one found in an allegory.

While all those who employ the term agree that it refers to a speculative search for a deeper reality, Diodore—and this is true for all the Antiochenes—insisted the second reality had to be linked with the literal meaning of the original text. It is the task of *theoria*, then, to discover the inner relationship between the two poles. If both are not historically grounded, Diodore considered the correlation to be an allegory where a commentator has interpreted the text in light of what he or she is imagining it to mean. This is an example of what contemporary Scripture scholars now term an *eisegesis* or the imposition of one's own understanding of the meaning upon the text itself. The crucial question here is, of course, whether this intuited meaning is what God intended to be derived from the text and, if so, how one authenticates it.

A fragment from Diodore's extant works can exemplify for us how Diodore interpreted a scriptural text according to his literal, historical, and rational method. In it he is discussing the passage where Adam asserts: "This one is now bone from my bones and flesh from my flesh. She will be called 'woman,' for out of 'her man' she has been taken" (Gen. 2:23).

From many indications, it is possible to see that Adam was filled with abundant grace, and this [present case] being not the least of all. For while the woman was being formed from him, he was not aware of this. How [could he be], seeing that he was asleep? He recognized her [only] after God had brought her to him, when he declared in a prophetic way that a woman will no longer come to be from man

34. Olivier, xcii. The translation from the French is my own.
35. William Telfer, ed. and trans., *Cyril of Jerusalem and Nemesius of Emesa*, Library of Christian Classics 4 (Philadelphia: Westminster, 1955), 358 n. 3.

in the same way that Eve did from him. For he says "this being is now bone from my bones." In our day, this "being" is brought forth by being generated, as Symmachus and Theodotion[36] have explained. This "being," however, is only once declared to be "bone from my bones." For all other [human] beings proceed from a man and a woman in a sexual liaison. Why then [does he specify] "from his rib?" [It is] that they may rejoice to honor one another not only because of everything in human life thought to be beautiful but also because of their formations as woman and man united in one flesh. Yet the statement, "For she was called woman because she was taken from her man," does not seem to flow as a consequence [from what has proceeded]. For if Eve is indeed a woman because she is Adam's rib, then [all] other women will certainly not be from men [in this sense]. On the other hand, according to the commentators, these words state that the Fall is connected with generation. Scripture, however, [in its statement "for out of her man she has been taken"] does not use the word "woman" but "man" [understood] in its generic sense. For it employs the word "man" with the feminine article [the Greek signifying thereby that it includes both men and women] without any refinement.[37] A similar indifference [regarding sex] underlies [the statement] "Eve is from the man." This seems in my opinion to better preserve the argumentative character of the narrative.[38]

Several characteristics of the Antiochene exegesis are clearly exemplified here. Diodore's comments reveal that he was primarily interested in determining the sacred writer's intent by examining the text closely. He noted how the feminine article is used with the Greek word for "man," signifying that it is to be understood as man in a generic sense. He rejected the interpretation that Eve has been called a woman because she proceeded from the side of Adam. He reasons that, if true, this would not apply to all other women who have been generated by a woman and man together. He explained Eve's formation from Adam's side in Pauline terms as being indicative of their unity in one flesh. When Diodore mentioned

36. As the hostility between Judaism and the early Church grew, the Jews abandoned the Septuagint in favor of new versions by Symmachus and Theodotion. Diodore is referring here to what appears to be comments that they must have made about the present text.

37. The literal translation is: "Scripture uses the word 'man' indifferently, employing an aspirated pronunciation of the word." Diodore interpreted the official Septuagint version that speaks of the woman being taken ἐκ τοῦ ἀνδρὸς αὐτῆς (from her man) to be the equivalent of ἡ ἄνθρωπον.

38. Diodore, PG 33:1566. For other examples of Diodore's exegetical method as it was applied to the Psalms, see Olivier, xciii-ciii.

that Adam stated "in a prophetic way that women will no longer come to be from men in the same way that Eve did from him," he admitted that the verse is prophesying about an event that will come to be at a later time. Finally when he cited Theodotion and Symmachus, he indicated that he must have examined their translations on Genesis. So what he has basically done is to apply critical reasoning to the text and to explain it in light of other applicable passages from Scripture.

John Chrysostom

Chrysostom's reputation for having an unparalleled knowledge of Scripture is well deserved. Even if one did not have the witness of his contemporaries, this can be surmised from the continual way he wove scriptural quotations into his writings. Chrysostomus Baur calculates: "his treatises and approximately six hundred sermons contain not less than eighteen thousand Scripture citations."[39] An examination of these reveals how he has woven into a text different verses from Scripture, so as to clarify, amplify, and strengthen the point that he wanted to make.[40] In so doing, Baur believes, "Chrysostom's commentaries on the New Testament are considered even in our own day, from a literary and exegetical point of view, the best and most useful that the Greek patristic age has bequeathed to us."[41] However, Chrysostom was not so much a professional exegete as a priest and bishop motivated by a desire to instruct and challenge his listeners by means of his pastoral writings. He did not so much exegete the Scriptures, as did Theodore in his commentaries, as he sought to highlight and substantiate in a critical analytical way the points he was striving to get across to his congregation or readers.

39. Chrysostomus Baur, *John Chrysostom and his Time*, 2 vols. Trans. M. Gonzaga (Westminster, Md.: Newman, 1959–60), 1:316.

40. For two recent works that elaborate on John Chrysostom's method of exegesis, see J. N. D. Kelly, *Golden Mouth: The Story of John Chrysostom—Ascetic, Preacher, Bishop* (London: Duckworth, 1995) and Amy Smyth McCormick, "Example of Antiochene Exegetical Tradition: John Chrysostom's Homily #50," *Patristic and Byzantine Review* 12 (1993): 65–82. See also Peter Gorday, *Principles of Patristic Exegesis: Romans 9–11 in Origen, John Chrysostom, and Augustine*, Studies in the Bible and Early Christianity (New York: Mellen, 1983) for a study into the principles of exegesis that Chrysostom employed in einterpreting Romans 9–11.

41. Baur, 1:322.

Chrysostom held that all of Scripture was divinely inspired. Baur observes that Chrysostom "says repeatedly that in the Holy Scripture there is nothing without purpose, not a syllable, not an iota, not the smallest dash. . . . In his eyes, Scripture proofs are stronger and surer than any proofs founded on reason."[42] His outlook on inspiration also led him to believe that, in addition to moral and dogmatic truths, the Scriptures manifest scientific and historical facts and social roles. This may explain why he was so willing to accept the Psalms as prophetic.[43] His understanding of verbal inspiration was similar to the opinion held by others of his day, both Christians and conservative rabbis.

Chrysostom proposed the same kind of distinction that Diodore made between a type and an allegory. The type is based on *historia,* that is on what the author actually intends, whereas the allegory is the product of an exegete's imagination. This has been expressed in Chrysostom's interpretation of Paul's remark in Galatians 4:24 that Abraham's wife and his slave woman foreshadow the two testaments: "(Paul) called this type an allegory in a misuse of language. What he is affirming is this: the *historia* itself not only manifests what is apparent but also proclaims publicly some other matters. On this account it has also been called an allegory. But what has it made public? Nothing else than everything that is now present."[44] In other words, Chrysostom believed that Paul has not used the term allegory in its strict sense. Rather he should have specified that he was employing a type when he compared the two women to the two covenants, for he was comparing the historical reality of Sarah and Hagar with that of the two covenants to highlight the existence of the future relationship between the Jewish and Christian Testaments.

Chrysostom's scriptural analyses are invariably insightful and stimulating, yet he was not beyond imposing his own beliefs upon a passage. There are times when he faced problems and responded to them, in the words of Baur, by tracing "them back to mere variations, which he neither contradicts nor corrects."[45] And there are other times when he would be selective in the texts that he chose to corroborate his particular viewpoint

42. Ibid., 1:318–19.

43. For an example, see Chrysostom, PG 55:531–32.

44. Chrysostom, PG 61:662. For a study into Chrysostom's exegesis of this passage, see Robert J. Kepple, "Analysis of Antiochene Exegesis of Galatians 4:24–26," *Westminster Theological Journal* 39 (1977): 243–46.

45. Baur, 1:319.

and rationalize away those that ran counter to this. For instance, as the following brings out, he appealed to the second creation account in Genesis and to Paul's statement about women being the glory of men as confirming his contention that women do not share in the power God had entrusted to men.[46] He reconciled Genesis's first chapter about God creating man and woman as equals with what the third chapter has affirmed about women's subjection to men.

> [The author of Genesis] taught us [the meaning of] this in a cryptic manner. For since he had not yet apprised us about [their] fashioning and had not said from whence the woman came, he said: "Masculine and feminine He made them." Do you see how he has related what had not yet come to be, as though it had? Spiritual eyes can see this. Those possessing carnal eyes cannot grasp what is being seen, while those having spiritual eyes can see what is indeed invisible and immaterial.[47]

In other words, Chrysostom believed that the first Genesis account of Adam and Eve's creation is but a general anticipatory statement of what is really to happen when God does create. It is the second account that he believes an interpreter must examine to determine what has been revealed about the relationship of women to men. When Chrysostom stated that one needs a spiritual outlook to be able to recognize this relationship between the two accounts, he doubtless believed this. Since his interpretation has a rational ring to it, it appears somewhat plausible. But to those objecting to it, it seems to be a rhetorical device, for it implies that a person who does not agree with Chrysostom's view has not acquired a truly spiritual vision. Chrysostom may be influenced here by the view of those, such as Origen, who affirmed the existence of two creations, for it fit in well with his own interpretation. But even if this is so, it is important to note how his interpretation differs from an allegory. Chrysostom is here referring to an event that would take place when creation actually did occur.

The above interpretations highlight how Chrysostom exegeted a Scripture passage. He justified his belief that Eve was created to be subordinate to Adam by appealing to what he believed to be the literal meaning of Genesis 3:16 and 1 Corinthians 11:7. He showed himself also to be willing to confront the earlier creation account in Genesis where the text suggests that women too have been created in God's image. He offered an

46. Chrysostom, PG 54:589. See also 53:74.
47. Ibid., 53:85–86.

explanation of how this text can be reconciled with his interpretation. Though one can challenge this interpretation, the point here is that Chrysostom was attempting to demonstrate through a rational analysis of the Genesis and Pauline texts what he believed their authors to be saying. He relied, too, on the power of reason to draw conclusions from what is affirmed there regarding the role of women in society.

Theodore

Of all the Antiochenes, Theodore has been the one whose method of exegesis has been most commented upon. While this is due in some measure to the fact that so few of Diodore and Nestorius's writings have come down to us, it is, however, not the complete answer, for a considerable body of commentaries that Chrysostom and Theodoret have written are extant. The primary reason for Theodore's appeal seems to be that he has fine-tuned the Antiochene exegetical method and is considered its foremost exponent. This has won a place for him in the history of exegesis as a true forerunner of the historico-grammatical method that has become, together with form criticism, so central to contemporary exegesis. Thus it is not surprising that in the past ten years or so, two major works have been published: a posthumous treatise by Rudolf Bultmann[48] and a study by Dimitri Zaharopoulos on Theodore's Old Testament exegesis.[49] When taken with the earlier studies of Pirot,[50] Greer,[51] and Devreese,[52] these can provide a critical up-to-date evaluation of Theodore's exegetical thought.

According to patristic sources, Theodore wrote commentaries on nearly all of Scripture and was universally respected as one of the outstanding patristic exegetes of his day. If there is truth to Leontius of Byzantium's sarcastic remark that Theodore was writing commentaries as a youth, this would mean that Theodore was in his late teens when he began his scholarly career. Vosté suggests that his works can be grouped,

48. Rudolf Bultmann, *Die Exegese des Theodore von Mopsuestia*, ed. Helmut Feld and Karl Hermann Schelkle (Stuttgart: Kohlhammer, 1984).

49. See Zaharopoulos.

50. D. Louis Pirot, *L'Oeuvre exégétique de Théodore de Mopsueste* (Rome: Pontificii Instituti Biblici, 1913).

51. See Greer, *Theodore*.

52. Robert Devreese, "La méthode exégétique de Théodore de Mopsueste," *Revue Biblique*, April 1946: 207–41.

generally speaking, into two periods: those written on the Old Testament up to the time when he was ordained a priest in 383 and those on the New Testament starting around 400. But since so many of his commentaries have been lost, with almost no factual information about when they were written, it is hard to assess how well-founded these opinions are. Fortunately, though, enough passages have survived so that one can speak confidently about his hermeneutical and exegetical principles, especially in light of the critical studies that have been made concerning his habitual method of exegeting a text.[53]

Theodore's General Views on Scripture

Theodore lived at a time when Christians were still struggling to reach a consensus as to what Jewish and Christian books belonged to their respective canons. Since Theodore has not specified what he believed should be included, scholars have had to speculate as to which works he thought were divinely inspired. On this basis, he appears to have accepted as authentic those Hebrew books that the Jews in Palestine had determined to be part of their sacred canon, for he never alludes to the Jewish apocrypha in his extant works.[54] But because he did not know Hebrew except for "the few scraps of information he was able to gather from intermediary sources,"[55] he had to rely upon the Septuagint, which he believed to be faithful to the original.[56] He appears, nevertheless, to have consulted with other versions, whenever the textual reading of the Septuagint was suspect.

As a result of his critical examination of the Septuagint, Theodore questioned the conventional wisdom of those who regarded the Jewish Scriptures as comprising a single book. For him they were a collection of works that were written at different periods, with dissimilar and at times contradictory outlooks and traditions. They embodied distinct stages in the way that God had progressively revealed Himself and His will. Theodore also rejected the opinion of those who treated the whole psalter as if it were a repository of prophecies concerning Christ. He believed only

53. J.-M. Vosté, "La chronologie de l'activité litteraire de Théodore de Mopsueste," *Revue Biblique* 34 (Jan. 1925): 54–81.

54. See Zaharopoulos, 54–55.   55. Ibid., 58.

56. See ibid., 60–65.

Psalms 2, 8, 45, and 110 directly referred to Christ and his Church. He was willing, however, to grant that there could well be passages that foreshadow Christ as their antitype in the sense that Christ is their true end and fulfillment. Theodore also challenged the titles that were assigned to the Psalms, contending that some of these dated from the time of the Maccabees.[57]

Despite the fact that Theodore regarded the Septuagint as a reliable work,[58] this did not prevent him from also pointing out that certain books like Job and the Song of Songs were based on human origin, wisdom, and experience. From the patristic literature now available, Theodore's subjection of these to internal criticism is thought to be the first time their historicity was investigated. His critique of Job, however, was later cited at the Fifth General Council at Constantinople in 553, where the charge was introduced that he denied Job was an inspired work. But from the fragments that have survived from his commentary[59] and from passing remarks by Išoʻdad of Merv, a ninth-century East Syriac writer[60] who was a faithful adherent of Theodore's thought on this question, it seems what he had actually concluded after his analysis of the book of Job was that it had been written by some anonymous Jewish author who had integrated into his work a pagan folk tale about a celebrated just man in order to make his story more appealing.[61]

While it now seems that Theodore considered Job to be inspired in its final Hebrew version, he did exclude the Song of Songs from the canon, considering it after a close rational examination to be a love song celebrating Solomon's marriage to an Egyptian princess. Furthermore, he opposed the common view of the day that the Song was an allegory of Christ and his Church. This indicates his deep-seated antipathy for allegory and his

57. See Pirot, 137–40.

58. Greer (*Theodore*, 99) affirms: "Nowhere do we find Theodore speaking of the Septuagint as a miraculously inspired translation, having as much authority as the original. His view of the Septuagint is, in a sense, summarized by his comparison of it with other Greek versions."

59. For a commentary on Theodore's work on Job, see J.-M. Vosté, "L'oeuvre exégétique de Théodore de Mopsueste au II Councile de Constantinople," *Revue Biblique* 38 (July 1929): 382–95; (Oct. 1929): 542–54.

60. For Išoʻdad's commentaries, see C. Van den Eynde, trans., *Commentaire d'Išoʻdad de Merv sur l'Ancien Testament*, CSCO 156/Syr. 75 (Louvain: Dubecq, 1955).

61. For a treatment of this question, see Zaharopoulos, 46–47 and Pirot, 131–34.

willingness to take a stand against what most other Fathers were teaching whenever this was, in his opinion, what an objective reading of the text required.[62]

As regards the New Testament canon, he probably excluded, as Chrysostom and Theodoret did, the book of Revelation, the second letter of Peter, the second and third letters of John, and the letter of Jude.[63] When he came to interpret those passages in the Gospels where Jesus is said to be fulfilling Jewish prophecies, he understood these to be instances of accommodation. He believed that the evangelists were pointing out a similarity—not the actual fact that this is what prophet had in mind when he uttered his prophecy. Theodore believed that the evangelists saw how appropriate certain Old Testament prophecies were to Jesus and used these to bring out in a emphatic way Jesus' messianic vocation. Theodore asserts that Paul too employed the same kind of accommodation when he introduced various verses from the psalms into the third chapter of his letter to the Romans: "(Paul) was using the citation not as if it was being said in a prophetic way, but as adapting the very things that David said in a summary fashion about those who have fallen to the point that he is [now] making. Just as we in our ecclesiastical discourses also make use even today of citations which our reason can harmonize with what we are presently asserting."[64]

Theodore's Views on Inspiration

As regards his understanding of biblical inspiration, Theodore accepted the Jewish conviction that God had revealed Himself and His will to His people through their prophets and sacred writings. He considered these an infallible source for knowing truth. In his commentaries on the prophets, Theodore looked upon inspiration as a movement whereby God implanted certain ideas and images within a sacred writer's mind: "For (the prophet) calls God's activity the word of the Lord as it enables the prophets to receive by means of a prophetic grace revelations of what is to be."[65] Then at a later date—when and why it happened is uncertain—Theodore appears

62. For a discussion of this, see Zaharopoulos, 33–34 and esp. 49–52; as well as Pirot, 134–37.

63. For a treatment of this, see Zaharopoulos 55–56.

64. *Pauluskommentare aus der Griechischen Kirche*, ed. Karl Staab (Münster: Aschendorff, 1933), 117.

65. Theodore, PG 66:308.

to have moved away from his belief that everything in the Scriptures is inspired to one where he sought to distinguish between what the Spirit was revealing and the role that the sacred writer played in the whole process.[66]

Whether Theodore changed his view or was simply clarifying his thought, he began to describe inspiration no longer as a conceptual communication of some revealed truth, but as an ecstatic state in which a sacred writer psychologically senses an immediate encounter with God's Spirit.[67] He realized that there was a dynamic interplay between the Spirit's inspiring activity and the human make-up of the person being inspired. This means that the content of what the Spirit wanted revealed is filtered through the sacred writer and is thereby inevitably modified. Grasping this, Theodore saw the need in his Gospel prologues to treat the evangelists as being more than simple stenographers passively recounting what the Spirit inspired them to write. This led him to examine such factors as the Gospel author's purpose in writing and his personal memories of events. In his commentaries on the minor epistles of Paul, in fact, Theodore reached the point where he so stressed Paul's autonomous role it is hard to assess what collaborative role he believed the Spirit played in the exposition of Paul's thought.[68]

This shift of emphasis away from the Spirit's role to that of the spiritual writer indicates, therefore, that Theodore was likely aware of the distinction between what God was actually revealing in an inspired moment and what the inspired person affirms it to be in its final modified form.[69] Perhaps as he reflected on how Jesus as the assumed man interacted with the Word in a prosopic union, he realized its ramifications for the way the Spirit inspired a sacred writer. Or perhaps it was the other way around. Whatever may have led him to a recognition that the writer had a crucial role to play in inspiration, this provided him, at any rate, with a justification whereby he could freely scrutinize a text and, if reason permitted it, to question and even oppose widely and long-held traditions.

Theodore's Exegetical Method

Generally speaking, Theodore appears to have followed a set exegetical procedure. In the prologue of his commentary, he would weigh such

66. See Zaharopoulos, 82.   67. See ibid., 98.
68. See ibid., 178.   69. See ibid., 90.

issues as the author of the work, its date, its historical setting, its purpose, and its major insights, and then offer a concise summary of its content. In his commentary on the text itself, he would very carefully note variant readings and the impact that a conjunction, preposition, and punctuation might have on the meaning of the text. Though his remarks on why he chose a particular word are suggestive and at times profound, they are judged today to be of little value in determining the true text and its meaning. His exegesis, nevertheless, is significant for the careful, critical way he proceeded, rather than for what he specifically proposed.[70]

For Theodore, it was of primary importance to ascertain what an author meant by his or her terms. He did this by trying to determine how a word was to be understood in its particular context but also in light of how it was used in other passages. He also paid special attention to how an author's thought advanced in a passage. To all of this, he applied common-sense reasoning to sort out what meaning was actually being affirmed. So while accepting that Scripture is a divinely inspired, infallible account of how God has revealed not only who He is but how one is to live in accordance with His will, Theodore also realized that one had critically to sort out and justify from the text itself what God is actually revealing in and through the Scriptures. He is equivalently saying that it is not what one feels or intuits or imagines that a particular text means, but what one can rationally support by well-founded arguments.

While Theodore is to be commended for introducing a critical element into his exegesis, he is also open to the charge that his own overall theological synthesis has subconsciously affected his interpretation. Greer points out well how Theodore has arrived at his overall theological stance when he sums it up as follows: "As a generalization, we may say that Theodore draws his theology from the text, organizes it somewhat systematically, and then reimposes the more sophisticated theological system upon the text. This is certainly legitimate; and, in fact, the rabbinical system of explaining one text by another is really little more than what Theodore is actually doing."[71] While Theodore's general synthesis will be discussed in a later chapter, the point needs to be made here that it does have an influence on how he interprets a text. While Theodore's honesty would guide

---

70. See ibid., 119 and 126.

71. Greer (*Theodore*, 104) believes that the "very basic notions of his [Theodore's] theology are ultimately derived from the Pauline epistles themselves."

him to be objective in his analysis of a text, he did approach a passage from a perspective that would condition—but not predetermine—his interpretation. For instance, his understanding of divine transcendence prevented him from admitting even the possibility of a natural union between the divine and the human natures in Christ. It is a case where one pre-judges a situation in light of what a person expects to find there. As the English word "mindset" brings out so clearly, the human mind is "set" in the sense of being conditioned to discern a particular pattern in reality.

Theodore's Exegesis of John's Gospel

When commenting on John's Gospel, there must have been times when Theodore would be aware that there were conflicts between his literal reading of a text and his general theological system. For instance, John often intimates the merging of the eternal with the temporal. He also insinuates in his prologue and in his account of the seven "signs" that Jesus and the Word are substantially united with one another. Theodore could not miss that John's emphasis upon the ontological and the mystical runs counter to his own historical and functional perspectives. While his synthesis highlights how the "assumed man" acted in human as well as divine ways and grew as a human being during his union with the Word, John stresses how Jesus is divine. It is an instance where a person espousing what is today called a "low" Christology is brought face to face with one who is expressing a "high" Christology. So Theodore's commentary on John is important for answering the questions of how really objective Theodore was as an exegete. Did he go wherever his critical reason led him, or did he attempt to rationalize John's thought forcing it to conform in a Procrustean manner with what he was convinced had to be true?

There are many passages in John where Theodore could easily reconcile his viewpoint about the union between the Word and the "assumed man" with the way John described the union. In fact, he has drawn his terminology about "inhabitation" from John. He is able in most instances to distinguish which nature is being referred to in a specific text. But there are occasions where he had to have been perplexed by John's clear-cut statements about Christ's divinity, as when John has Jesus affirm in 10:30, "I and the Father are one." To his credit, Theodore confronted the issue head-on. The issue is not the divinity of Christ, which he held, but the correct way to state how the divine and human natures in Christ can function as one. His response here reveals his method of exegesis and the influence of his systematic dogmatic outlook. He observed how the word "one" can be understood in various ways, such as signifying an "equality," or a "similarity," or a "consensus." Its meaning has to be determined from the context in which it is being used.

From his analysis, it seems Theodore believed that the term "one" ought to be understood as a consensus where Jesus' assumption by the Word and the perfect union of his human will with the Word's enabled God's power to flow through his human acts in such a unified way that it appears to be one power. Theodore implied this when he asserted that Christ and the Father are one "in the sense of power (*virtus*), insofar as his (Christ's) power is greater and more powerful than all others; and this appears from the interpretation of the words."[72] While such an answer may strike one as twisting Scripture to reflect Theodore's christological viewpoint, it is a possible rational interpretation. While this will be discussed later, it suffices to state here that Theodore was convinced that John was depicting how the Word and the "assumed man" function together. He evidently wanted to remain with the way the Gospels, especially the evangelists, portray the union, without getting into an explanation of the metaphysical nature of the actual union present there.

One last issue needs to be mentioned concerning how Theodore would interpret a text: his attitude toward the positions taken by other scriptural commentators. From his careful study of Theodore's method of exegesis, Dimitri Zaharopoulos remarks that "if we may judge from his extant biblical commentaries, (Theodore) never appeals to the authority of the earlier church fathers, but frequently attacks other commentators with derision."[73] While it is true that Theodore felt free to follow wherever his critical analysis of a text would point him, even if this led him into public opposition with traditional teachings, he always adhered to the conciliar doctrines of Nicea and Constantinople I and would doubtless value the opinion of another whenever this was based on objectively grounded rational arguments connected to a literal reading of a text. His scorn would be directed toward those advancing a purely allegorical explanation or a crude literal interpretation of a text.

72. *Theodori Mopsuesteni Commentarius in Evangelium Joannis Apostoli*, ed. J.-M. Vosté, CSCO 115–116 / Syr. 62–63 (Louvain: Officina Orientali, 1940), 153.

73. Zaharopoulos, 138 n. 96.

Theodore's Understanding of Types

In addition to the literal and accommodated senses of a text, Theodore also acknowledged the legitimate presence of types within the Scriptures. He accepted this because of his underlying belief in a providential hand guiding events towards their fulfillment in Christ. As with Chrysostom, Theodore expressed his understanding of a type in his commentary on Galatians 4:24, where he remarked that Paul's comparison of Sarah and Hagar with the two covenants may be termed an allegory: "[Paul] calls the comparison made by juxtaposing events which have already occurred with present events an 'allegory.'"[74] But he believed that Paul was really speaking of a type. Theodore thus understands the comparison of the slave / free relationship existing between the two women as pointing to what is the present relationship existing between the Jewish and Christian covenants.[75]

Knowing a type, however, does not enable one to interpret its meaning by itself. One must also be familiar with its antitype, or archetype, which reveals how the type is to be fulfilled.[76] So when one compares the correspondence between persons (such as Adam and Christ), or actions (such as baptism and a birth into a resurrected life), and events (like the Exodus and the acquiring of a spiritual freedom) that can be historically compared and contrasted with one another, one can enrich his or her understanding of the two "poles" as they shed light upon each other. For as Theodore understood it, the New Testament not only guarantees that the relationship between the type and antitype really exists but also enables one to realize how the latter is the eschatological fulfillment of the

74. *Theodori Episcopi Mopsuesteni in Epistolas B. Pauli Commentarii*, ed. H. B. Swete, 2 vols. (Cambridge: Cambridge UP, 1880 and 1882), 1:79. Froehlich offers a clear English translation of Theodore's commentary on Galatians 4:22–31 on pages 95–103. For an elaboration on how Theodore has interpreted this passage, see Kepple, 240–43. In the conclusion of his study, Kepple notes that, while allegory and typology are logically distinct, they belong at the opposite ends of the same continuum.

75. Greer (*Theodore*, 108–9) concludes: "Theodore defines typology . . . as the comparison of two poles against an historical, eschatological background, with the belief that a real relationship between the two exists, and that the second is the fulfilment of the first, and with the conviction that each pole has its own reality."

76. Zaharopoulos regards typology as "not an interpretation of biblical texts but an historical comparison of events. It is the external correspondence of the events themselves in the two Testaments that has to be compared and brought forward" (131).

first and provides grounds for speculating further about the relationship. For example, the Adam-Christ typology of which Paul had approved raises the issue of how Christ is the fulfillment of Adam. If Adam were initially fashioned immortal, Christ would then be fulfilling what Adam was before he sinned and thus restoring humanity to the state it lost. But if Adam were first created mortal (which seems to be Theodore's position) and started a historical, educative process that all must undergo, then Christ is the fulfillment of what Adam was only in potentiality.

Further insight can be gained into Theodore's understanding of the kind of relationship existing between a type and its antitype by his remarks on how the Church and its sacramental life function as symbols and types prefiguring the future life promised for those believing in Christ. Those who have been baptized into a new life in the Church and who nourish this life through the eucharist are living a life that foreshadows the promised future life that only Christ has actually achieved at present. Theodore expressed these ideas often in his catechetical homilies, for example: "We will delight in the blessings of the Kingdom, while (Christ) wants those who approach Him by religion and faith in this world to have celestial things typically. There is a certain likeness to the celestial things to be procured in the Church where he wanted those who believe in him to live."[77]

Theodore observed that it is important for those receiving the sacraments to be aware of what is happening. For since baptism and the eucharist are types of future spiritual realities, they need to be explained: "For every sacrament is an indication by signs and symbols of invisible and ineffable things. It certainly cries out for a revelation and explanation of such things, if the one who is prepared to approach is to know the power of the sacraments."[78] In explaining what this power can effect, Theodore described it thus: "Likewise this phrase 'In the name of the Father and of the Son and of the Holy Spirit' is an indication of the gifts given by baptism: a birth that leads one to renewal, immortality, incorruptibility, impassibility, immutability, deliverance from death and slavery and all evils, an uplifting freedom and a participation in the expected blessings which

77. Raymond Tonneau with Robert Devreese, trans., *Les Homélies Catéchétiques de Théodore de Mopsueste* (Vatican City: Vaticana, 1949), 341–43. Since the Syriac text here is not legible, I have translated it from Tonneau's French translation.

78. Ibid., 325. The translation from the Syriac is my own.

are ineffable."[79] It is to be noted here that these gifts do not entail a mystical sharing in God's life as such but rather are gifts radically transforming and liberating one's human life from mortality to immortality.

Because Theodore has used traditional language to describe the effects of baptism, it is not easy to determine to what extent he believed these are being experienced in this present life, for he was constantly affirming that it is in hope that a believer expects to achieve these. Theodore was doubtless stressing the idea of hope because of how he conceived the kind of union existing between God and His creatures. This point will be discussed later. Suffice it to say that, since Theodore regarded redemption as the attainment of a future state of immortality and immutability presently possessed only by Christ, he could not assert that a baptized person now enjoys that kind of resurrected life—even partially. Just as a woman cannot be affirmed to be partially pregnant, the same ought to be affirmed of a person who is said to be partially immortal. For one is either mortal or immortal at any given moment. Yet despite his unwillingness to grant the actual possession and enjoyment of an immortal life in our present earthly life, Theodore did hold for a real potentiality that will later be actualized.

Theodore's understanding of how the future life is experienced only in hope should not lead one to conclude—falsely—that he was simply using merely rhetorical terms when he was speaking about the life that the Church bestows at baptism and later nourishes through the eucharist. For he taught in his catechetical homilies that the Church in general and its sacraments in particular are effectual means enabling one to be assured of a future immortal and immutable life in heaven. This is seen expressed in the following: "Because we are not yet in [possession of] these heavenly gifts, it is by faith that we now press on until we ascend to heaven. . . . We are commanded in this world to celebrate the types and symbols of those things to come, in order that, as people who through the liturgy possess in a parabolic way the delight of heavenly things, we might possess an assured hope of those things that are expected by us."[80] Baptism and the eucharist provide one, as it were, with the graces and guarantees that God will be faithful to His promises in a way similar to those exchanging American paper money are assured that its value is being backed by the

79. Ibid., 439.
80. Ibid., 493.

United States Government. One does not have the real value at hand, seeing that the paper in itself is worthless. But it has a potentiality for being fully redeemed at a later date.

From this overview of Theodore's understanding of how baptism and the eucharist serve as types, one can see how Theodore regarded a type as having a necessary connection with its antitype since it points to a fulfillment that its antitype shows is already assured. For it is God who established the relationship and guarantees that the end result will occur in the future. While the scriptural types are absolutely determined, the sacramental are provisional, as they depend upon the free participation of human beings who may choose not to proceed along the path that God has mapped out. Both types, nevertheless, point out clearly what are their fulfilment. For they are both revealed in and sanctioned by the Gospels and Paul.

Theodore's Hermeneutical Mindset

In concluding this section, it is helpful to highlight the hermeneutical principles guiding the way Theodore exegeted a text: 1) that the Scriptures are divinely inspired; 2) that God has willed a plan for salvation that can be discovered by applying one's reason to what Scripture reveals; 3) that a scriptural text needs to be interpreted in a literal, historical, and rational way, if one is to be able to determine the role the sacred writer has played in expressing and modifying what God is revealing; and 4) that a type and its antitype have to be firmly grounded in a literal interpretation of a text and also be confirmed as such by Scripture. Theodore was consistent and rigorous in the specific ways that he applied these principles as criteria, especially when he employed them to determine an authentic type. He found only a relatively few types that could actually measure up to his standards.[81]

Two major reasons seem to account for why Theodore developed his exegetical criteria as he did: the training he received from both Diodore and Libanius as well as the rational bent of his own personality. These factors inclined him toward a highly critical, systematic approach to exegesis that left him wholly indifferent, if not hostile, to those unable to

---

81. Zaharopoulos states that "Theodore refused to recognize more than three 'types' which satisfied the strict criteria stipulated by him" (131).

justify their interpretations of Scriptures with well-founded arguments. He was especially negative toward the allegorists' intuitive, imaginative interpretations.[82] He expressed this when he described the allegorists as being those who "indeed overturn everything, wanting to make no distinction between the historical content of divine Scripture and nighttime dreams."[83]

Nestorius

Nestorius is even more difficult than Diodore to evaluate as an exegete, for although we have what appears to be three separate works bound into a single volume, called the *Bazaar of Heracleides*, these are mostly apologetic and historical in their content. They depend primarily on the strength of their rational arguments. When Nestorius does introduce scriptural passages, they are used as ways to buttress his own position or to refute Cyril's. Yet in spite of the paucity of evidence, it is not unreasonable to conjecture that, if he had been educated at the School of Antioch, he too would have been well trained in Scripture. Since he has been acclaimed to have been an eloquent preacher and a widely admired ascetic, he probably employed his knowledge of Scripture, like Chrysostom, principally for oratorical and apologetic purposes. Like Chrysostom, he appears not to have been a "professional" exegete in the same mold of Diodore, Theodore, and Theodoret.

Because of the apologetic purpose of Nestorius's *The Bazaar of Heracleides*, one can provide little direct textual evidence of how he would exegete scriptural passages. He alluded to Scripture but always in defense of his christological position or in situations where he explains scriptural texts in light of his own theological outlook. For instance, he discussed Christ's birth, baptism, moral struggles and temptations, and obedience unto death, as well as Christ's roles as the second Adam and the one who brings atonement. He also explained how his understanding of the prosopic union can be reconciled with Philippians 2:1–7 where Christ is said to be in the likeness of God and to have taken on the likeness of a servant.

82. For a discussion of this, see Joanne McWilliam Dewart, *The Theology of Grace of Theodore of Mopsuestia*, Catholic University of America Studies, Christian Antiquity 16 (Washington: The Catholic University of America Press, 1971), 150.

83. Swete, TEP, 1:74. The English translation is my own.

But he was not strictly exegeting these passages.[84] He was employing them as scriptural proof-texts that substantiate his theological theses and systematic stance. They indicate that he understood a text in a literal and rational way.

Theodoret

Theodoret was much more a professional exegete than Nestorius. Like all his predecessors, he employed the same basic hermeneutical principles as discussed above. But in applying these principles, he tends in his extant commentaries to be briefer, more circumspect, and less controversial than the other Antiochenes, often simply paraphrasing what a scriptural text is stating. In fact, as Wallace-Hadrill has noted, "in their treatment of the minor prophets, Theodore and Theodoret do not always agree, and that the latter sometimes stands nearer to Cyril than Theodore."[85] Being a good scholar, Theodoret showed himself aware of what other exegetes, theologians, and philosophers were holding and appears to be faithfully summarizing their views. Considering the hostile clouds of suspicion and opposition hovering over Antiochene theology and exegesis after the Council of Ephesus, as well as the bitter personal attacks being leveled against him up to Chalcedon, Theodoret's conservative stance and succinct comments are readily understandable.

Conclusion

While the origins of the Antiochene exegetical tradition are shrouded in uncertainty, it seems to have evolved along lines close to that being developed by the conservative rabbis in Palestine. It shared many of their hermeneutical principles and their antipathy towards Philo's allegorical method of interpreting Scripture. Like the School of Alexandria, it admitted the possibility that one can find moral, theological, and mystical meanings within a scriptural text, but disagreed with the Alexandrians

---

84. See Rowan A. Greer, "Image of God and the Prosopic Union in Nestorius' Bazaar of Heracleides," Lux in Lumine: Essays for W. N. Pittenger, ed. Richard A. Norris, Jr. (New York: Seabury, 1966), 50–52 for an elaboration of how Nestorius interpreted chapter 2 of Philippians.

85. Wallace-Hadrill, 39.

over the exegetical role of allegorical interpretations.[86] The Antiochenes were all opposed with some variations to a method that downplayed the literal in favor of the allegorical by allowing a person to substitute one's imaginative insights rather than accept at face value what a writer intended to convey in a particular context.

While the Antiochenes were committed to a literal, historical exegesis of a text, they also recognized the possibility of finding through a "theoretic" speculation a deeper or, in Diodore's terms, a more lofty meaning hidden within a particular text. They admitted the legitimate usage of types that point to someone or something in the future. They believed that God in His providence predetermined that this relationship should occur and has revealed its existence through the Scriptures. But here they parted company with Origen and those following him by distinguishing a type from an allegory. They required that the type and its future antitype be grounded in *historia*. An allegory may propose a meaning that is both inspiring as well as insightful, but if it is not corroborated by the actual intent of an author and, at least for Theodore, also confirmed by a later Scripture passage, it is not a meaning being revealed by God.

The Antiochenes, therefore, took history seriously. They were convinced that God spoke through reality. With such an outlook, one can readily understand why they would have bristled at the charge of those who dismissed a meticulous literal reading of the "body" of a text as the way that "simple" people read Scripture. Also they were skeptical of the value of pagan philosophies, considering Origen's willingness to introduce Philo's fusion of Jewish and Greek viewpoints into Christian exegesis as hindering, if not in fact perverting, what God is revealing in Scripture. While in no way opposed to the reality of a spiritual world, they recognized a danger that the values of both the "body" of a text and the human body are downplayed in so stressing the spiritual and mystical over the material. Because of their stalwart defense of Christ's complete human nature, they realized how fundamentally critical was the need to establish a solid connection between a spiritual interpretation and the "body" of a scriptural text. To maintain that one was able to prescind from the literal and historical basis of a text struck the Antiochenes as practicing an irresponsible method for treating God's revealed word.

86. For a comparison of the two schools of exegesis, see Guillet, 257–303.

The Antiochenes believed that the true key for unlocking the deeper spiritual message contained in a text was what they called *theoria*. By this they meant the speculative power of the intellect to perceive within historical facts a real spiritual relationship between two poles that God intended should be apprehended together (but in different ways). In applying *theoria* to a text, Chrysostom and Theodoret were faithful in general to the principles that the School of Antioch espoused, but they were also much more flexible than Theodore in how a specific text ought to be interpreted. While Theodore was open to the possibility that a text might point typically to another reality, he was, in practice, so demanding in applying his criteria that he admitted the existence of relatively few types sanctioned by Scripture.

As modern commentators have recognized, Theodore stands out as the most penetrating and interesting of the Antiochenes, at least on the basis of the commentaries now available. They applaud him not because he provides any insights into the meaning of Scripture but because he so fine-tuned the Antiochene hermeneutical principles and exegetical criteria that they could be applied in a rigorously critical way. His emphasis on determining a text's reliability, its historical context, and the actual intent of its author makes him the exegete in patristic times who comes closest to our present-day scholarly standards.

What is especially fascinating in Theodore's approach is how his general systematic theological synthesis became blended with his exegesis. While one can question how much his theoretical view has affected his interpretations, it is evident that Theodore came to his systematic outlook on the basis of what he found present in Scripture itself. The elements he uncovered there were woven into a coherent pattern that seemed to him to fulfill the basic beliefs of Christianity. This in turn assisted him when he came to exegete a scriptural text. He applied his critical reason to understand the author's intent in light of his theological synthesis and was ready to break with other Fathers, even his own Antiochene compatriots, if the situation so required. His strong-willed, independent cast of mind bowed only before the Scriptures, conciliar decrees, and the power of a well-ordered reason.

So with this general awareness of how the Antiochenes approach a scriptural passage in light of their hermeneutical principles, we turn now to scrutinize in more detail how the Antiochenes explained the Genesis and the Pauline passages regarding the "image of God."

2

THE ANTIOCHENE TRADITION REGARDING

THE "IMAGE OF GOD"

HE PREVIOUS CHAPTER has provided some knowledge of the exegetical tradition and methods that the Antiochene Fathers employed. We move now to the heart of our concern: how they interpreted the meaning of the phrase "to be made in the image according to the likeness of God" (Gen. 1:26). Like all the other Fathers, they treated this verse as though it were a rich mine from which one could unearth invaluable nuggets of theological and anthropological truths. They judged this to be a revealed, and therefore dependable, source from which they could delve into such questions as: what are the elemental relationships between God and humans beings, between men and women, and between humans and the rest of creation, and how creatures can come to know who is their God and what are the ways to encounter God in life. Yet while the Fathers have generally agreed that human beings have been truly gifted with a uniquely privileged position within the created universe because of their being created in God's image, they offered widely divergent views as to how humans image God and where actually this image can be said to reside within themselves.

The Antiochene outlook regarding image contrasts notably, at least in emphasis, with what the Alexandrian School and Augustine espoused. It is also one rarely, if ever, mentioned in theological literature, though it coheres with the current understanding of most exegetes of the Jewish Scriptures, who interpret the passage as portraying the royal function of humans as God's representatives in the world.[1] Our probe will begin with a survey of what contemporary exegetes hold to be the meaning of the phrase to be created "in the image according to the likeness of God." Then in order to provide a background against which the Antiochene, especially Theodore's, viewpoint can be compared and contrasted, Irenaeus's outlook will be presented in some detail. This will be followed by the Antiochene understanding of image, with the emphasis centered upon Theodore's opinion because it is both highly complex and the one that is most stimulating theologically.

Contemporary Scriptural Exegesis

In their commentaries on Genesis 1:26–27, scriptural exegetes today discuss, generally speaking, three interrelated issues: (1) the meaning of the terms "image" and "likeness" in Hebrew; (2) the origin of the terms, and (3) their possible meaning in the Genesis passage. Because the primary focus of this study is not scriptural, our main interest is to present the opinions of those scholars who can be cited as spokespersons for the major interpretations of what the redactor of Genesis actually intended when he introduced the term "image" into the Genesis text.[2]

First, Geoffrey Bromiley in *The International Standard Bible Encyclopedia* believes that the Hebrew words for "image" and "likeness" are an example of what he calls to be a "synonymous parallelism," where the words do not differ in meaning from one another.[3] Reginald Fuller, however, sees particular

1. See J. Richard Middleton, "The Liberating Image? Interpreting the *Imago Dei* in Context," *Christian Scholar's Review* 24 (Sept. 1994): 13. He believes that "the last thirty years have seen the royal interpretation of the imago Dei come virtually to monopolize the field."

2. For contemporary works other than the standard biblical commentaries, dictionaries, and encyclopedias, see the references contained in Middleton, 8–25.

3. Geoffrey W. Bromiley, gen. ed., *The International Standard Bible Encyclopedia* 2 (Grand Rapids, Mich.: Eerdmans, 1979), 803. A similar conclusion is found in N. W. Porteous's article on "Image, Imagery" in *The Interpreter's Dictionary of the Bible*, gen. ed. George A. Buttrick (New York: Abingdon, 1962), 3:683. Porteous writes: "The linguistic evidence which has been thus summarily reviewed would suggest that there is not much difference in meaning between the two nouns or, indeed, as used here, between the two particles." From this he concludes: "This disposes of the dogmatic interpretation which

nuances in the two terms, with the Hebrew word for "image" (ṣelem) denoting an exact reproduction or duplicate of another, and the word for "likeness" (dĕmût) signifying a resemblance.[4] He regards the term "likeness," therefore, as both qualifying and restricting the meaning of "image." According to him, the author or redactor of Genesis is asserting that Adam is to be looked upon as a "copy" of God, but not exactly so. While asserting that other usages in the Hebrew Bible oppose Fuller's interpretation, Walter Vogels thinks: "The word [dĕmût] suggests a likeness between the role of God as creator and the human role as pro-creator. The word ṣelem on the other hand is more concerned with power and stresses that the human person shares in the power of God."[5] In Vogels' understanding, the two words connote the double function God has entrusted humans: to procreate and co-create with Him, with the mission of transmitting "this likeness to new partners with whom God can continue to communicate."[6]

As regards the origin of the term "image," Edward Curtis in his article on the "Image of God" in *The Anchor Bible Dictionary* points out that in Egyptian and Mesopotamian literatures, the image of a god was looked upon not as the "picture" of a particular god but as a temple, where this god could be both encountered and truly worshiped.[7] If the image were

---

goes back to Justin and Irenaeus that the 'צלם' is reason, which man retained after the Fall, whereas 'דמות' is 'justitia originalis,' which he lost." For a detailed study on what the prepositions "in" and "according to" mean in the context of the three Genesis passages dealing with "image" and "likeness," see Walter Vogels, "The Human Person in the Image of God (Gn 1,26)," Science et Esprit 44/2 (1994): 190–92. His conclusion is: "This suggests, as most scholars accept, that there is no real difference between the two prepositions and that the meaning of the two terms is not influenced by the preposition used" (192).

4. Bruce Vawter, "Genesis," in *A New Catholic Commentary on Holy Scripture*, gen. ed. Reginald C. Fuller (New York: Nelson, 1969), 175. The same view is expressed in R. Clifford and Roland Murphy's exegesis of Gen. 1:26–27 in the *New Jerome Biblical Commentary*, ed. Raymond Brown et al. (Englewood Cliffs, N.J.: Prentice, 1990), 11–13; and also Edward Curtis's article "Image of God" in *The Anchor Bible Dictionary*, ed. David Noel Freedman (New York: Doubleday, 1992), 3:389–91.

5. Vogels, 194.

6. Ibid., 201.

7. Curtis, 389–91. For a brief summary of how the Egyptian and Mesopotamian understanding of image as referring to the king may have evolved to become part of Genesis, see John L. McKenzie's entry on "image" in his *Dictionary of the Bible* (New York: Collier, 1965), 384; Jacques Fantino, *L'homme image de Dieu chez saint Irénée de Lyon* (Paris: Cerf, 1986), 43–44; Middleton, 18–21; and Lily Ross Taylor, *The Divinity of the Roman Emperor* (Middleton, Conn.: American Philological Assoc., 1931).

not present, then no cult could be offered, but on those occasions when it was, the worshipers would employ a morning ceremony, called the "Opening of the Mouth." By means of this rite, they believed that they could ritually animate the image and thus be able to present their cult and petitions to their god. Curtis suggests that this cultic practice may explain the background looming behind Genesis 2:7 in which God is said to have fashioned the figure of a "man" out of the clay of the ground and then animated it by breathing life into it.[8]

Closely allied with this practice is the ancient Egyptian and Mesopotamian view that considered the pharaoh or king to be either an embodiment of god or his unique representative and thus an image of the god. It is an attitude present in the Roman emperor worship and perhaps even in Jewish and Christian times where king and emperor were thought to be God's specially anointed.[9] In fact, it may underlie the viewpoint that regarded the violent smashing of the emperor Theodosius I's image during the tax revolt at Antioch in 387 as a regal and personal offense. If the author of Genesis had in mind the ancient regal understanding of image when he declared that Adam was created in God's image and likeness, he would, of course, be adapting it to convey the meaning that all human beings, and not merely the king, stand in a special, unique relationship to God. Because the Jews looked upon Yahweh as a transcendent God, the author's intent would be to portray the functional role that humans are to play within creation. They would be, as it were, the "place" where all other creatures could come in contact with God and offer their worship. If this is the author's purpose, then the meaning of the phrase "the image of God" has less to do with

---

(Paris: Cerf, 1986), 43–44; Middleton, 18–21; and Lily Ross Taylor, *The Divinity of the Roman Emperor* (Middleton, Conn.: American Philological Assoc., 1931).

8. Curtis holds that it was fear of idolatry that prevented the use of the term "image" in the period before the Exile. But afterwards, when idolatry was no longer a problem, Jewish writers were free to employ the imagery. Curtis writes: "In the new religious context created by the Exile and return, the 'image of God' motif was again taken up and developed both in the intertestamental period and in the NT" (391).

9. For an analysis of image as a mandate to rule, see Middleton, 13–25. In 12 n. 11, he makes an important distinction between the overwhelming agreement today by Jewish and Christian scripture scholars on a royal interpretation of Genesis 1:26–27 and the reasons they advance for this interpretation. He then proceeds to enumerate how feminists, environmentalists, and those opposed to the *status quo* strongly object to this today. For a study relating the Roman imperial cult to the divinity of kings in the Near East, see the appendices in Taylor.

what God looks like than with the position and role humans play in the created order of things.[10] In other words, the term "image" in Genesis 1:26–27 is to be understood in not a graphic but a cultic, functional sense—a sense, as we will see, that mirrors Theodore of Mopsuestia's opinion.

While Curtis's interpretation offers an interesting possible explanation of the literary background of the term "image" in Genesis, it is still not clear in what precise way the author of Genesis understood how human beings image God. In his article in *The Interpreter's Dictionary of the Bible*,[11] N. W. Porteous notes that physical resemblance cannot be totally excluded. For Adam is said in Genesis 5:3 to have given birth to Seth, "in his likeness, after his image." Yet as John McKenzie in his *Dictionary of the Bible* points out, the Jews of ancient times considered it be almost an article of faith that any attempt to picture Yahweh by an image was rejected, for it was tantamount to reducing him to the level of nature and thus bringing him down to the level of the gods who were worshiped through images.[12] Yet this did not prevent the Hebrew sacred writers from affirming that God manifested Himself as well as His will through human beings, such as the prophets, and also through events, such as the Exodus.

Porteous lists a variety of possibilities of how human beings can be said to image God in several purely spiritual ways: because of their "personality," "self-consciousness," "self-determination," "reason," "ability to pass judgment," "freedom of the will," "moral capacity" and "immortality."[13] In commenting on the interpretation of the way "image" is used in Ezekiel, Porteous observes that for Ezekiel "the image of God means personality, provided we remember this must not be understood in the sense of the autonomous, self-legislating self of the philosophers."[14] He believes that this may be significant because Ezekiel was a priest and all the references to image in Genesis belong to the priestly tradition. McKenzie also offers a similar view: "In the OT Yahweh is distinguished from the other gods by the designation 'living;' He is an extremely vigorous and sharply defined personality who plans, desires, achieves, and responds

10. Curtis, 391.   11. Porteous, 683.
12. McKenzie, 384.   13. Porteous, 683.
14. Ibid., 684. The present emphasis fits in with Karl Barth's psychological interpretation that regards image as signifying the personal capacity of human beings to be addressed by and respond to God's Word. For a summary of Barth's and the Reformed perspective on image, see Anthony A. Hoekema, *Created in God's Image* (Grand Rapids, Mich.: Eerdmans, 1986), 42–65.

personally to the words and deeds of men. In this 'living' quality man resembles Him."[15] To sum up both views in another way, humans image
God by their ability to relate to others in a vital, rational, and free way
and can become thereby immortal in body as well as in soul.

Other scholars refuse to apply "the image of God" to human spiritual
faculties.[16] Fuller maintains that the author of Genesis would not possess
our understanding of the human psyche and would therefore find it impossible to comprehend how image can be said to relate to the rational
soul and its faculties. He insists that "it is man himself, not merely his nature, that is in the image and likeness of God; the author's conception is
existential rather than essential."[17] In other words, it is the whole person
who is in the image of God rather than some specific aspect to the exclusion of others. According to Curtis, such a holistic view of image is truly
"consistent with the way humanity is viewed throughout the Hebrew
Bible."[18] It is a Semitic outlook that the Antiochenes also share.

In his article, "The Image of God: Masculine, Feminine, or Neuter?"
Henry F. Lazenby offers an interesting interpretation of how image refers
to the whole human nature. He combines Genesis 1:27a "God created
man in his image; in the divine image he created him;" with 1:27b "male
and female he created them."[19] He suggests that image is applicable to
"humankind" not only in a generic sense but as male and female cooper-
ating with one another in such a way that their working together effects a
true unity of purpose and of meaning. Moreover since all possess within
themselves masculine and feminine qualities, both need to be integrated,

15. McKenzie, 385.

16. Middleton laments that "A simple word study would thus lead to the preliminary
observation that visibility and bodiliness are minimally a necessary condition of being *tse-
lem elohim* or *imago Dei*" (11). For another detailed study of this from the perspective of
how the ancient Jews understood person, see Graham J. Warne, *Hebrew Perspectives on the
Human Person in the Hellenistic Era: Philo and Paul* (Lewiston, N.Y.: Mellen, 1995), 55–85.

17. Fuller, 175. In his exegetical commentary in *A Catholic Commentary on Holy Scripture*, ed. B. Orchard, et al. (New York: Nelson, 1953), E. F. Sutcliffe reminds us that "in the
Old Testament categories soul and body are so intimately one that the body is the soul
in its outward form, its external expression" (183).

18. Curtis, 390. For a modern Jewish interpretation that includes the body within
the notion of image, see Byron L. Sherwin, "The Human Body and the Image of God,"
in *A Traditional Quest* (Sheffield, England: Sheffield Academic, 1991), 75–85. He shows
how this viewpoint is a direct rejection of medieval Jewish thought on image.

19. Henry F. Lazenby, "The Image of God: Masculine, Feminine, or Neuter?" *Journal of the Evangelical Theological Society* 30.1 (Mar. 1987): 66–67.

if a person is to become fully human and thus able to enter into a relationship with God.[20] Vogels dismisses such an interpretation, noting that at the beginning of Genesis 5, Adam is referred to as a person fashioned in the likeness of God who has sired his son Seth according to his image (Gen. 5:3). He insists that image is assigned to human nature as such, and not in a collective sense to men and women together.[21]

Pauline Understanding of Image

A change of view toward the meaning of "image" occurs in the New Testament, particularly in the Pauline writings. Saint Paul employed the term in reference to Christ "who is the image of God" (2 Cor. 4:4). Porteous sums up the significance of this, when he notes: "Nothing could make clearer the tremendous impact of the revelation of God in Christ than the fact it has almost completely obliterated the thought of man as being in the image of God and replaced it with the thought of Christ as being the image of God, that being understood in the sense of perfect correspondence to the divine prototype."[22] He elaborates upon this by noting how "Paul's identification of Christ with man as "in the image of God" of Gen. 1:26 springs, not from a cosmological, but from a soteriological, concern."[23] In other words, "image" for Paul refers not to Christ's pre-existence as "the image of the invisible God, the first-born of all creation" (Col. 1:15), but to the primary and central role that Christ plays in the achievement of human salvation and final glory. As will be seen, this is an outlook that Theodore has adopted.

Yet there are authentic passages in Paul where he looks upon humans as also being made "in the image of God," understanding it to be a dynamic element within a person that grows towards fulness as one becomes more "conformed to the image of his Son" (Rom. 8:29) and "transformed into the same image from glory to glory" (2 Cor. 3:18). McKenzie interprets these two passages as stating that the "image of glory" is "not to be found only in the attributes of grace and virtue, but ultimately in the resurrection which alters the physical form of man also into the glory of Christ."[24] So while conceiving the dignity of image as assigned primarily

---

20. Lazenby, 66–67.

21. See Vogels, 198–201 and also 201–2 for a bibliography on how image can be interpreted in a royal sense.

22. Porteous, 684.   23. Ibid.

24. McKenzie, 385.

to Christ, Paul does acknowledge that it can also be attributed to other human beings and indicative of the glory that is awaiting them at their bodily resurrection in a future life. Or to state this differently, humans may be "images of God" in a typical sense but Christ is the archetype.

Summary

This brief overview of contemporary exegesis seeks to make one point, namely how extremely rich in content and vague in meaning is the phrase that Adam was formed "in the image and likeness of God." The same wide divergence of opinions is encountered in the opinions of several leading Fathers who have attempted to incorporate image into their theological syntheses. They divided into two camps in regard to image. The first proposed that it is a spiritual reality residing in the highest reaches of the rational soul,[25] for under the influence of Neoplatonic thought, they believed that one can reflect and share in God's transcendent nature only in a spiritual way. This led them to regard image as either a state or an ability to become more like unto God, in a word "divinized," by means of contemplating the Word and acting like God. While this viewpoint has helped to develop an understanding of grace, it also resulted in an unintended downside: it effectively minimized the role that God intends the human body to play in the economy of salvation.[26] It is

25. For a study of how Origen understood image, see Henri Crouzel, *Théologie de l'image de Dieu chez Origène Théologie* 34 (Paris: Aubier, 1957); and for a study on the role that the "image of God" later played in the Origenist controversy, see Elizabeth A. Clark, *The Origenist Controversy* (Princeton: Princeton UP, 1992), 43–84; for Gregory of Nyssa, R. Leys, *L'image de Dieu chez Grégorie de Nysse: Esquisse d'une doctrine* (Paris: Desclée, 1951), and H. Merki, *Von der platonischen Angleichung an Gott zur Gottähnlichkeit bei Gregor von Nyssa*, Paradosis 7 (Freiburg: Paulusverlag, 1952); for Cyril of Alexandria, Walter J. Burghardt, *The Image of God in Man according to Cyril of Alexandria* (Washington: Catholic University of America Press, 1957); and for Augustine, John E. Sullivan, *The Image of God: The Doctrine of St. Augustine and Its Influence* (Dubuque: Priory, 1963). For summaries of these view from the early church, see Lars Thunberg, "The Human Person as Image of God," *Christian Spirituality: Origins to the Twelfth Century* 1, ed. B. McGinn and J. Meyendorff (New York: Crossroad, 1985): 291–312; and especially A.-G. Hamman, *L'homme, image de Dieu* (Paris: Desclée, 1987) and George A. Maloney, *Man the Divine Icon* (Pecos, N.M.: Dove, 1973).

26. For a summary of the Alexandrian and Cappadocian views as to what role the body plays, see Lars Thunberg, *Microcosm and Mediator: The Theological Anthropology of Maximus the Confessor*, 2d ed. (Chicago: Open Court, 1995), 113–18. McGinn, *Christian*

against this kind of spiritual outlook that the Antiochenes, in particular Theodore, have written in defense of the body playing a primary and essential role within one's understanding of image.

The Antiochene Tradition

While those belonging to the Alexandrian school were heavily influenced by Philo's Platonic views regarding the human being as a soul existing in a body and his distinction between the "first" and "second" creations (supposedly described in Chapters One and Two of Genesis), the Antiochene tradition, which was scripturally and semitically based, offered a far different theological view.[27] It maintained that humans were a unified composite of body and soul and identified the "image of God," not as Philo did with the "first" creation, but with the person of clay fashioned at the "second" creation.[28] It is about this latter view—which has two different em-

---

Spirituality, states well the weakness of those who exclude or minimize the role of the body within image: "The concentration on the soul, or inner person, as the true image and the difficulties that thinkers in this tradition had in expressing the substantial union of body and soul led to systematic ambiguities that encouraged depreciation of the body and sometimes skewed the sanity of ascetical observances" (328). Middleton also affirms the same view: "Although few modern interpreters come to the Genesis text with the ascetic predilections of Origen or Augustine, nevertheless this unwarranted limitation of the image continues to perpetuate an implicit devaluation of the concrete life of the body in relation to spirituality" (11). The same can be said of Anthony A. Hoekema's outlook on image in *Created in God's Image*. Although he argues that image refers to the whole human composite and insists that it has a structural as well as a functional sense, he says little about the body's role. He sums up his view: "The image of God in man must therefore be seen as involving both the structure of man (his gifts, capacities, and endowments) and the functioning of man (his actions, his relationships to God and to others, and the way he uses his gifts)" (73).

27. It should be noted too that not all those belonging to the Alexandrian tradition held the same position as Origen regarding the location and meaning of image. Procopius of Gaza (465–530), an opponent of Theodoret, for one held an outlook similar to Theodore's regarding human beings as the bond of the universe and the symbolic representative of God to whom all the rest of creation must show reverence and service. See Procopius, PG 87:123.

28. This may also explain why in their exegetical interpretation that the Antiochenes are suspicious of what they believe to be an over-emphasis upon the spiritual or allegorical meaning of a text to the detriment of its "bodily" meaning. For a brief summary of those early Fathers who held that image refers to the whole human person, see Burghardt, *Image of God in Man*, 15–19. I believe his statement including Chrysostom

52

phases—that now needs to be considered.[29] However, before these are addressed, it will first be helpful to highlight the thought of Irenaeus because of his similarity with what will be encountered in Theodore.

Irenaeus

Irenaeus was born around the middle of the second century and is acclaimed to be the outstanding theologian of his era.[30] In his letter to Florinus,[31] he asserted in intimate, first-hand details that he had listened as a youth to Bishop Polycarp of Smyrna. This definitely suggests that he was born in or around Smyrna, but more importantly, his statements about Polycarp being familar with John and others who had seen the Lord indicate that he was aware of the apostolic teaching.[32] Sources also report Irenaeus was a presbyter at Lyons in Gaul who was sent to Rome to mediate a question about Montanism. Upon his return to Lyons, he succeeded Photinus as the bishop of the city. Later he sought to reconcile Pope Victor with Asiatic bishops over the date of Easter. He is reported by a late (and questionable) document to have died as a martyr.[33]

Irenaeus's major surviving work, the *Adversus haereses*,[34] is an important patristic document. Besides being useful for the data it provides about

among those who "exclude the body from a share in the image" (18) needs to be nuanced. Chrysostom regards image as a power entrusted to men as such, including their bodies.

29. While the ante-Nicene Fathers strongly maintained that humans were created in the image of God in a non-anthropomorphic way, they reveal very little elaboration on this subject, at least in those works presently available to us. A few, (e.g. Cyprian's *De Bono Patientiae* in PL 4:634; and Lactantius's *Divinae Institutiones* in the *Corpus Scriptorum Ecclesiasticorum Latinorum* 19, [Lipsiae: G. Freytag, 1890], 147) refer to the whole person as being made in the image of God, but without explaining what they mean by "image" and "likeness."

30. For two contemporary studies regarding Irenaeus's views on image, see Hamman, 49–76, and Fantino.

31. An English translation of the most pertinent part of the letter is found in Johannes Quasten, *Patrology*, 4 vols. (Westminster, Md.: Christian Classics, 1986), 1:287.

32. See A. Roberts and J. Donaldson, ed., *Ante-Nicene Fathers* (Christian Literature Publishing, 1885; reprint, Peabody, Mass.: Hendrickson, 1994), 1:416.

33. Quasten, 1:288.

34. For the critical edition, see Adelin Rousseau and Louis Doutreleau, eds., *Contre les Hérésies* Book 4, SC 100.1 and 2; Book 5, SC 152–53; Book 3, SC 210–11; Book 1, SC 263–64; Book 2, SC 293–94 (Paris: Cerf, 1965, 1969, 1974, 1979, and 1982). All the following citations to *Adversus haereses* will simply state the book, chapter, and section numbers.

the Gnostic belief systems, it is invaluable for the present study, as it indicates what was being taught at the end of the apostolic period regarding "image." Irenaeus is acknowledged, moreover—despite his skepticism towards speculative theology—to be the first Christian theologian to formulate a coherent, dogmatic synthesis. In addition to this, his understanding of *imago Dei* is of interest because he is thought to have relied upon the anti-Gnostic works of Theophilus of Antioch.[35] While this is difficult to prove because these works of Theophilus have not survived, there are a number of similar points between both Irenaeus and Theodore's understanding of humans as God's image (but not their opinions on likeness). Their concurrence may point to the presence of a common tradition, possibly coming from Antioch[36] or to Theodore's possible dependance or familiarity with Irenaeus's and Theophilus's writings.

In his treatment of Irenaeus's remarks about Adam being created according to God's image and likeness, Jules Gross begins by noting how Irenaeus has often employed the terms "image" and "likeness" as synonyms.[37] But when Irenaeus responded to the Gnostic belief that material beings image the thirty eons present in the Pleroma,[38] he did distinguish between the two terms, as Jacques Fantino in his detailed analysis of Irenaeus's passages on image and likeness shows.[39] By his denial that the material world can correspond with the spiritual world in the Pleroma, Irenaeus indicated that he considered "image" to be a material reality possessing a visible form either the same as or similar to one present in its exemplar. Since a purely spiritual being cannot be imaged in a quantitative way—seeing that it is immaterial and invisible—this means that a spiritual being can be truly imaged only when it is united with a material

---

35. For a discussion of this, see Friedrich Loofs, *Theophilus von Antiochien Adversus Marcionem und die anderen theologischen Quellen bei Irenaeus*, Texte und Untersuchungen 46 (Leipzig: J. C. Hinrichs, 1930) and R. F. M. Hitchcock, "Loofs' Theory of Theophilus of Antioch as a Source of Irenaeus," *Journal of Theological Studies* 38 (1937): 130–39 and 255–265, as well as a summary in Quasten, 290.

36. See Hamman, 75.

37. Jules Gross, *La divinisation de chrétien d'apres les pères grecs* (Paris: Gabalda, 1938), 145.

38. For a discussion of Valentinian's view of the 30 eons, see Hamman, 50–53.

39. Fantino, 82. In his first chapter, he summarizes well the Jewish, Gnostic, and early Christian writers' views on image. See also Hamman, 9–61 for his summaries of the scriptural, Gnostic, Alexandrian, Cappadocian, and Latin positions and an analysis of the principal comments by Irenaeus regarding image and likeness in Books 3 and 4 of the *Adversus haereses*.

body,[40] as in the case of the human soul being joined with its body. This is also expressed in Irenaeus's explanation of why no one could discern how humans image God, for the reason became evident only after the Word became visible in flesh.[41]

> In the past, man was said to have been made to the image of God, but this was not apparent. For the Word according to whose image man was made was still invisible. It is for this [reason] that he easily lost his likeness.[42]

"Image," therefore, refers to a material being that is similar to the reality that it is revealing because of some trait or form that it has in common with its exemplar, such as between a statue and its model.[43] But Irenaeus also understood image in a broader way when he regarded events and persons in the Old Testament as being images of Christ and his church.[44] Taken in this sense, image can therefore be thought to be equivalent to a type prefiguring its prototype. While the image present in a statue is a concrete form like to or similar to what can be discerned within another reality, an image-type affirms, in a derived sense, the existence of a some kind of correspondence or special relationship between the type and its archetype, such as Adam being an image of Christ.[45]

In addition to being visibly able to reveal and represent its exemplar or archetype, an image can furthermore connote the process that was involved in the way an image was fashioned;[46] e.g. a son who inherits from his parents characteristics similar to their own. Taking into account these understandings of image, Fantino affirms that Irenaeus has conceived of image as an anthropological category that attests to a relationship existing between a visible, material being and its prototype, a relationship that is not coincidental but intentionally caused by God.[47] When image is applied to Adam, Irenaeus understood it as referring to the whole of human nature: "For by the hands of the Father, that is by the Son and the Holy Spirit, man, and not [merely] a part of man, was made in the likeness of

---

40. See Fantino, 83 and 88–91; and also Hamman, 67.

41. See Hamman, 64–65.

42. *Adversus haereses*, 5:16:2. The translation here and in the following citations are my own.

43. See Fantino, 99.

44. See ibid., 95–96.

45. See ibid., 96–97 and 99. This understanding of image as a type most likely underlies the Antiochene view regarding a type.

46. See ibid., 91.

47. See ibid., 89.

God. Now the soul and the spirit are certainly a part of man, but certainly not the [whole] man."[48]

Image points, therefore, to the whole human nature that Adam and all other humans share with the incarnate Word's humanity. Since it refers to what is natural to all human beings, it was not "lost" at the moment Adam sinned.

But when the Spirit joined with the soul is united to [God's] handiwork, the man made in the image and likeness of God became spiritual and perfect because of the outpouring of the Spirit. However if the Spirit is absent from the soul, he who is such is indeed of an animal nature and, being left carnal, will be imperfect. For the one possessing the image of God in his formation but without receiving the likeness from the Spirit is an imperfect being.[49]

Before discussing what Irenaeus meant when he refers to humans having a "likeness" with God, one needs to consider how he regarded humans having a "similitude" with God. Fantino believes that Irenaeus understood this latter term as affirming the general, analogous correspondence that can be said to be present between a human being and God.[50] For example, human beings can be said to be reasonable and free in ways that are analogous to how God acts. Fantino links these abilities to act freely and reasonably with the cooperative role humans have been called to play in the attainment of their own salvation.[51] But since these abilities to act in ways analogous to God's are natural to humans, they too have remained, as image has, after Adam sinned and lost his likeness to God but in diminished form.[52]

While Irenaeus looked upon image as signifying the same human nature all of humanity shares with the incarnate Word, he regarded likeness as indicating the presence of a spiritual relationship to God. Fantino believes the meaning of the term can be found in one of the connotations that the Greek term *homoiōsis* can have: namely as an "assimilation."[53]

48. *Adversus haereses*, 5:6:1.

49. Ibid. For a study into the role of the Spirit in regard to Irenaeus's understanding of the *Imago Dei*, see James G. M. Purves, "The Spirit and the *Imago Dei*: Reviewing the Anthropology of Irenaeus of Lyons," *The Evangelical Quarterly* 68.2 (1996): 99–120.

50. See Fantino, 91 and 106–7.

51. See ibid., 116–17. See also Hamman's treatment of "image" and "liberty" on 69–71.

52. See Fantino, 117.

53. Ibid., 113. Fantino points out on 110–21 that there are many occasions when Irenaeus distinguished between *image* and *likeness*.

When understood in this sense, it signifies the process whereby someone can become "like" another. As applied to humans becoming assimilated to God, it signifies an individual's state of holiness that has been produced by God's Spirit. Since it is a gift bestowed by the Spirit justifying one spiritually in the eyes of God, it is not a state connatural to human nature and can be lost, if an individual does not remain obedient to God's will.[54] On the other hand, a person's "likeness" to God is also capable of undergoing a spiritual deepening of one's state of holiness.[55] One can now understand what Irenaeus means when he asserts that a person who lacks a likeness with God is imperfect. The "perfect" individual is one possessing both his natural and spiritual endowments.

For Irenaeus, it is because of Christ's relationship to the Father that humans have been able to recover their divine likeness, in addition to their liberation from Satan and death.[56] As long as an individual remains faithful to God, the Spirit will transform such a person progressively until he or she procures immortality, incorruptibility, filial adoption, and entrance into the kingdom of the Father.[57] This growth in one's likeness to Christ highlights the essential role that human freedom must play in the process. In other words, while a sharing in a likeness to God is ultimately a gift of the Holy Spirit, it presumes that there is also present a person's own collaboration and consent, if one's divine likeness is to be both acquired and maintained.[58]

When Fantino comes to interpret how having a likeness with God's Spirit enables one to become more like Christ, he illustrates it in terms of the Spirit dwelling within a person and elevating one to a state of divinization.[59] He understands this divinization not as removing, as did the pagans and Gnostics, the boundary line between a creating God and His creatures, so that one loses one's identity in God, but rather as raising a person to a level where one becomes a child of God. Although Irenaeus has never used the Greek word for divinization (*theopoiesis*), Johannes Quasten[60] and Jules Gross[61] believe with Fantino that his soteriological outlook implies this, particularly when he described becoming like unto God as a gift of

---

54. See Fantino, 116; and also Hamman, 68.
55. See Fantino, 116–17; and Hamman, 73–75.
56. See Fantino, 112–13.   57. See ibid., 117
58. See ibid., 104 and 117; and Quasten, 1:310.
59. See Fantino, 112–14.   60. Quasten, 1:311.
61. Gross, 158.

the Holy Spirit that enables humans to become "conformed to the Word of God." "By assuming the quality of the Spirit," humans are rendered "similar to the invisible Father."[62]

Granted that much depends upon what one means by divinization, it is important to distinguish here between a state where a person shares directly in God's life while maintaining at the same time one's own individual identity, and one where a person has acquired an immortal and an immutable life but one without an ontological participation in the divine life. As will be established later in Chapter Six, Theodore and Nestorius insist upon the latter, while denying the former. So while granting that Irenaeus has clearly affirmed that a person enjoying a likeness with God is spiritually related to God and can act in ways similar to Christ's that will entitle a person to live a future, immortal life as a child of God, it needs to be established that Irenaeus understood his view of being "like unto God" as stating what the Alexandrians, Gregory of Nyssa, and Augustine later meant by divinization.

The term "likeness," therefore, should be understood as having a soteriological significance.[63] While one's image with God cannot be lost because it connotes what all human beings possess by their nature, one's likeness with God can be lost and was lost by Adam. When this occurred, humans did not cease to be images of God who still function freely and reasonably. They have been able, however, to recover their likeness to God thanks to Christ in His role as the perfect image of God who possesses a true likeness with God.[64] While no one can attain the very same likeness to God that Christ enjoys as the Word incarnate, one can regain the likeness that Adam initially acquired at creation and grow in this divine likeness.[65] In brief, "likeness" in Irenaeus connotes a spiritual way of relating to God that differs from the way human nature images Christ as the second Adam.

Closely connected to Irenaeus's viewpoints on God's image and likeness is his teaching on recapitulation. This is a term and an idea that he borrowed from Saint Paul and made the centerpiece of his theology.[66] He understood recapitulation as Christ's gathering up of all human beings

---

62. Quasten (1:311) cites these three phrases without specifying their source. For an extended treatment of the point Quasten is making here, see Gross, 144–59.

63. See Fantino, 117–18 and 121.   64. See ibid., 89 and 115–16.

65. See ibid., 116–17; and Gross, 149–50.

66. See Quasten, 1:295–97; Fantino, 295; and Gross, 151.

within his own person, as Adam originally did, in a corporate sense. So when Adam sinned as the head, he caused the loss of God's likeness for all the rest of humanity. Similarly, Christ, by recapitulating the whole human race, has restored them to their original relationship of likeness with God. It is here one can discern how Irenaeus's understanding of the three terms "image," "similitude," and "likeness" are interrelated. It is because humans are by their human nature images of Christ that they can be said to become like unto God, provided that they live as Christ has done in obedience to God's will.

In brief, Irenaeus stands out in the early church as the first Father to develop a theology of "image." Relying upon Scripture and the Christian tradition for his data, he regarded image as applying to the whole of human nature insofar as it reveals and represents Christ as the incarnate Word. Because of his likeness with God and because of his recapitulation of all humanity within his person, Christ has been able to restore the spiritual relationship with God that Adam originally enjoyed but then lost with God. Other humans can also grow in their spiritual likeness with God, provided that they too freely consent to the lead of Christ's Spirit in their own lives. Their transformation into their likenesses will be fulfilled when they too achieve an incorruptible body in a future life.

Diodore

Very little is known about Diodore's early life, other than that he was born c.330 to a distinguished family in Antioch. He is believed to have first studied theology there under Eusebius of Emesa and then undertaken a classical education at Athens.[67] On his return to Antioch, he became, in succession, a monk, then a priest c.362, and afterwards the head of a monastery in or around Antioch. It was about this time that Chrysostom and Theodore began their studies under Diodore. In 372 Diodore was banished to Armenia and, while there, carried on a correspondence with Basil the Great. Upon the death of Valens, he returned in 378 to Antioch and was shortly afterwards chosen to be the bishop of Tarsus. In this capacity, he attended the Council of Constantinople in 381. After his death in c.394,

---

67. For a treatment of Diodore's life and works, see Quasten, 3:397–401; and Christoph Schäublin, *Theologische Realenzyklopädie*, ed. F. Shumann and M. Wolter (Berlin: de Gruyter, 1990), 8:763–67.

his reputation for being an outstanding pillar of faith was assailed.[68] Cyril of Alexandria accused Diodore and Theodore as precursors of Nestorianism. Except for his works on the Psalms and possibly on Astronomy and several pages of fragments[69], almost all his vast literary output was destroyed after his condemnation in 499.

From the few fragments that have survived from Diodore's vast corpus, there is one that discusses his understanding of image.[70] Granted that it is indeed authentic and that Diodore's thought can be judged by a single passage, it reveals that he understood image as being a function that God bestows upon man *qua* male.

How, then, is man (ἄνθρωπος) God's image? [It is] by his ability to rule and exercise authority. The voice of God is the witness [to this], saying: "Let us make man (ἄνθρωπος) according to our image and likeness," and adding the way [this is so] "and let them rule over the fish of the sea and the birds of the air and the beasts of the earth" etc. Therefore just as God governs over all, so does man (ἄνθρωπος) govern over earthly beings. What then? Does the woman not also rule over the aforementioned? Though governing all others, the woman, nevertheless, has man (ἀνήρ) as her head. The man (ἀνήρ) is not subject to the woman. The blessed Paul rightly says that only man (ἀνήρ)is the image and glory of God, while woman is but the glory of man (ἀνήρ).[71]

For Diodore, therefore, image refers to the power that God has bestowed upon humans to rule in His place over the material world. He based his interpretation on the verse in Genesis that follows the statement that man (ἄνθρωπος *qua* human being) has been created in God's image and likeness. It contains God's command to Adam and Eve to govern material creatures as His authoritative proxies on earth. While this right to exercise dominative power is basically spiritual, it is not found to be inherent in the soul as such. It is rather a personal office delegated fully to men *qua* males. Diodore believed that Paul affirmed this when he designated man *qua* male to be God's image and women "the glory of man."

68. For a fair treatment of what can be gleaned about Diodore's thought, see D. S. Wallace-Hadrill, *Christian Antioch: A Study of Early Christian Thought in the East* (Cambridge: Cambridge UP, 1982), 119–22.

69. Rudolf Abramowski has published these in "Der Theologische Nachlass des Diodor von Tarsus," *Zeitschrift für die neutestamentliche Wissenschaft* 42 (1949): 19–69.

70. Diodore, PG 80:107–10.

71. Ibid., 33:1564–65.

John Chrysostom

Despite being unparalleled in the number of biographies written about him, very little is known about John Chrysostom's (c.350–407) early life. He was born into a well-to-do Christian family, his father being a high government official who died when he was but an infant. His mother insisted upon his acquiring a good education. He most likely studied under the leading rhetorical teachers of his day, the pagan Libanius.[72] After he was baptised, he joined the inner circle surrounding the bishop Meletius, Flavian, and Diodore, until he felt more and more inspired to live a life dedicated to perfection. He left Antioch for a mountain outside the city where he spent four years under the guidance of a monk and afterwards two more years by himself.[73] During this time, he so immersed himself in Scripture that he is said to have known every verse from memory.

When his health seriously deteriorated, Chrysostom realized he had to return to Antioch for the care he needed. After his condition improved, he was ordained a deacon by Meletius in 381; and a priest by Flavian in 386.[74] Over the next ten years, his eloquent, dramatic sermons and his passionate zeal as a religious reformer quickly gained for him widespread acclaim throughout the Christian world. His fame made him the Emperor Arcadius's (395–408) choice to be the patriarch of Constantinople when this office needed to be filled in 398. When he was installed, he immediately provoked a firestorm of critical opposition because of his sermons on social justice and the reforms that he tried to implement. His enemies spanned a wide spectrum of outraged and influential figures,[75] such as the

72. For a discussion of whether Chrysostom studied under Libanius, see Chrysostomus Baur, *John Chrysostom and His Time*, trans. M. Gonzaga, 2 vols. (Westminster, Md.: Newman, 1959–60), 1:22–28.

73. For summary of Chrysostom's time as a monk, see Baur, 1:104–14.

74. Socrates (*Historia ecclesiastica*, trans. A. C. Zenos, NPNF, Second Series, ed. Philip Schaff and Henry Wace, [1890; reprint, Peabody, Mass.: Hendrickson, 1994], 2:139) asserts that Chrysostom was ordained a priest/presbyter by Evagrius, the successor of bishop Paulinus. This is difficult to justify, since Chrysostom preached in the major basilica which was at that time under Flavian's control.

75. Socrates, 139–40 and 144–51; Sozomen, 403–9; and Theodoret, *Ecclesiastical History*, NPNF, Second Series (1892; reprint, Peabody, Mass: Hendrickson, 1994), 3:152–53. Socrates records many instances where he believes that Chrysostom's peremptory and caustic manner of dealing with his adversaries was a contributing factor to his

Empress Eudoxia, prominent bishops, and disaffected monks. These banded together to depose him in 403. But after one day, widespread popular discontent compelled the Emperor Arcadius to revoke the decree expelling him. Then in the following year, his opponents succeeded in driving him from office by accusing him of having assumed, after his previous deposition, the patriarchical chair without official authorization to do so.[76] He died during a forced march which seems to have been deliberately ordered to fatally weaken his frail health.

View of Image

John Chrysostom espoused the same understanding of image as did Diodore: "[man (ἄνθρωπος)] is said to be the image in light of his preeminence and dominion, not for any other reason. For God made him to rule over everything on the earth. There is nothing greater than man (ἄνθρωπος). For all things are under his power."[77] He also excluded the possibility that image is spiritual in nature, for this would mean that angels who are invisible would have to be called images.[78] Though Chrysostom spoke of men (qua ἀνήρ) alone as being the image of God, he qualified this in other places by noting that man's "image of God" strictly speaking applies only to Christ. In a response to the query "who is the image of God," he stated: "Take care to assign [this] to Christ alone. For as you see the Father through him, then if you ignore his glory, you will also have no knowledge at all of the Father's glory."[79] Chrysostom made, however, no attempt to elaborate on how Adam and Christ are related to each other as the image of God or more specifically why God had empowered Adam to rule on earth as His image. The topic appears not to have been a serious concern for him. We will consider in a later chapter how Chrysostom viewed the role of women in this governance.

---

downfall. Theodoret asserts that Chrysostom was wronged. But out of personal respect for "the high character of those who wronged him," he did not wish to give names.

76. See Socrates, 150, and Sozomen, 412. On the day that Chrysostom was being forced into exile, some of John's supporters are said to have set fire to the church near the senate-house.

77. Chrysostom, PG 53:72. The same idea is expressed also in PG 53:78: "[Image] refers not to the dignity of one's substance, but to a kind of dominion."

78. Ibid., 62:317–18.

79. Ibid., 61:456.

Theodore of Mopsuestia

Of all the Antiochenes, Theodore of Mopsuestia (c.350–428) is considered to be the foremost exemplar of their theological teaching.[80] Very little can be said about his early life, other than that he was born c.350.[81] He apparently was a fellow student and close friend of Chrysostom at the school of Libanius. The two became monks under the guidance of Diodore and Carterius. Some time later when Theodore's ardor for the ascetical life had cooled, he left. However, he was persuaded, so it seems, by a letter from Chrysostom urging him to return.[82] He was eventually ordained a priest by bishop Flavian in 383 and remained at Antioch until 392 when he was appointed bishop of Mopsuestia. He died in 428, generally respected for his learning and orthodoxy.

After his posthumous condemnation in 553 at the Second Council of Constantinople, almost all his writings were lost, except for a few works that have survived in Syriac translations and one Latin commentary that was attributed to Ambrose.[83] Various fragments that reveal his thought concerning the meaning of image have also survived in Greek.[84] Since the ideas contained in this Greek manuscript correspond with those found in Theodore's surviving writings and in the later works of Syriac writers who have acknowledged their dependence upon him, there seems to be no reason for not accepting this ninth-century florilegium as authentic. Françoise Petit, however, notes one failing on the part of the redactor: He was "more careful in his calligraphy than in his orthography or grammar"—

---

80. For a critical summary of his theology, see Aloys Grillmeier, *Christ in Christian Tradition From the Apostolic Age to Chalcedon (451)*, trans. J. S. Bowden, 2d rev. ed. (Atlanta: John Knox, 1975), 421–39.

81. For a treatment of Theodore's life and works, see Quasten, 3:401–23.

82. The consensus of scholars favors Chrysostom's letter to a Theodore ("Two Letters," NPNF, First Series [Grand Rapids, Mich.: Eerdmans, 1956], 9:87–116) as being addressed to Theodore of Mopsuestia. See also Baur, 1:120–23.

83. *Theodori Episcopi Mopsuesteni in Epistolas B. Pauli Commentarii*, ed. H. B. Swete, 2 vols. (Cambridge: Cambridge UP, 1880 and 1882), 1:xiv-xv.

84. Edward Sachau, ed., *Theodori Mopsuesteni Fragmenta Syriaca* (Leipzig: G. Engelmann, 1869). For other passages of Theodore's *Commentary on Genesis*, see R.-M. Tonneau, "Théodore de Mopsueste, Interprétation (du Livre) de la Genèse (Vat. Syr. 120, ff. I-V)," *Le Muséon* 66 (1953): 45–64; as well as the fragments contained in PG 66:109–13. See also Françoise Petit, ed. and trans., "L'homme créé 'à l'image' de Dieu: quelques fragments grecs inédits de Théodore de Mopsueste," *Le Muséon* 100 (1987): 269–81.

a failure entailing the need at times to conjecture the meaning of a particular text.[85]

A very serious difficulty arises in any attempt to establish Theodore's
view on image. Not only must it be reconstructed from several fragments
but it is so different from the others and so involved that it is not easily
summarized. To address these issues, it is necessary, first of all, to learn
what he says about how Adam and Christ are God's images and then how
the two are interrelated. This viewpoint will then be shown to be corroborated by later East Syrian theologians who have espoused Theodore as
their theological mentor. This section will be concluded with a discussion
of how we can synthesize Theodore's statements about image into a coherent whole.[86]

Adam as the Image of God

In an excerpt that has come down to us from his commentary on Genesis, Theodore rejected the opinions that the idea of "image" was connected with an ability to rule or reason or think. He writes: "I have especially to marvel at the inherent contradictions of those who speak wisely
[but] ridiculously saying that 'man has been made according to the image
of God somehow according to an ability to rule, and somehow according
to an ability to reason, and somehow according to an ability to think.'
Those [maintaining this] need to understand that only man (ἄνθρωπος)
is said to have been created the image of God."[87] He then proceeded to
quote passages from Genesis and the Book of Noah where man (ἄνθρωπος) is affirmed to be created in God's image and from Paul where "Man
(ἀνήρ) ought not to cover his head, being the image and glory of God."
(1 Cor. 11:17) He argued that if image pertains to an ability to rule and to
reason, then it should also be applicable to those spiritual powers alluded

85. F. Petit, "L'homme," 269.

86. For a summary of Theodore's understanding of image, see Richard A. Norris,
Jr., *Manhood and Christ* (Oxford: Clarendon Press, 1963), 140–48; and for a clear exposi-
tion of how "man" as the bond of the universe relates to his role as "image of God, es-
pecially as regards its anthropological ramifications, see Nabil el-Koury, "Der Mensch als
Gleichnis Gottes: Eine Untersuchung zur Anthropologie des Theodor von Mopsuestia,"
Oriens Christianus 74 (1990): 62–71.

87. Françoise Petit, ed., *Catenae Graecae in Genesim et in Exodum* 2. Collectio Coisliniana in Genesim, Corpus Christianorum Series Graeca 15 (Brepols: Turnhout, 1986), 71.

to in Colossians 1:16, Ephesians 3:10 and 6:12, Daniel 10:21, and Psalm 135 (136):8–9. But there is no indication whatsoever that they and the sun, moon, and stars are to be called "images of God." He concludes from this:

How therefore was it possible according to any of these [ideas] for man to be called an "image" along with many other beings with whom he shared [this honor] when he alone is said to have been created according to the image of God? In light of [all] this it is clear to us that there is fittingly only one reason for man alone to be called [the image]—a reason he does not share with those not sharing this designation.[88]

Here Theodore separates himself from those who look upon image as associated not only with the activities of the rational mind but also with power to rule. By rejecting the latter, he revealed his difference with and independence from what Diodore and Chrysostom were maintaining. He relied upon what the Scriptures were stating in an explicit way about "image." It is affirmed only of "man" in the generic sense of this term except for 1 Corinthians 11:7 where Paul speaks of man as the image of God explicitly as male. It is, as Theodore notes, never applied to the various angelic powers that are mentioned elsewhere in Scripture, such as the "thrones," "dominations," and "principalities." Theodore detected in this lack of specific endorsement an indication that the term "image" ought not to be regarded as simply a spiritual power.

In another passage about "image," Theodore interpreted it as applying to man (ἄνθρωπος) as a human being composed of both body and soul. He enlarges further upon this by maintaining that God's bestowal of image upon human nature in this sense demonstrates the preeminence that humans enjoy over all other creatures and the role that they exercise as the "bond" uniting the spiritual and material worlds to each other within the entire cosmos. In fact, he grounds humankind's superiority within their role as the bond uniting all of creation within the universe. In addition, because humans image an invisible God whose transcendency impedes any knowledge of Him, they also serve as the way that other creatures are expected to manifest their love and worship for God. In other words, humans mediate God to all others and provide a cultic focus for them to worship God. Their care for the needs of humans is the way that they show their glory to God. We see this expressed in a Syriac fragment published by Edward Sachau.

88. F. Petit, "L'homme," 72.

This is the excellence of man's[89] coming to be, that he came to be in the image of God. For just as in the case of these other things, by his repetition he made known the excellence of each one and its reason for coming to be, so he twice established that He made man in the image of God, in order to manifest that this is indeed a matter of excellence in his fashioning, that it is in him that all beings are gathered together, so that through him as by an image they might draw near to God by obeying the laws that were laid down by Him by means of the service toward him, pleasing the Lawgiver by their diligence to him.[90]

As to how humans serve as the bond of the universe, Theodore has described this in an early passage of Genesis when he wrote:

For (God) fashioned Adam with an invisible, rational, and immortal soul and a visible and mortal body. By the former, he is like unto invisible natures; and by the latter, he is akin to visible beings. For God willed to gather the whole of creation into one, so that, although constituted of diverse natures, it might be joined together by one bond. He [then] created this living being which is related by its nature to the whole of creation. He created Adam to be this bond.[91]

Theodore, therefore, conceived of image as indicating the functional roles that Adam plays within creation. Because his roles pertain to his visible nature that bonds the material universe to his body and the invisible world to his soul, they must also apply to all men and women who share the same human nature. Besides having an essential unitive role to play within the whole cosmos, Adam as representative of human nature also had a revelatory function, as is seen in the following where Theodore compared God's creation of the universe with an all-powerful king's foundation of a new city:

If some king, after having constructed a very great city and adorned it with numerous and varied works, ordered upon the completion of everything that his image, having been made the greatest and most remarkable, be set up in the middle of the entire city as proof of his founding of the city, the image of the king who built the city would necessarily be venerated, with all in the city confessing their gratitude to their city's founder for having given them such a place to live. So also the Artisan of creation has made the whole cosmos, embellishing it with diverse and varied works and at the end established man to serve as the image for his household, so

---

89. The Syriac word is the generic word for "man."
90. Sachau, TFS, 24–25 in the Syriac and 15 in the Latin.
91. Ibid., 7 in the Syriac and 5 in the Latin. For a treatment of Adam's cosmic function as God's image, see Norris, *Manhood*, 142–45.

that all creation would by their care for and veneration towards him render the honor due to God.[92]

For Theodore, therefore, Adam's visible human nature reveals the existence of the God who created everything. It also possesses another role to fulfill. It is meant to act like a shrine wherein other creatures can fulfill their duties to God and honor Him by caring for human needs. Since God is transcendent, created beings have need of an authentic visible image that manifests God as well as provides a place where they can worship God. This is an outlook on image that reflects a similarity with Edward Curtis's suggested opinion that the Jewish author of Genesis had modified a Mesopotamian and Egyptian conception of image. It also evokes a comparison with the historical account of the Emperor Theodosius I's reaction to the news that his imperial image had been smashed during the tax revolt at Antioch. This may be, therefore, an instance where Theodore saw an ancient practice supporting his exegetical understanding of what Paul was saying about the functional roles that Christ plays as God's primary image.

But first one needs to consider what happens to Adam's dignity as God's image when he disobeys God's solemn command not to eat of the tree of the knowledge of good and evil. In the first instance, Theodore indicates that Adam's role as image not only is a dignity bestowed on man as ἄνθρωπος but also involves a responsibility to live up to his revelatory, cultic, and unitive functions. Because he acted contrary to God's will, Adam became an image of Satan.

Our Lord God fashioned man[93] in His image from the earth and honored him in many other ways. He especially honored him by calling him His image whereby man alone is called God and the son of God. If he had been wise, he would have remained with the One who was for him the source of all good things that he possessed. But he accepted and completed the image of the devil who had risen as a rebel against God and wanted to usurp for himself the glory due to Him.[94]

Theodore repeated the same idea but added the notions of how Adam

92. See Swete, 1:lxxx, for a summary of the Pauline passages that Theodore most likely drew upon in elaborating his views on "image."

93. The Syriac word for "man" throughout this passage means literally a "son of man" or simply "human being."

94. Raymond Tonneau with Robert Devreese, trans., *Les Homélies Catéchétiques de Théodore de Mopsueste* (Vatican City: Vaticana, 1949), 333. The translation here and those in the following citations are my own.

lost the honor of being God's image and how his sin was responsible for introducing death into human existence.

We did not belong to Satan from the beginning and from the time of our fore-fathers, but to God who created us while we were not and made us in His own image, and that it was through the iniquity and the wickedness of the Tyrant and through our own negligence that we were driven towards evil, and lost also the honor and greatness of our image, and because of our sinfulness we have further received the punishment of death.[95]

Image, therefore, is intimately tied in with the necessity to live voluntarily according to God's will. To rebel as Satan did means that humans reflect the image of Satan. By their disobedience they sundered their relationship to God, and, when death appeared, they could no longer serve as the bond uniting creation with God.

One final quotation from Theodore's catechetical homilies will indicate how "men"(again in the generic sense of referring to humans beings) recover the honor of being God's image. It also points to why God has decided that humans are to be His image and will serve as an introduction to the next section affirming how Christ is God's primary image. The point to be stressed is that Theodore understood image as having a soteriological significance. Christ fulfills the roles originally entrusted to Adam but dishonored by him. Christ is the one chosen by God to restore humanity to its unblemished dignity as God's image, so that it can become immortal in heaven.

. . . and we are, as we were at the beginning, in the image of God. We had lost the honor of this image through our carelessness but by the grace of God we have re-taken this honor, and because of this we have become immortal and we will dwell in heaven. Indeed it is in this way that the image of God ought to rejoice and ac-quire the honor that is due to the One who by promise was to be called and was to be in His image.[96]

Christ as God's Image

As the quotation above brought out, Theodore regarded the role of image as being primarily fulfilled in Christ who is "the image of the invisible

---

95. *Commentary of Theodore of Mopsuestia on the Lord's Prayer and on the Sacraments of Baptism and the Eucharist*, ed. and trans. A. Mingana, WS 6 (Cambridge: Heffer, 1933), 28. I have checked Mingana's translation against the Syriac text and adapted it slightly.
96. Ibid., WS 6:30.

God." His understanding of image derives from Paul. In a surviving Latin passage, Theodore insisted against those who believe that image can only be spiritual that every image has to be visible to others by its very nature.

We see His invisible nature present in him (Christ), as in an image. For he has been united to God the Word and will judge the whole world when he appears, as it is right, according to his own nature, coming in the future age from heaven in great glory. . . . Blessed Moses also says of man (homo) that "God made him to His image," and likewise blessed Paul that "man (vir) ought not to cover his head, being the image and the visible glory of God." Image, however, could never be said of men (homines), if it were proper [only] to the divine nature. Moreover, these [interpreters who hold image to be spiritual] have not seen that every image, when seen, shows what it is not seen. It is impossible, therefore, to make an image that is not seen. For it is evident that images are ordinarily fashioned by their makers either for honor or affection, so that they may be a [source of] remembrance of those not seen for those who are able nevertheless to see.[97]

In the next citation, Theodore elaborated upon how Christ as God's image fulfills a revelatory and cultic function because of the way the divine and the human natures are united in him. In fact, this union is the reason why Christ functions in the other two ways as God's image. It is a long quotation but an illuminating one for understanding Theodore's position on image.

Christ fulfills the role of image in two ways. Those who love certain individuals very often set up their images after their death and deem this as providing them some solace over their death. By looking at their image, they think that they see, as it were, their [loved] one who is neither seen nor present, appeasing thereby the flame and force of their desire. Also those who have the emperors' images within their cities seem to honor by cult and adoration those (emperors) who are not present, as if they were present and seeing all this. Both of these [analogies] are fulfilled in the case of Christ. For all his followers who pursue virtue and promptly fulfill what is due God love him and greatly honor him. And even though the divine nature is unseen, they still show love to him who is seen by all. For they all think of him as one who is seen by means of him and always present to him. They fully honor him as [God's] imperial image, seeing that the divine nature is, as it were, in him and is seen in him. For if the Son is indeed the one said to be dwelling in him, then the Father is also with him. For everyone believes that He is altogether inseparable from the Son. And the Spirit is not absent in that He came to him in the form of an anointing and is always with the assumed one.[98]

97. Swete, 1:261–62. The translation from the Latin text is my own.
98. Theodore, PG 66:991.

Before seeing how our reconstruction of Theodore's thought is also present in the teaching of East Syrian theologians who adhere faithfully to his teaching, there is a need to consider some other brief fragments that distinguish between image and likeness in a way that may seem to differ from what has just been proposed as Theodore's thought on image. The texts will first be presented and then discussed together.

Rightly then has (Moses) also added [the term] "likeness" to [the phrase] "according to the image." When indeed God bestowed on man (ἄνθρωπος) the function of image, [it is] as I have said, for such a reason [that] he has also rightly given him [ways] to imitate divine attributes but [in a manner] far inferior to [God's] substance and to the extent that [every] image is inferior to its archetype's image and yet bearing [some] imitations and reflections of that one's majesty.[99]

The second is just one line: "For this (attribute) exists in God in an unlimited way, but in us as in an image according to the measure that has been given to us by the Maker."[100] In the next, Theodore observed: "We reflect and imitate in a certain way this power of critical discernment of (human) acts, insofar as we function as image, which is in fact far inferior to its archetype. But it suffices in a certain imitative way to lead us to perceive the grandeur of God's attributes in relation to this."[101] Finally in a passage that is partially defective, Theodore suggested that there exists a likeness between a human being and the number of persons in the Trinity. (Its full significance will be seen when Narsai's understanding will be discussed below.) "And by the designation of 'image' what sort of [lacuna] is affirmed so that the divine nature may be understood as one. Then as regards what is meant by 'according to our likeness,' we take it to be a sign of the number of those persons within the divine nature."[102]

It is admittedly difficult to speculate on Theodore's thought on the basis of these few brief fragments. But his comments on how humans manifest a likeness to God do not contradict what has been so far reconstructed to be his position on image. Adam's and even Christ's human roles as God's image reveal in a true but a limited, inferior way the transcendent Creator and redeeming God. Because they stand as God's image, one can also look upon their spiritual activity as providing some analogous insight into how God acts and in a passage that is similar to an

99. F. Petit, "L'homme," 276. 100. Ibid.
101. Ibid., 278.
102. Sachau, TFS, 22 in the Syriac and 14 in the Latin.

analogy that Augustine has also proposed, how human spiritual activities point to the three divine Persons in the Trinity. But note that Theodore does not assert that human activity is exactly like God's: he switches from speaking of this as strictly a *homoiōsis* (likeness) to a *mimēma* (imitation) and qualifies this imitation in a carefully restricted way. He does so in order to avoid giving the impression that God acts exactly like humans. In brief, Theodore seems to understand the term "image" in the sense of being a symbol and "likeness" of providing some ideas of the imitative ways that humans can profess something analogously about God.[103] He does not understand it as referring to a spiritual relationship with God and a participation in His life, but, as has been noted above, sees it in the way Irenaeus argued human spiritual activity can be said to manifest a "similitude" with God's manner of acting.

The East Syrian Teaching on the Image of God

In this section, the views of two East Syrian writers will be discussed. The first is Narsai, a fifth-century exegete and theologian;[104] and the second is the East Syrian exegete and theologian Išoʻdad of Merv, who lived and wrote around the middle of the ninth century.[105] Their stated views on image are useful for confirming and elaborating upon the present study's reconstruction of Theodore's thought.

Narsai

In the fifth century, Edessa (now the Turkish city of Urfa) began to supplant Antioch as the center of theological thought for the Antiochene tradition.[106] Its school, then known as the Persian school, likely dates back

103. Richard A. Norris, Jr. (*Manhood and Christ* [Oxford: Clarendon, 1963]) relates "image" primarily to a human representation of God founded on resemblance that is "defined externally, without reference to the themes of participation or natural affiliation" (142). From this, he believes that "Theodore argues to a quite distinctive characterization of the nature of man's office as image."

104. For a biography of Narsai, see Philippe Gignoux's *Homélies de Narsai sur la Création*, PO 34/3–4 (Paris: Brepols, 1968), 419–23.

105. *Išoʻdad of Merv, Commentaire d'Išoʻdad de Merv sur l'Ancien Testament, I. Genèse*, ed. Ceslas van den Eynde, CSCO 156 (Louvain: Durbecq, 1955).

106. See R. Lavenant's article on "Edessa" in EEC 1:263.

at least until the time of Ephrem (c.306– 84).[107] When Narsai, a Syrian Christian from the Persian lands, was elected head of the school in about the middle of the fifth century, he became a strong, vocal mainstay in defense of Diodore, Theodore, and Nestorius.[108] When Narsai was forced to flee for his life, he sought refuge in the Persian empire where he established a school at Nisibis. This quickly became the theological center for the East Syrian Church and was celebrated for its efforts to translate and promote Theodore's thought.

Narsai's teaching on the "image of God" is explicit and richly delineated in verse. He maintained that "The Creator willed to call it (the human soul) and body His image."[109] But he was also careful to point out, as Theodore has done, that God "called [Adam] an image of His majesty in a metaphorical sense. For everything created is vastly inferior to the divine essence. [God's] nature is so immeasurably exalted over that of creatures

107. Barhadbshabba 'Arbaia (Cause de la Fondation des Écoles, trans. A. Scher, PO 4 [Turnhout: Brepols, 1908], 377) asserts that Ephrem founded this school in 363 A.D. Arthur Vööbus (History of the School of Nisibis, CSCO 266, Subs. 26 [Louvain: CSCO, 1965], 8) also cites the opinion of E. R. Hayes, who believed that a school already existed before Ephrem arrived at Edessa. He questions the reliability of the sources on which Scher and Hayes were dependent, but he believes that "there is no cogent reason for us to reject the tradition altogether. It may contain a historical kernel." In regard to Ephrem's view on image, we find this expressed in his Commentary on Genesis (CSCO 153:17) where he maintains that image pertains to Adam because of his freedom and his dominion over creatures. He understands that this is exemplified in three ways. First, just as the power of God is present in all things, so has Adam's dominion been placed over all. Secondly, Adam possesses a pure soul that can receive into itself all kinds of virtues and divine charisms. Thirdly, the human mind can direct the rational part of its soul to any point and arouse images of anything that it wants. In other words, image for Ephrem is a spiritual power that is like God's in its ability to exercise dominion within the universe as well as to acquire all virtues and at least be able to conceive of all created things. This view of image, if it is authentic, commands interest because it comes out of a Syriac tradition that shows little or no influence at all from Greek philosophical thought. Beginning in the fifth century, Theodore's understanding of image will start to supplant that of Ephrem among the East Syrians. For a discussion of Ephrem's views, see Nabil el-Khoury, "Gen. 1,26 dans l'interprétation de Saint Éphrem, ou la relation de l'homme à Dieu," Symposium Syriacum 1976 (Rome: Pontificium Institutum Orientalium Studiorum, 1978).

108. Narsai's homily in defense of the three doctors attests to this. See F. Martin's "Homélie de Narses sur les trois Docteurs nestoriens," Journal Asiatique 14 (1899): 446–92; and 15 (1900): 469–525. Edessa was also noted as a center where Greek and Syriac texts were rapidly translated into each other's languages.

109. A. Mingana, ed., Narsai doctoris syri homiliae et carmina (Mosul, Iraq, 1905), 2:251.

that it does not possess, as do corporeal beings, a visible image."[110] In other words, the *imago Dei* refers to the whole human being, not in a photographic way but in a metaphorical sense. As the following indicates, he understood image, like Theodore, to be a symbol that expresses and shares in God's power. He verbalized this in language clearly dependent upon Theodore: "The Creator set His image in the world, the city of the kingdom, and by a visible image He makes known the power of His transcendent divinity."[111]

Like Theodore, Narsai envisaged an intimate connection between human beings as the image of God and the bond uniting the material and spiritual dimensions of the universe. Narsai telescoped both of these outlooks when he declared: "[The Creator] has fashioned and skillfully made a double vessel, a visible body and a hidden soul—one man.[112] He depicted the power of His creatorship in him as an image: mute beings in his body and rational beings in the structure of his soul."[113] Narsai specified more clearly how humans function as both image and bond in the following: "[The Creator] has exalted his image with the name of image, in order to bind all [creatures] in him, so that they might [thus] acquire love by knowing Him by means of knowledge of His image."[114] As Theodore did, Narsai looks upon human beings as divinely appointed media through which other creatures can know, love, and serve God. Humans bind the spiritual and corporeal worlds on a horizontal plane and unite these vertically to God by enabling them through their image function to know and love God.

Narsai refined this twofold understanding of the meaning of image even more. Doubtless reflecting the teaching of Theodore as well as Colossians 1:15, he carefully pointed out that Christ, not Adam, is in point of fact God's primary image: "[The Creator] has called the first Adam by the name of image in a secondary sense. The image is in reality the Messiah, the Second Adam. Thus 'Come, let us make man in our image' was fulfilled when

---

110. Frederick McLeod, ed. and trans., *Narsai's Metrical Homilies on the Nativity, Epiphany, Passion, Resurrection and Ascension*, PO 40, Fasc. 1 (Turnhout: Brepols, 1979), 39.

111. Mingana, *Narsai doctoris*, 2:100. The translation is my own.

112. The Syriac word is the generic word for human being. Unless otherwise noted, any further reference to "man" is to be presumed to be such in this section.

113. Mingana, *Narsai doctoris*, 2:239.

114. McLeod, *Narsai's Metrical Homilies*, 39.

the Creator took His image and made it a dwelling place for His honor. The promises to Adam came to be in reality in the Messiah."[115] For Narsai, the bestowal of the name of image upon Adam is thus a foreshadowing of that time when God will dwell within Christ, His primary image. He showed that Adam's image is a type representing Christ as the true image.

Narsai provided two interesting texts that describe how Christ actually functions as God's true image. In the first, he looked upon Christ as restoring the bond of love that Adam loosened by his sin.

(The Word) assumed him (Christ) for the peace of rational beings as the first fruits for us all, in order that He might bind in him the love which Adam loosened by [his] transgression of the divine command. He honored the whole nature of rational beings by assuming him, because He made those related to him by nature to share in his honor.[116]

And in the next quotation, Christ is said to function in heaven as the one imaging God to the angels and the elect:

By the yoke of his love will be united together angels and men, and they will celebrate him as the image of the hidden king . . . They continually worship in the temple of his body that One who is hidden in him and offer therein the pure sacrifices of their minds. In the haven of his body come to rest the impulses of their thoughts, as they become worn out in search for the transcendent incomprehensible One. For this reason, the Fashioner of the universe chose him from the universe, that by his visible body he might satisfy the need of the universe. A creature needs continually to search out for what is transcendent and to discover the meaning and intent of what is secret. Because it is impossible that the nature of the hidden One appear in an open way, He limited their inquiries to his visible image.[117]

One final point needs to be made about Narsai's view on how humans have been created "in the image and likeness of God." While insisting that humans do not have a natural likeness to God, Narsai does note similiarities that can afford some insight into who God is.

A figure, signifying the name of the Divine Essence, is found in the generation [of Adam's soul] . . . Its likeness faintly resembles [and] signifies the Persons [of the Trinity]. Its nature resembles the Father; and its [mental] word, the Son; and [its]

---

115. Gignoux, 602. The English translation is my own.

116. McLeod, *Narsai's Metrical Homilies*, 130.

117. Ibid., 176. I have translated this from the Syriac text. For a very similar passage, see Thomas of Edessa, *Tractatus De Nativitate Domini Nostri Christi*, ed. Simon Joseph Carr (Rome, 1898), 39.

life, the Spirit. Its nature does not have a natural likeness to the Nature of the transcendent One, but only a typical likeness.[118]

This provides a context for understanding what Theodore meant when he affirmed that humans manifest a "likeness" with the Trinity. There exists a resemblance between a human being's mind and rational faculties and the nature and Persons in the Trinity. This suggests what was observed above in our treatment of Theodore. Narsai is using "image" to express the symbolic role that humans, especially Christ, play within creation, while understanding the "likeness" that can be said to exist between humans and God as providing grounds for pointing out how humans and God are alike in a limited typical/archetypal ways.

Išoʿdad of Merv

The final Syriac source to be mentioned is Išoʿdad of Merv, an exponent of Theodore's literal, historical, and grammatical method of exegesis. When he treats of the Genesis 1:26 passage, he listed pages of interpretations for the meaning of the phrase, "image of God" in a rambling manner indicating that he is drawing these from different contexts without attempting to sort them out in a logical and rational order.[119] He first likened God to a king who has placed his image in the center of the city he has built and adorned. Then after a long series of general meanings, he noted how God has made humans to be akin to the visible and the invisible worlds, so that these latter may not only honor them as God's image but love them because of their affinity with them. He then proceeded to reject the position of those holding that "image" and "likeness" are applied to men (*qua* human beings) by reason of their rational natures and domination. Angels are recognized as being either intelligent or inanimate powers able to dominate nature, but neither of these is ever called an "image of God." Išoʿdad then offered several ways that humans can be thought of as being "images" of God. First, they alone symbolize both the unity and persons within the Trinity. For example, he compared the soul to God the

118. Mingana, *Narsai doctoris*, 2:239. This analogy is similar to what Augustine proposed as his final understanding of how human nature is an image of the trinitarian God in Book Ten (xi.18) of his *De Trinitate* where memory, understanding, and will "constitute one thing, one life, one mind, one essence."

119. Išoʿdad of Merv, 49–53.

Father, the mental word engendered by the soul to the Son, and its spirituality to the Holy Spirit. Secondly, human beings are called image because they synthesize the world, for they enclose and unite in themselves the entire creation of spiritual and corporeal beings. Thirdly, human beings are like unto God by their operational power, though they differ in the media from which they fashion things, humans using matter and God nothing. Fourthly, they are like unto God by reason of the way their mind can grasp all of creation in heaven and earth in an instant, while the divine nature exists everywhere already. Fifthly, they are like unto God by the royal and judiciary power they exercise. Sixthly, they are called image because from their race will later come the man Jesus Christ, who will be the image of the invisible God.

While Išoʿdad did not identify from whence he has drawn these different explanations, he is evidently indebted to Theodore and/or those Syriac Fathers who acknowledge him as their mentor. He would seem to have compiled these from writings that he had at hand and would be expressing—out of context—different usages of "image." He has missed, however, uniting all of these ideas in a coherent whole as Theodore and Narsai appear to have done.

Nestorius

As remarked earlier, it is difficult to affirm exactly what Nestorius held regarding "image" if one is to judge solely on the basis of what has survived of his writings.[120] But now knowing what Theodore held, one can situate his few passing remarks about image within a context. Each of his passing comments about image will be first presented and then related to Theodore's overall thought. In his *Sermon Against the Theotokos*, Nestorius observes in passing: "Because humanity is the image of the divine nature, but the devil overthrew this image and cast it down into corruption, God

---

120. The best treatment that I have read about Nestorius's view on image is Rowan A. Greer's "The Image of God and the Prosopic Union in Nestorius' *Bazaar of Heracleides*," *Lux in Lumine: Essays for W. N. Pittenger*, ed. Richard A. Norris, Jr. (New York: Seabury, 1966), 46–59. While I disagree with his opinion that Nestorius's use of the image of God separates him from Theodore (58), I concur with his fundamental assessment of how "The words *prosôpon* and 'image' are used as equivalents" (50) and that both taken together express Nestorius's understanding of how the natures in Christ are united.

grieved over his image as a king might grieve over his statue, and renewed the ruined likeness."[121] While this language is close to Theodore's view of image, Nestorius did not develop his thought on image. It suggests that he understood image as referring to the whole of humanity and was familiar with Theodore's passage likening God's image to that of a king's image in the center of a city that he has established. However in this passage and the few remaining works that have survived, Nestorius made no reference to image as the bond of the universe.

In his discussion of the verse "Therefore he who shall be born shall be called the son of God" (Lk 1:35), Nestorius observed that the Son:

> . . . is the Holy One who is to be created; so that in the creation he calls [him] 'holy' and 'Son', denoting the image and the likeness which the first man received in the Creation and which he kept not. For, as the image of God, he ought to have kept himself for God without spot and without blemish, and that by willing what God wills, since he had the *prosōpon* of God.[122]

Nestorius associated "the image and likeness of God" here with the notions of the "holiness" and *prosōpon* that Adam initially possessed but lost. If he had willed what God wants, he would have remained in union with God and continued to image God to others. From what we have seen in Theodore, Nestorius would appear to be highlighting here how Adam and Christ as God's images have a responsibility to live their lives in a holy way. Adam did not, but Christ did by faithfully and lovingly obeying the will of God as His image or *prosōpon*. What Nestorius has meant by *prosōpon* will be examined much more in depth in a later chapter. Suffice it to say at this point that it denotes how a person appears visibly as God's image to others with some reference to one's underlying nature or, in the case of Christ, his divine and human natures. In the present case, Nestorius has simply contrasted the ways that Adam and Christ have fulfilled their revelatory roles as God's image.

We can see this expressed more fully, but unfortunately rather obscurely, in the next quotation that seeks to explain how the first and the second Adams fulfill their roles as God's image.

121. Richard A. Norris, Jr., trans. and ed., *The Christological Controversy*, Sources of Early Christian Thought (Philadelphia: Fortress, 1980), 124.

122. Nestorius, *The Bazaar of Heracleides*, ed. and trans. Godfrey R. Driver and Leonard Hodgson (Oxford: Clarendon, 1925), 59. See also 69. Since I have not been able to consult the Syriac text, I have used the English translation provided here.

As God appeared and spoke unto Adam in *schēma*, and as it was none other, so will God be [seen] of all men in the natural *schēma* which has been created, that is, that of the flesh, appearing and speaking in his own image and the image in the Archetype. So that on the one hand God appeared in the image, since he is not visible, on the other hand the image is conceived as representing him who appeared not. For it is not [the fact] that the image is his being, but that on the other hand the very image and *prosōpon* [are] the humanity of the divinity and the divinity of the humanity.[123]

Since this translation by Godfrey Driver is unfortunately awkward and requires some understanding of *schēma* (which will be discussed in Chapter Five), it needs some elaboration. For Nestorius, *schēma* denotes a person's external, changeable appearance. So when he referred to a human *schēma*, he was affirming how God has manifested Himself in a visible way through Adam, who is the prototype of Christ, who is the archetypical image of God. Image and *prosōpon* are, therefore, the ways that an inner reality manifests itself through its *schēma* or its present appearance. The visible appearance of Christ reveals both his complete humanity and his complete divinity. One can say that the divinity exists within his humanity and vice versa that the humanity exists within the divinity. Rowan Greer explains the relationship thus:

Therefore the image of God is the perfect expression of God to us as men. The image of God, understood in this sense, can be thought of as the divine *prosōpon*. God dwells in Christ and perfectly reveals himself to men through him. Yet the two *prosōpa* are really one because both the humanity and the divinity are the image of God.[124]

The next citation is also difficult to grasp out of context, especially as the translation is not smooth. It reinforces the view that one's role as image entails an obligation to conform one's own will to God's. Nestorius believed that this was how Christ, as the archetypical image, lived. Christ therefore exemplifies how those who are images in a typical sense are to live out their lives.

For this appertains only to the image of God and to him who preserves the image of God, to will the same as God the Father. . . . He raised up his very soul unto God, conforming that which was according to his will to the will of God in order that he

123. NES, 60. I have not been able to consult the Syriac text to determine whether the confusion pertains to the translation or the text.
124. Greer, "The Image of God," and Norris, 50.

might be the image only of the Archetype, and not of his being; for the image according to its own [being] is without likeness and its own proper likeness is that of the Archetype.[125]

As I understand what is being said, Christ's human will images (in the sense of visibly pointing to) the perfect conformity that the Word manifests toward His Father. The conformity of his human will may not be equal to the Word's, but it does reveal how all human beings are to enter into union with God. Greer sums this up well in his article showing the relationship between *prosōpon* and image in Nestorius: "God forms Christ in his own image, but this formation is possible only because Christ exercises his free will as a man in obedience to God's will. Perhaps the most moving aspect of the Antiochene theology is the way in which there is conveyed a sense that Christ's battle is a type of our own, and his life so deeply an ensample for us, that we can see ourselves in him."[126]

Since only a limited amount of material has survived whereby one can know Nestorius's view of image, it is difficult to judge whether and to what extent Nestorius shared, besides Theodore's revelatory and voluntaristic outlooks on image, his cosmological viewpoint of humans as the bond linking the two worlds of visible matter and invisible spirits. His only possible references to this are his statements that "[God] has renewed all creation in Christ and has made known and shown to us what the Maker is,"[127] and "since men were in need of the divinity as for our renewal and for our formation anew and for [the renewal] of the likeness of the image which had been obliterated by us."[128] Yet this is understandable, granted Nestorius's apologetic focus in writing *The Bazaar of Heracleides*. He likely saw no reason for including it because of his concern to prove how Christ's human will was united with the Word's in their prosopic union. Greer affirms this view thus: "The answer seems to be that he really does not discuss the image of God save in close conjunction with his Christology."[129]

Theodoret

Before examining Theodoret's writings to determine his view on image, I was expecting he would follow Theodore, as Nestorius seems to

125. NES, 65–66.
127. NES, 58.
129. Greer, "The Image of God," 55.

126. Greer, "The Image of God," 53.
128. Ibid., 183.

have done. Thus it was surprising to discover that he chose, as did Diodore and Chrysostom, to interpret image as the power entrusted to males to rule over the material world. While he doubtless chose this because he believed it to be true or, at the very least, the best available interpretation, his differences with Theodore might indicate that he received his exegetical training at a different monastery school than the famed School of Antioch. For, by the time Theodoret began his theological education, Theodore would have been long departed from the city of Antioch, having been appointed the bishop of Mopsuestia in 392, the year before Theodoret is said to have been born.

In a fragment published in Migne, Theodoret outlined numerous opinions expressed about the meaning of "image."[130] He began by rejecting the position of those holding that image resides in the invisible soul: "For if the image of God would be an invisible element of the soul, then much more the angels and archangels and all the bodiless and holy natures . . . would be called images of God."[131] He immediately follows this with a total rejection of those maintaining that the human body strictly images God: "For they are evidently senseless (views)."[132] For they fail to realize that the Scriptures are employing accommodated language when they speak of God's visible appearances. After this, he discussed what some other doctors have asserted about image, speaking favorably about their position without saying whether or not he agreed with them. It is clear that he was presenting, without mentioning them by name, the viewpoint that Theodore and, possibly, Nestorius favored.

Some of the teachers have understood it thus: that, after having made creation to be sensible and intellectual, the God of the universe formed man (ἄνθρωπος) last of all, placing him as a certain image of Himself in the midst of inanimate and animate, sensing and intellectual beings, in order that the inanimate and the animate beings might care for him as a certain tribute [due Him]. Intellectual natures manifest their good will for the Fashioner by the care [they show] for him.[133]

When Theodoret addressed the issue of whether humans have been created in the image of God according to their power to dominate over the irrational world, he simply observes that there are other kinds of ways that humans can be said to imitate God, such as in fabricating things,

---

130. Theodoret, PG 80:103–8.
131. Ibid., 80:104. The translation from Migne is my own.
132. Ibid.   133. Ibid., 80:104–5.

making judgments, and thinking discursively of all sorts of possibilities.[134] As the following indicates, he viewed being "in the likeness of God" in the same way as Theodore: "Thus when man creates, he imitates in some way his Maker, as an image imitates its archetype. For an image exhibits similarities with its archetype."[135] The fact that he chose to speak of an "imitation" rather than a "likeness" is likely a confirmation that he is referring to Theodore.

Since the fragment ends here, one needs to move on to another passage to discover Theodoret's own position on image. He professed here the view of Diodore and Chrysostom that image refers to man's ability as a male to rule as God's plenipotentiary.

Man (ἀνήρ) is the image of God, but not in a bodily or spiritual sense but only in relationship to his ability to rule. He has been called, therefore, the image of God insofar as he has been entrusted with the rule over all beings without exception on earth. Woman, however, since she has been placed under the power of man is the glory of the man, as it were, an image of the image. For she also rules over other creatures, but she has been ordered to be subject to man.[136]

Conclusion

As the survey at the beginning of this chapter has traced, there exists a wide disparity of viewpoints among the Scripture exegetes and Fathers of the Church regarding the meaning of the phrase "to be created in God's image." While all concede that it indicates that Adam and Eve possessed not only a special but even a unique relationship with God, they disagree over whether it must be entirely spiritual and, if so, how it includes the body as a co-element with it.[137] The Alexandrians, the Cappadocians,

134. Ibid., 80:106–7. For a different conclusion, see E. Montmasson's "L'Homme créé à l'image de Dieu d'après Théodoret de Cyrrhus et Procope de Gaza," "Échos d'Orient" 15 (1912): esp. 158–60. I believe that Montmasson has missed the significance of how image relates to humans as the bond of the universe and how Theodoret's remarks on image as dominion need to be interpreted in light of the distinction that Theodore appears to have made between "image" and "likeness."

135. Theodoret, PG 82:105.

136. Ibid., 82:312.

137. For a detailed study of some of the attitudes present in the early Church toward the human body, person, society, and sexual renunciation, see Peter Brown's masterfully written *The Body and Society: Men, Women, and Sexual Renunciation in Early Christianity* (New York: Columbia UP, 1988). Though he makes no reference in this work to the

and Augustine readily maintain that the body is good, serving as the temple in which the image resides, but they restrict image to the highest reaches of the mind, maintaining emphatically that only a spiritual reality can image and participate in the spiritual, transcendent nature of God.[138] They appear to be following the intellectual lead of Philo, Origen, and Plotinus.

As regards the Antiochenes, the extant writings, particularly those of Diodore, Theodore, and Nestorius, are relatively sparse. Yet when taken together with Chrysostom and Theodoret's statements about image, they provide us with enough material to depict their approaches to the meaning of image. It would seem that they derived their viewpoints from a literal reading of the scriptural passages on image. By insisting that image must refer to the whole composite of human soul and body, they also give another indication that they belong to a Semitic exegetical tradition. They might also have been opposed to the viewpoint of those locating image in the highest reaches of the rational soul because it served as a possible way for explaining how a person could become mystically united to God and truly divinized. They would likely regard such an approach as an example of how pagan philosophical ideas regarding divinization has directed theology, rather than the other way around. For them it would be an inversion of what ought to be the approved theological method—a reliance on what the Scriptures factually reveal.

The Antiochenes themselves, however, divided into two camps over their explanation of how image pertains to the whole human person.

---

patristic opinions regarding the image of God, this is understandable, granted the vast scope of Brown's inquiry. But his approach with its focus upon continence, celibacy, and life-long virginity, I find, can suggest a partial, if not distorted, view of how the Fathers—theoretically at least—valued the body in relationship to the whole person and society. For I believe that not merely their ascetical outlook regarding a need to channel their passions in creative ways as Christ did—which admittedly some failed to do—but also their teachings concerning the image of God and the significance of the incarnation and the resurrection for the body also have to be taken into account. Otherwise one may miss the crucial role that the body was meant to play, in practice as well as in theory.

138. Those insisting that the image of God was to be sought in the highest reaches of the soul admit that the Incarnation and Jesus' bodily resurrection both point to the body as an essential element that must be attended to within any Christian explanation of salvation. But from the few comments of those Fathers who held that the image resided in the *nous*, it is evident they did not see any need to reconcile their outlook on image with the role of the body in salvation. They seem satisfied simply to state that the image of God resides in the body. See Burghardt, *Image of God*, 102–3.

Diodore, Chrysostom, and Theodoret understood image to be the power that God has, as it were, officially delegated to man *qua* male to rule over the whole material universe. While granting that women also have a share in this power, they insisted on the basis of a literal interpretation of Genesis 1:26–28 and 3:16 in light of 1 Corinthians 11:7–9 that women are nevertheless to be considered subordinate to men. They reached this conclusion because they saw that image was referred in Genesis to "man" in the generic sense of the term. Since they interpreted the context as signifying that the "image of God" is connected with the authority humans can have over creation, they had to grant that women too share in this power. But because Paul in 1 Corinthians explicitly asserts that man as a male is God's "image" and women the "glory of man," they believed that only men as such have been truly and fully created in God's image.

Employing the same hermeneutical principles, Theodore and Nestorius, however, arrived at a conclusion that appears at first glance to be different but is actually a fuller explanation than that put forward by the other Antiochenes. They admitted that by being created in God's image humans represent God's power and person on earth, but Theodore and, so it seems, Nestorius explained image in terms of the threefold unitive, revelatory, and cultic roles that humans ought faithfully to exercise as types of Christ within creation. Theodore derived his understanding of "image" from Paul, not Genesis. As we will discuss in Chapter Six, this will lead to a problem about whether or not women are to be considered created in God's image, for it is not certain whether he took a stand on this issue. If he did, he would seem logically to be forced to maintain women as God's image because of his emphasis upon image as associated with human nature as a whole.

Theodore expressed the threefold functions of image when he combined the notion of humans as God's image with that of human nature as the bond uniting the spiritual and the material worlds. While it is possible that Theodore is dependent here upon Nemesius and/or the cultural, Stoic world-view of the day for this outlook, affirming, as it does, humans as bonding the spiritual world by their soul and the material by their body, all indications are that his view stems from his literal and rational understanding of what Paul affirmed about Christ as God's image. Being a person with a systematic bent who wanted to make a coherent sense out of the various places in Scripture, his key to the meaning of image, so it seems, is in the three functional roles Paul portrays Christ as playing in salvation. He would have regarded the cultural, Stoic viewpoint of humans as the bond of the universe as confirming what is contained in Scripture.

Theodore considered image as possessing a typical/archetypical meaning. Adam images God as a type in relationship to the principal roles Christ plays within salvation history. Theodore readily agreed with Diodore, Chrysostom, and Theodoret's understanding of image as a symbol of the power that Adam possessed as God's representatives on earth, for besides being justified by a literal reading of Genesis text, it foreshadowed the power Christ will acquire and exercise as the Lord of the universe. But Theodore realized too that Christ's power flowed from his humanity's union with the Word's divinity. He saw that, since the nature of an image is to make something visible to others, Christ's and Adam's bodies are meant to play a revelatory role within salvation history. For Theodore, to emphasize image as solely a spiritual reality was to miss an essential element in the Christian understanding of salvation. It failed, furthermore, to address the Pauline emphasis upon the central mediating role of Christ's bodily resurrection and upon his role as the *plērōma* who will recapitulate all of creation in himself and return it to his Father at the end of time.

While it is true that Theodore's overall synthesis has been reconstructed out of isolated fragments, it coheres with and makes sense out of what Nestorius, Narsai, and Išoʻdad of Merv have left us about image. Narsai in particular was helpful for substantiating the view that Theodore considered Adam to be a type foreshadowing Christ's unitive, revelatory, and cultic roles as God's primary and perfect image. So also were Nestorius's passing references regarding image as entailing a responsibility to maintain a relationship of holiness with God by faithfully living up to one's roles as image. Nestorius's primary concern was to establish that Christ had a human will that fully cooperated with God's will. Theodore and Nestorius saw clearly the connection existing between the archetypical union of the two wills in Christ and a typical union that ought also to be present between other humans and God.

Theodore and Nestorius expressed the voluntary aspect of image when they portrayed how both Adam and Christ lived out their roles as God's image. When Adam sinned, he became an image of rebellion against God's will. He not only cut off his relationship with God but also, when death began to sever the mortal body from its immortal soul, could no longer function as the bond of the universe. But while he blackened and distorted his image of God, his sin could not destroy his role as image since he is a type that foreshadows Christ as God's perfect image. It is Christ who truly reveals who God is and enables all of creation to enter into communion with God and to worship Him as He desires in and through his human body. By his union with the Word and by recapitulating all creation in his humanity, Christ is the sole mediator between God and the universe.

For Christ to be the perfect mediator, Theodore and Nestorius insisted, Christ had to have a true, fully human nature. They realized that this meant that there also had to be, besides a union of two natures in Christ, a perfect union of their human and divine wills. Since the union of natures in Christ is unique, then in the minds of Theodore and Nestorius the only way that all other human beings can be united to God through their sharing with Christ is by uniting their wills to God's as Christ did. This emphasis upon the role of will within image calls attention to a difference between themselves and those who regarded a virtuous life as a necessary preparation for entering into and growing in a mystical union with the Trinity. As will be seen in a following chapter, they believed that the union can occur only on a level of wills united in love, not of a nature that has been divinized. They insisted upon living a life of virtue as the necessary way to enter into communion with Christ, for their understanding of what kind of union can exist between creatures and a wholly transcendent God precluded a mystical (in the sense of a direct and immediate) union that puts one on the same divine level as God.

With the exception of John Chrysostom, who stood apart from the question, the Antiochenes faced a fundamental problem when they had to confront the two questions of what kind of relationship existed between Christ's human nature and a transcendent God and therefore between all other creatures and God, and of how one can rightly speak of this union when there was no agreement regarding what is now referred to as the *communicatio idiomatum* proper to Christ's person. This was, of course, a serious dilemma for Theodore, who had combined the notion of image with that of human nature's mediating role as the bond linking the spiritual and material worlds with each other and with God—a role Christ is destined to fulfill as the one who will recapitulate the universe at the end of time. While all the Antiochenes clearly defended the view that Christ's human nature is consubstantial with that of humanity and with the soul of angels and the body of material beings, they ran into a buzz saw when they were pushed to justify how the divine and the human natures have been united within the person of Christ. So there is a need to determine more clearly the unitive function of Christ's role as God's primary image. Such an inquiry will also determine to what extent the Antiochene Fathers have introduced metaphysical terms and ideas into their religious and theological outlooks.

3

THE INFLUENCES UPON THE SCHOOL

OF ANTIOCH

IODORE, CHRYSOSTOM, AND THEODORET'S under-standing of image as a symbol of God's ruling power over the material creation may well be the original intent of the priestly redactor of Genesis, but Theodore enlarged upon this functional role by seeing Adam's image, as Saint Paul has done, as a symbolic "type" who foreshadows Christ. He thus shifted the search for the meaning of image away from what the author of Genesis intended to how Christ was portrayed in the New Testament. By centering his attention upon Christ as the primary fulfillment of God's image, Theodore was able to speculate as to how Christ's revelatory, unitive, and cultic functions might be potentially present in Adam. Whether or not Paul is the source of Theodore's understanding of how Adam *qua* human being serves as the image of God, Theodore does portray Adam as the one who reveals the existence of God, unites the spiritual and material worlds to human beings and to God, and serves as the way that other creatures are to honor God by caring for all those who are created in His image.

Perhaps abetted by the Stoic worldview of humans as the bond uniting the created worlds of spirit and matter, Theodore also saw how the notion of image is intimately connected with Christ's role as the mediator who will recapitulate the universe and return it to His Father.[1] Because of his belief in and ardent defense of Christ's full, integral human nature, Theodore was easily able to assert Christ's consubstantiality with other humans and all the rest of creation, but he experienced a serious problem when he turned to discuss how Christ's humanity is actually united to the Word's divinity. For neither Nestorius nor he could affirm, because of their understanding of the terms involved, how Christ's humanity can be declared to be "hypostatically" or "consubstantially" united with the divine. When this was combined with their understanding of what divine transcendency entails, they were severely limited as to what they could assert about how Christ unites both his humanity and the rest of creation to God's Word. For God belongs to a "totally other" level of existence that no creature can bridge. As we shall see later, Theodore and Nestorius opted for the idea of a uniquely graced union where the Word's and Jesus' natures and wills function as one in Christ.

Since Theodore understood "image" as signifying a unitive role that Christ plays within the divine economy, this requires a clear understanding of what kind of union he conceived of between Christ's human and divine natures and between God and the rest of creation. But before attempting to delve into his explanation of these questions, we first need to explore how the terms ὑπόστασις (hypostasis), οὐσία (ousia), πρόσωπον (prosōpon), and φύσις (phusis), which became the vocabulary for expressing how Christ was both human and divine, were envisaged in general at the end of the fourth and the beginning of the fifth centuries. Since the Antiochenes were most likely influenced by the meanings that the Councils of Nicea (325) and Constantinople I (381) had accorded these four terms, we will examine how each council had understood these terms as expressing what they believed to be contained in Scripture. Their evolving understanding will serve as a backdrop for clarifying what the Antiochenes meant when they employed these terms.

Afterwards we will consider the extant late fourth-century work on human nature by the Christian philosopher Nemesius.[2] His philosophical synthesis has interest for us on several scores. First, since Nemesius

1. See Col. 1:15–20 and 1 Cor. 15:24–28.
2. For a translation with an informative introduction, notes and commentary, see William Telfer, ed. and trans., *Cyril of Jerusalem and Nemesius of Emesa*, The Library of Christian Classics 4 (Philadelphia: Westminster, 1955).

is acknowledged today as belonging to the Antiochene tradition, his work provides us some insight into what metaphysical ideas were current in Antioch at the beginning of the fifth century. Second, his work manifests a familiarity with the whole spectrum of Greek philosophical schools and indicates that the philosophy of the day was highly eclectic. And last, it is especially relevant for our study because it contains a clear allusion to Theodore. For these reasons, Nemesius' views are especially valuable in that they provide us with a way to compare and contrast Theodore's understanding of the metaphysical terms he employed and what kind of union he was proposing when he discussed the union between Christ's human and divine natures. All this will be helpful for determining how Theodore's Christology is intimately related to his understanding of how Christ functions as God's "image" and the bond of the universe.

Educational Influences

Before we probe into the background issues noted above, one other has to be briefly addressed: whether the education that Theodore and John Chrysostom received first (so it appears) at Libanius's famed rhetorical school and then later at Diodore's catechetical school had a philosophical component that might have oriented and inclined them toward a specific viewpoint.[3] While it is clear that Libanius's sophist training undeniably provided a professional education for the elite, it appears from the few facts known about the kind of classes offered there—and the same can be said about the school of Diodore—that his students received little or no in-depth formal training in philosophy. The two philosophical courses that seem to have been offered concerned logic and moral theory, particularly as regards a knowledge of the virtues. If there were other courses, or if Theodore and Chrysostom had read on their own the prevalent Neoplatonic writings, especially in the collections of philosophical opinions called doxographies, they would have been exposed to what is now recog-

3. For recent studies into education in the ancient Greek world, see Ilsetraut Hadot, *Arts libéraux et philosophie dans la pensée antique* (Paris: Études Augustiniennes, 1984) and George Kennedy, *Classical Rhetoric and Its Christian and Secular Tradition* (Chapel Hill: U of North Carolina, 1980). Three other works that are dated but still important studies are: Henri I. Marrou, *A History of Education in Antiquity*, trans. George Lamb (New York: Sheed, 1956); A. Harrent, *Les Écoles d'Antioche: essai sur le savoir IVe siècle apres J-C* (Paris, 1898); and John W. H. Walden, *The Universities of Ancient Greece* (New York: Scribner's, 1912).

nized to have been fundamentally an eclectic outlook toward metaphysics. From what is known specifically about the kind of education that Libanius's training would have offered to Chrysostom and Theodore, we can surmise that they would have been well schooled in how to express their thoughts, arguments, and encomiums in orderly, elegant, and persuasive language.[4] It would have also inculcated well-tested rhetorical principles and methods on how to marshal arguments in full support of one's position so as to best one's opposition. A sophist education[5] also seems to have sought to instill within its students a highly critical attitude toward traditional positions that were being accepted unquestioningly. We see this exemplified in Theodore, who often challenged traditional beliefs that he believed had not been well thought-out.

If we can judge from the few records we possess, the School of Diodore seems to have been primarily, if not totally, dedicated to the study of Scripture and, also likely, to liturgical practice.[6] The remarks that are extant in the writings of the Antiochenes indicate that they were hostile to the pagan philosophers as defenders of paganism. They would be among those who questioned what Athens had to offer Jerusalem, especially as they believed that philosophy was unable to solve such fundamental questions as: what was the origin of life, the cause of human weakness, the reason for human freedom, the right way to live one's life, and the nature and certainty of a future life after death. According to their way of thinking, the various pagan philosophical schools could only speculate about the answers to such questions.

Cultural and Conciliar Understanding of Metaphysical Terms

Since John Chrysostom, Theodore, and Nestorius were concerned solely with mining the truths God has revealed through Scripture and tradition,

4. For studies on the kind of training that Libanius would have offered, see A. J. Festugière, *Antioche païenne et chrétienne: Libanius, Chrysostome et les moines de Syrie* (Paris: De Boccard, 1959); Paul Petit, *Les étudiants de Libanius* (Paris: Nouvelles Éditions latines, 1957); and J. H. W. G. Liebeschuetz, *Antioch: City and Imperial Administration in the Later Roman Empire* (Oxford: Clarendon, 1972).

5. See James Jarrett, *The Educational Theories of the Sophists* (New York: Teachers College P, 1969).

6. See the following chapter's treatment on the kind of schooling that Diodore's training would likely have imparted.

they manifested little interest in their writings about philosophical questions. Yet they were undoubtedly influenced by the metaphysical ideas that had permeated the Greek culture and had become part of the language of their day.[7] We can detect this presence in the terms that they and the other Fathers used to express what the New Testament has revealed about God as triune and Christ as both divine and human. Since the terms ὑπόστασις, οὐσία, πρόσωπον, and φύσις, which they employed for these theological concepts, run a wide gamut of meanings, we now need to consider in general the various meanings that they possessed in Scripture and in Late Antiquity. This will provide us with a useful, if not a necessary, background for understanding first what the Fathers meant in their conciliar documents when they employed these words and then in the next chapter what meaning the Antiochenes have attached to these terms. This is important because part of the conflict between Cyril and Nestorius was semantic in nature; that is, that they conceived of ὑπόστασις, πρόσωπον, and φύσις in notably different ways.

The General Meanings of Trinitarian and Christological Terms

Since ὑπόστασις, is the critical term in the controversy between Nestorius and Cyril, we will first begin with this word and then proceed to the others.[8] If one takes ὑπόστασις as derived from the transitive verb ὑφίστημι,[9]

7. For a treatment on how much influence Hellenistic thought had upon the Fathers in general, see Edwin Hatch, *The Influence of Greek Ideas and Usages upon the Christian Church*, ed. A. M. Fairbairn, 5th ed. (1895; reprint, Peabody, Mass.: Hendrickson, 1995). Hatch ends his study of the influence of Greek thought upon the early church by expressing his opinion that Hellenistic thought shifted the Fathers' attention away from leading a moral and spiritual life to their assenting intellectually to a body of doctrines proclaimed by a majority. While Greek terms played a critical role in shaping the Fathers' terminology, I think that they gradually narrowed the meaning of what for them was the common cultural understanding of the terms. They did this to reflect their beliefs in what the New Testament and their own traditional Christian language were affirming about the Trinity and the union of natures in Christ.

8. I am indebted here to G. W. H. Lampe, ed., *A Patristic Greek Lexicon* (Oxford: Clarendon, 1961); Helmut Köster, *Theological Dictionary of the New Testament*, ed. Gerhard Friedrich, trans. Geoffrey W. Bromiley (Grand Rapids, Mich.: Eerdmans, 1968), esp. vols. 6 and 8; and H. G. Liddell and R. Scott, ed., *A Greek-English Lexicon* (Oxford: Clarendon, 1961).

9. Köster, 8:573. In his treatment of *hypostasis* Helmut Köster objects to those who derive different etymological meanings from ὑφίστημι and ὑφίσταμαι.

it moves from signifying first "origination," then "sustenance," and later even the notions of "actualization," and "plan." If it is, on the other hand, from the intransitive verb ὑφίσταμαι, it can connote a wide range of meanings: a "source," "original existence," "being," "state of being," "reality," "nature," "substance," "substantive existence," "subsistent entity," "concrete entity," "individual," "settling," "property," "statement," and finally a "person." The earliest examples of ὑπόστασις point to a medical and scientific origin.[10] Stoicism was the first school to introduce the scientific usage into philosophy.[11] It originally understood the term ὑπόστασις as a subsisting unformed being prior to becoming a specific being, as well as the actual coming into existence of primal matter. It later stressed the latter meaning as primary.

Although ὑπόστασις and οὐσία are quite close in meaning, they are clearly differentiated conceptually. Where οὐσία is by nature primal and eternal matter as such, its ὑπόστασις is a real being that has entered into existence.[12] Its reality, however, is not immediately apparent but can be recognized as present beneath its appearance.[13] Among the Neoplatonists, the term became synonymous with οὐσία.[14] From his study of how the term was employed after New Testament times, Köster detects no consistent evolution in the meaning of the term among the Fathers until the fifth century. He observes that: "One has rather to consider at every step the corresponding usage in the period concerned."[15]

The word πρόσωπον possesses fewer meanings than ὑπόστασις.[16] Its principal meaning is that of a "face" or "expression" or one's "individual outward being." It connotes, however, that what appears is real and

10. Ibid., 8:572.

11. Ibid., 8:575.

12. Ibid. Köster elaborates on the significance that this has for translating *hypostasis* in Hebrews 11:1. He contends that Luther's translation of *hypostasis* as being "sure confidence" is untenable. It ought to be rendered as the "reality" guaranteeing faith and the "reality of the goods hoped for." For Köster the term stands for "the 'reality' of God which stands contrasted with the corruptible, shadowy, and merely prototypical character of the world but which is paradoxically present in Jesus and is the possession of the community" (576).

13. See Köster, 8:586. Köster describes *ousia* as primal matter that is present under its hypostasized form and quality.

14. Ibid., 8:575.

15. Ibid., 8:589.

16. See Lampe, 1186–89, and E. Lohse's treatment in the *Theological Dictionary of the New Testament*, ed. Gerhard Friedrich, trans. Geoffrey W. Bromiley (Grand Rapids, Mich.: Eerdmans, 1968), 768–79.

not something that is false or transitory. It was employed too to signify a "surface," a "form" and, because of its resemblance to a human face, to the "mask" worn by an actor and then extended to one's "role" in a drama or to one's "position" within his or her community. In the Septuagint πρόσωπον was selected to translate the Hebrew word for "face," but as "face" understood in a synecdochical sense as connoting the whole person.[17] When employed in the phrase "to see God's face," the phrase meant that one has been specially graced to encounter God's presence within a cultic setting.[18] In the New Testament it expresses a "personal presence" and implies the "whole person."[19] In the first few centuries c.e., it was employed too as a legal term, affirming a person who possessed legal rights. In this sense, a child or a slave would not be considered a πρόσωπον.[20]

In the patristic period the term πρόσωπον slowly evolved in its meaning because of protracted trinitarian and christological controversies. Among the anti-Sabellian writers it was interpreted as being synonymous with ὑπόστασις but without any of the latter's metaphysical connotations. It was used also to express the concrete disclosure of an abstract οὐσία,[21] and, in this sense, as an individual. As will soon be discussed, Nestorius seems to have understood πρόσωπον in way similar to Cyril's view of ὑπόστασις.[22] Cyril, on the other hand, understood Nestorius's use of πρόσωπον as signifying that Christ had assumed the divinity in the way that an actor took on a character role in a drama, so that one could not "confess that the Word of God suffered in the flesh and was crucified in the flesh."[23]

The final term, φύσις, includes everything that has been given to a being at its original constitution.[24] As Köster observes, to speak of a "φύσις is already to go beyond the sphere of naive description and implies a judgment on its actual constitution or true nature."[25] To inquire

17. Köster, 6:771. 18. Ibid., 6:773.
19. Ibid., 6:776. 20. Lampe, 1187.
21. Ibid., 1188.
22. See Aloys Grillmeier's comments on this equivalency in his work on *Christ in Christian Tradition: From the Apostolic Age to Chalcedon (451)*, trans. John Bowden, 2d ed., vol. 1 (Atlanta: John Knox, 1975), 508–9.
23. Norman P. Tonner, ed., *Decrees of the Ecumenical Councils*, vol. 1 (Washington: Georgetown UP, 1990), 61.
24. Köster, 9:252. 25. Ibid.

about a φύσις was to seek what belongs peculiarly and distinctively to its true constitution either from the beginning or the final product of its development. In this sense, it meant the definition of something. Aristotle appears to have been the first to employ φύσις as a philosophical term, with, however, a twofold sense. It can be considered in an abstract way as the true universal nature of a being that remains constant or in a concrete way as a specific, individual nature.[26]

The Evolution in the Patristic Understanding of Terms

As studies have pointed out,[27] the Antiochene Fathers were not philosophers but biblical exegetes and pastoral bishops who were concerned about promoting and defending what they believed to the authentic Christian tradition. While they may have been somewhat influenced by Greek metaphysical speculations that had pervaded the cultural thought and language of their day,[28] they were mainly dependent, in my opinion, upon how the Fathers at the Councils of Nicea and Constantinople I had understood ὑπόστασις, οὐσία, πρόσωπον, and φύσις. To substantiate this, we need now to discuss how these terms evolved in their meanings within conciliar documents.[29]

The Fathers at the Council of Nicea promulgated a creed that they insisted accurately affirmed what Scripture had revealed about the relationship existing between the Word of God and His Father. They added in a concluding paragraph to their creed that "those who say 'that there once was [a time] when he was not' and 'before he was begotten he was not' and that he came to be from things that were not or from another ὑποστάσεως or οὐσίας [which the Latin text simply translates both by

26. Ibid., 9:256–58.

27. Grillmeier's evaluation (424) of Theodore is typical: "He is primarily an exegete, 'the Interpreter', as he was called, and is so even in his dogmatic writings. He experiences the theology and presence of Christ as a liturgist. His speculative theology is therefore subsidiary, and not an aim in itself. His philosophy stands even further in the background. It makes itself felt primarily in his anthropology."

28. Hatch maintains that Greek philosophical thought exercised a direct influence upon doctrinal development in the early church (2). I believe, rather, that the Antiochenes were influenced by the way these terms had evolved within the Christian tradition.

29. For the most recent overall study of the creeds in English, the best is J. N. D. Kelly, *Early Christian Creeds*, 3d ed. (San Francisco: Harper, 1978).

the one word *substantia*] . . . these the catholic and apostolic church anathematizes."[30] The Fathers indicate here that they understood ὑπόστασις as synonymous at least in some equivalent sense[31] with οὐσία. The two terms were cited to emphasize against Arius and his followers that the Word was really God in the same sense as the Father. The Nicene Fathers' use of the two terms indicates that there existed some differences among themselves or in the current understanding of the day as to which term best expressed this. But by combining both, they are equivalently saying that ὑπόστασις should be interpreted in the sense of an οὐσία and vice versa.

In their creedal statement, the Fathers of the First Council of Constantinople did not repeat the final paragraph of the Nicene creed,[32] but in an official letter they professed their belief that the Father, the Son and the Holy Spirit have "a single Godhead and power and . . . in three most perfect ὑποστάσεις or more correctly in three perfect πρόσωπα, so that there is no place for the disease of Sabellius whereby the ὑποστάσεις are confused and as a result their peculiar characteristics too are destroyed."[33] The signifiance is that at Nicea, ὑπόστασις was considered synonymous with οὐσία. By Constantinople, it had become interchangeable with πρόσωπον. For the Fathers at Constantinople, οὐσία is that which is by the Father, the Son, and the Holy Spirit in their common triune nature. Ὑπόστασις (and πρόσωπον) is that which is uniquely characteristic of each individual divine "person."

In the same episcopal letter, the Fathers at Constantinople also rejected what they insisted were the errors of the Eunomians, Arians, and the Pneumatomachi. They were convinced that these three sects have mistakenly made "a division of οὐσία or φύσις or Godhead and the

---

30. Tonner, 1:5. The translations here and in the following citations from Tonner are my own based on the Greek text. For a theological treatment of the significance of the Nicene creed, see Grillmeier, 264–73.

31. As mentioned above, there can exist a conceptual difference between the two terms, *ousia* denoting primal matter as such and *hypostasis* emphasizing a being who exists but whose reality is not immediately apparent. The term *ousia* may also be used here in a non-metaphysical way simply to express the being or reality of the Trinity. For a recent study on how these two terms evolved in the writings of Basil of Caesarea, see Lucian Turcescu, "*Prosôpon* and *Hypostasis* in Basil of Caesarea's *Against Eunomius* and the Epistles," *Vigiliae Christianae* 51 (1997): 374–95.

32. See Tonner, 24 for the creed proclaimed at Constantinople I.

33. Ibid., 28.

introduction . . . of a φύσις with a different οὐσία."[34] Here we see that in the Fathers' conception a φύσις implied the presence of an underlying οὐσία in the sense that a φύσις makes an οὐσία more explicit as a species does a genus. The two can only be separated conceptually: one cannot have a φύσις that actually differs from its οὐσία.

While both Cyril and the Antiochenes firmly adhered to the decrees of Nicea and Constantinople I, their christological dispute reveals that they understood πρόσωπον, ὑπόστασις, and φύσις as related to each other in different ways. As we will learn, the Antiochenes looked upon πρόσωπον as externally manifesting a ὑπόστασις that embraces all the "elements" of an existing concrete φύσις together with its οὐσία. Such a viewpoint is clearly in keeping with conciliar documents where ὑπόστασις and πρόσωπον as well as ὑπόστασις and οὐσία (which cannot be separated from its φύσις) are affirmed as intimately related as synonyms. Cyril, however, used ὑπόστασις as the term that best describes the unity of the divine and human natures within the "person" of the Word. He took at face value both the statement in John's Gospel that the Word became flesh and the Nicene creed's declaration that the only-begotten Son who is of the same οὐσία as God became incarnated, suffered and rose up on the third day. He understood ὑπόστασις not in any metaphysical sense but simply as designating what scriptural and traditional language affirmed about the Word as the subject to whom Christ's human properties can be truly attributed.[35] On the other hand, when Nestorius wanted to distinguish to which nature natural properties should be attributed, Cyril interpreted his need to do so as a clear sign that Nestorius was holding for two distinct individual subjects under the umbrella term "Christ" or for a voluntary union between Jesus and the Word.

While our interest centers only on those councils whose terms might have influenced the Antiochene understanding, it is helpful to fill out the picture with what the Orthodox-Catholic position became after Nestorius's condemnation at the Council of Ephesus in 431. Because of a growing antagonistic division within the church, fed in no small measure by the ambiguities in Cyril's terminology, especially his references to "the one

34. Ibid.
35. Richard A. Norris, Jr. in his article "Toward a Contemporary Interpretation of the Chalcedonian Definition," *Lux in Lumine: Essays for W. N. Pittenger* (New York: Seabury, 1966), 62–79, esp. 74–75.

incarnate φύσις of God the Word," it soon became necessary to convene a general council at Chalcedon in 451. It was here that the Orthodox-Catholic terminology for referring to the unity of natures in Christ was definitively established. The Fathers at Chalcedon began their sessions by reaffirming the creeds of both Nicea and Constantinople I as well as the decrees of Ephesus. Then in what became the heart of their teaching, they solemnly declared: ". . . we all with one voice teach the confession of . . . one and the same Christ, Son, Lord, only-begotten, acknowledged in two φύσεις which undergo no confusion, no change, no division, no separation; at no point was the difference between the φύσεις taken away through the union, but rather the property of each φύσις is preserved and comes together into a single πρόσωπον and a single ὑπόστασις he is not parted or divided into two, but is one and the same only-begotten Son, God, Word, Lord Jesus Christ . . ."[36] So besides maintaining once again the equivalency of ὑπόστασις and πρόσωπον in the sense that Christ's πρόσωπον externally manifests the Word's ὑπόστασις which alone is the real subject acting in both divine and human ways, the council Fathers found it necessary to insist on a distinction between the Word's ὑπόστασις and Christ's human φύσις, and on the integrity of each nature with its own properties. They reaffirmed Cyril's insight that the union within Christ occurs not on the level of the two natures that always remained intact but on the level of the Word's ὑπόστασις. They had logically concluded, as Cyril had earlier done, from the statements made in Scripture and the established traditional way of speaking about Christ and his mother that the Word's is the subject to whom the properties of both natures can be rightly attributed.

The Second Council of Constantinople (553), noted for its condemnation of Theodore, Ibas, and Theodoret, expressed the same terminological outlook, as can be seen highlighted in the following decrees concerning the Trinity and Christ's union of natures:

If anyone does not confess one φύσις or οὐσία for the Father, Son and Holy Spirit, one power and authority, a ὁμοούσιον Trinity, one Deity to be adored in three ὑπόστασεις or πρόσωπα: let such a one be anathema[37]. . . . If anyone, when speaking in regard to the two φύσεις does not confess that our one Lord Jesus Christ was made known in his divinity and humanity, in order that by this to signify

36. Tonner, 86.
37. Ibid., 114.

a difference of φύσεις of which an ineffable union has been made without confusion, in which neither the φύσις of flesh changed over to the φύσις of the Word
(for each remained what it was by φύσις even after the union had taken place in a
hypostatic way . . . let such a one be anathema.[38]

Having shown an evolving conciliar understanding of the terms used in
the fourth and fifth centuries to express the Christian beliefs in the Trinity
and the reality of Christ as human and divine, we turn now to a consideration of what seems to have been the metaphysical outlook at Antioch
around the beginning of the fifth century. Although the Antiochenes were
primarily concerned with what the Scriptures and Christian tradition had
manifested about the meaning of life, they were exposed to all the major
metaphysical questions, ideas, and terms circulating in their cultural setting. To provide us with some insight into what this may have been, we are
fortunate to have a classic philosophical work written by a Christian author
belonging, as most agree, to the Antiochene tradition. Nemesius's work *On
Human Nature* affords us a source for assessing Theodore's views on human
beings as the bond uniting the spiritual and material worlds and on the kind
of union that he proposed for explaining how spiritual realities can be
united with material beings without each being altered in the process.

Nemesius

Nemesius's work *On Human Nature* quickly became a classical patristic synthesis of Christian anthropology. It is a combination of Christian
revelation with what he considered to be the prime philosophical insights
from Neoplatonism, Aristotelianism, Stoicism, Neo-Pythagoreanism, and
the medical writings of Galen (131–200 C.E.).[39] But, as William Telfer shows

38. Ibid., 117.
39. For a recent study that sums up the secondary literature currently available
concerning the ancient Greek philosophical systems, see Anthony A. Long, *Hellenistic
Philosophy: Stoics, Epicureans, Sceptics*, 2d ed. (1974; reprint, Berkeley: U California P,
1986); for the classic study demonstrating Philo's influence upon the early Fathers,
Harry A. Wolfson, *The Philosophy of the Church Fathers*, vol. 1, *Faith, Trinity, Incarnation*
(Cambridge: Harvard UP, 1964); and for a study showing the Fathers' dependence upon
Stoicism and Platonism, Ronald H. Nash, *Christianity and the Hellenistic World* (Grand
Rapids, Mich.: Zondervan, 1984); and for a study of their influence in the development
of the Christian doctrine of God, Robert M. Grant, *Gods and the One God*, Library of
Early Christianity (Philadelphia: Westminster, 1986).

convincingly in his notes and commentaries following each section of his edition, Nemesius has derived his philosophical opinions primarily from Neoplatonic writers and / or the doxographies of the day.[40] He has, however, acquired his medical facts and several of his anthropological opinions immediately from Galen. But no matter what sources he has employed, Nemesius has fashioned his own masterful explanation of human nature to such an extent that, as Telfer has rightly remarked, his work cannot be said to belong to any one specific philosophical school of thought (219).

Whenever Nemesius has introduced philosophical opinions of others, it is evident over time that he has chosen these because they cohere with and promote his apologetic purpose in writing. His intent manifests itself when he advances a Christian explanation to perplexing questions about human nature. We observe this in his work when he turns to the scriptural account about the fall of Adam to explain why humans are mortal and morally weak. It is also evident when he seeks to illumine the kind of union between the soul and the body by comparing it to the union between the Word and Christ's humanity. Since Nemesius appeals to faith explanations in instances where philosophy cannot answer what is the origin and end of human nature, Telfer believes that this supports the opinion that Nemesius directed his work to moderately cultured non-Christians who are somewhat acquainted with Christian beliefs (227).

As we now proceed to consider in detail Nemesius's opinions *On Human Nature*, our concern centers solely upon his views regarding human nature in general, its bonding role, the nature of the soul, the soul's union with the body, free-will, and divine providence—topics that mirror the same, or at the very least a similar, outlook on human nature that we find present in Theodore and Nestorius. After summarizing Nemesius's thought on these topics, we will then discuss which Greek philosophic opinions appear to have played a positive role in shaping Nemesius's thought on specific points. This will serve as a detailed background for the following chapter's consideration of how the Antiochene Fathers conceived of human nature and its union with the Word in Christ. This in turn will offer a backdrop for understanding Theodore's positions on

40. William Telfer, ed. and trans., *Cyril of Jerusalem and Nemesius of Emesa*, The Library of Christian Classics 4 (Philadelphia: Westminster, 1955), 260. Through the remainder of Chapter 3, page references to Telfer will be made parenthetically in the text.

Adam and Christ as the "images" of God who bind together all elements within the universe and on the way that Christ's human and divine natures function together.

Nemesius's Anthropological Understanding of Human Nature

Nemesius commenced his work by declaring that human nature is essentially composed of body and soul. He then proceeded to dismiss the opinion of those, such as Apollinaris, who state that the mind can be considered a third entity distinct from the soul (224). This distinction, as we will see, has ramifications for Christology and, as Nemesius's next point specifies more clearly, also for Theodore's view on the image of God. For in his second section, Nemesius noted how humans are situated on the boundary line "between the intelligible order and the phenomenal order" (229), for they are akin to irrational creatures because of their corporeal bodies and to incorporeal beings because of their rational faculties. Humans stand at the focal point where the two worlds or orders of creation intersect and are linked in a unique bond. Nemesius stated it as follows: "Thus God, everywhere fitting one thing to another harmoniously, bound them all together, uniting in one bond things intelligible and things phenomenal, by means of his creation of man" (234).

Nemesius looked upon the material world of creation as though it were a ladder. On the bottom step are the simplest of all the material creatures, whose chief function is to serve the needs of those more complex and higher up on the ladder than themselves. Because they serve as the link enabling the physical world to come into contact with the spiritual world beyond, humans are assigned the highest rung on the ladder of material creation,[41] but this honored position also imposes upon them a cosmic responsibility. To explain what this responsibility is and what happens when a person does not live up to it, Nemesius turned to the beginning of Genesis which describes how when Adam sinned, he became subject to

41. Ibid., 248–49. Nemesius observed that besides joining mortal creatures with spiritual beings and bringing rational beings into contact with those that are irrational, a human being bears in one's nature "a reflex of the whole creation and is therefore rightly called 'the world in little.'" Telfer notes (254) that Nemesius's description of humankind as a *mikros kosmos* is the nearest that an ancient writer has come to our modern term "microcosm."

death and enslaved to his bodily needs. His death also entailed a cosmic disaster, for it meant that he could no longer function as the bond linking the material and spiritual worlds with each other and with God (239–40). Instead of being the unifying element in creation, he became the cause for its cosmic dissolution.

Because Nemesius's aim was to show pagans that leading Greek philosophers agreed with his anthropological view of human nature, he was cautious about elaborating upon Christian teaching, for he was not writing as a theologian but as a philosopher. But this did not prevent him from mentioning that the reason humans have been so specially created is that God became human, enabling humanity thereby to "attain incorruption and escape corruption, [so that they] might reign on high, being made after the image and likeness of God, dwelling with Christ as a child of God, and might be throned above all rule and all authority "(255). While this passage on Christ's role in salvation is tangential to Nemesius's primary intent, it is valuable for its suggestion that Nemesius regarded the "image of God" to be a dignity bestowed on humans empowering them to reign on high with Christ. It is a view similar to that affirmed by Diodore, Chrysostom, and Theodoret, that men *qua* males have been entrusted with power over the material creation.

The Nature of the Soul

After asserting what he considered to be the make-up of human nature in general and its specific role within the universe, Nemesius turned to a closer study of the nature of the human soul. He first showed against the Stoics that it was an incorporeal substance. He then described the soul in Aristotelian terms as functioning as the form determining the body: "a body requires some principle keeping it together, assembling its constituents, and (so express it) binding and holding them in union" (262). He afterwards defined the soul as "a self-subsisting rational living creature, ceaselessly in motion, the indispensable integrator of a living body, implicated in the material universe, and yet no part or product thereof" (280). While insisting that the body cannot affect an incorporeal and immortal soul (292), Nemesius nevertheless made it a cardinal principle "that a human body must be the fit habitation for a human soul, so that the study of the nature of man is the study of the soul in union with its body" (293).

Nemesius next moved to the critical question of what kind of union can allow the soul not to lose its own identity as an individual, uncorrupted nature nor the body its corporeal identity. Nemesius excluded a union of juxtaposition, as though they were two partners in a dance, or one of mixture, as wine becomes mingled with water, or the Neoplatonic view that the soul uses or puts on the body, as though the body were a coat (294–95). His answer was simply to accept the solution proposed by Ammonius Saccas that "it is the nature of the *intelligibles* both to be capable of union with things adapted to receive them . . . and to remain, nevertheless, unconfused with them while in union"(295). In stating this, Nemesius is, of course, making a statement of fact rather than offering an explanation of why the soul as an intelligible being has to relate to the body in this way. As we will see later, both Theodore and Nestorius will incorporate this Neoplatonic answer into their view of how the Word is united to the human nature of Christ, but with their own twist on what term ought to be used to describe the union and how it ought to be understood.

To elucidate how the intelligible or spiritual reality of a human soul can coexist with a corporeal body without being changed by it, Nemesius offered two examples. First of all, he compared the union of the soul with its body to that of an idea and the "object" that it represents (296). Just as something or someone existing in the external world can become one with the mind's idea of it, with each maintaining its separate existence apart from the other, so too can the soul modify "whatever it indwells, in accordance with its own life, while itself suffering no reciprocal change" (298). Yet as the following indicates, there is an active relationship between the soul and the body:

Therefore, if the soul is said to be in a body, it is not so said in the sense of being located in a body, but rather as being in habitual relation of presence there, even as God is said to be in us. For we may say that the soul is bound by habit to the body, or by an inclination or disposition towards it, just as they say that a lover is bound to his beloved, not meaning physically, or spatially, but habitually.[42]

This passage brings out two points about the term "habitual" when applied to the relationship between the soul and the body. In a negative sense, it states that the soul cannot be thought to be circumscribed in a

---

42. Ibid., 299. In a note, Telfer remarks: "We may compare Nemesius' notion of the soul indwelling in the body by habit of predilection with that of Theodore of Mopsuestia that God indwells in the righteous, not by omnipotence, but by his favor (εὐδοκία)."

certain place. In a positive sense, it refers to a person's usual, customary way of acting toward one with whom he or she is in a standing relationship. It also connotes a continuing, concerned disposition and desire to do whatever will benefit one's co-partner. Nemesius stated his intent more fully by clarifying that the soul relates "sympathetically" with its body: "to wit, the community of feeling which is throughout the living creature, because it is one subject"(296–97). Since the soul supplies the energy source its body requires, it can, therefore, be thought of as participating in what the body experiences, for the two are united as one in the same living organism.

We find the same view expressed in Nemesius's treatment of the passions. This is a critical question for him, as it was for all the Neoplatonists, for it raised the issue of whether the passions affect the soul and, if so, how they can affect a soul that is said to be impassible.[43] Nemesius responded by attributing the passions to the embodied soul in general and only indirectly to its intellectual life because the soul suffers in sympathy with its body (276). Telfer remarks on this point that: "the vital power which is pre-requisite to feeling is acknowledged to be derived by the body from the soul. It is therefore legitimate to speak of the soul's 'sympathy' with its body, thus recognizing that while soul and body are not partners on equal terms, in this respect, they are partners."[44]

The second comparison that Nemesius offers to exemplify the kind of union between the soul and the body further illustrates the habitual relationship of sympathy between the two. He compared the union between the Word and Christ's humanity to that between the soul and the body.[45] In a note on this section, Telfer points out that many of the Fathers have reversed this parallelism, for they used the soul's union with the body to illumine the union between the natures in Christ (300). The reversal is important to note, for by comparing the union of natures to the way that the soul and the body are united suggests the Monophysite contention that Christ's humanity is united to the uncreated Word by "nature" and becomes one with it. Since it required years of controversy to bring this

43. Nemesius explains in great detail what he means by passion in Telfer, 346–48.

44. Ibid., 297. For a schematic outline of Nemesius's psychology, see Telfer, 346. He presents here an overview that Domanski has proposed as a way to examine Nemesius's psychological approach. Domanski argues that it is an Aristotelian scheme.

45. Telfer (297) also states that Nemesius held that Christ's soul came into existence when his body was conceived.

nuance to the fore, it was not likely that Nemesius was sensitive to this when he chose to reverse the comparison. As we will see, Theodore alludes to this analogy, and Nestorius rejected its applicability to the union between Christ's natures.

When Nemesius does explain how he understood the union of the two natures in Christ, he maintained as indisputable that the Word cannot be affected in any way by his union with Christ's humanity, seeing that his nature is immutable. In a sentence that became a bedrock axiom of the Antiochene theologians and that foreshadows by fifty years the Council of Chalcedon's most often quoted statement, Nemesius described how Christ's natures interrelate with one other thus:

> The Word mingles with body and soul, and yet remains throughout unmixed, unconfused, uncorrupted, untransformed, not sharing their passivity but only their activity, not perishing with them, nor changing as they change; but, on the one hand, contributing to their growth, and, on the other, nowise degraded by contact with them, so that he continues immutable and unconfused, seeing that he is altogether without share in any kind of alteration. (301)

Nemesius also expanded upon what he intended here, when he referred to "the opinion of certain men of note" (which Telfer interprets to be a respectful reference to Theodore of Mopsuestia) who maintain that the union is by divine favor.[46] He repudiated such an opinion out of hand, insisting that the union has to be "grounded in nature." He implied that God is certainly expressing his favor by uniting the humanity of Christ to the divinity of the Word, but he holds that the union has to be founded on something much more substantial than when two people act in ways that are pleasing to each other. In other words, the union cannot be merely a voluntary union where two wills are in loving agreement with one another. However, his insistence upon a union "grounded in nature" should not be taken in a Monophysite sense. For since he contends that the natures remain unconfused within the union, he would be opposed to the Monophysite dogmatic formula that there is one nature—divine—after the union. He was expressing his belief in a real, substantial union.

To sum up Nemesius' position regarding the union of natures in Christ and between the soul and the body, it is an "habitual" union "in nature" where the spiritual partner is actively "sympathetic" to the needs of

46. Telfer (303 and also 299) asserts that Nemesius's use of the anonymous plural should not be understood as referring to anyone else other than Theodore.

its corporeal co-partner. His rejection of a union where the natures lose their individual identities or are united by their will complements what his two examples suggest about the union. He considers the union between the Word and Jesus' humanity to be a substantial union where each nature remains intact, even as the divine energizes and sympathizes with the human without being altered in its nature. In brief, a "habitual" union is not to be understood as defining the kind of union that exists between two natures that are spiritual and corporeal. Rather it is describing the *way* (or the *how*) a spiritual being is lovingly disposed towards its corporeal partner, energizes it, but is not altered in any way in the process.

Free Will

In his final sections, Nemesius treated three main points: the ability of the will to choose and act freely, the fallacy of a deterministic destiny, and the meaning and scope of providence. The last two questions are really corollaries connected with free will, for, if everything is fated to fulfill a foreseen, pre-determined destiny, a person is not truly free to act. But if one is actually free to determine oneself, in what sense, then, can God be said to exercise divine providence over everything, not merely in general but also over the particular free acts of humans? These questions were critical ones for Nemesius, for in writing an apologetic work to non-Christians, he had to address areas where pagan beliefs ran counter to what Christians believe about God's providence.

The issue of free will was especially critical for those who adhered to the Antiochene tradition. For unlike the Alexandrians who stressed a mystical path to union with God, the Antiochenes were more voluntaristic in their outlook on the role that the will plays in the attainment of salvation. For, if a person is to be judged on how well he or she has lived an upright life in accordance with divine laws, then he or she must be liable for what one is personally responsible. Nemesius, however, because of his focus on philosophical anthropology, only alluded to what the Antiochenes would stress: the soteriological importance of one's free will. For they realized that Jesus had to be endowed with human free will, not only so that he might be truly and fully human but also so that he, as well as all other human beings, might play—together with God's grace—his own personal role in gaining a future immortal and immutable life.

Nemesius began his treatment of an act of free choice by pointing out that it is not simply a voluntary act, or an act of desiring, wanting, or deliberation. He described it as "a kind of plan, followed by deliberation, which ends in a decision"(393). In other words, it includes rational as well as voluntary elements. To act in a free way is possible because God created the immortal soul mutable (417–20). This ability to change enables a person to do not only good but evil and, if evil, then to repent (420). When he discussed the question of the human proclivity for evil, Nemesius taught that it can be sufficiently explained by one's upbringing in an environment that leads to the acquisition of bad habits.

When taken together with Nemesius's stress upon the role that human free will plays in the drama of salvation, his teaching about the will's proclivity to sin has opened Nemesius to the charge that he was a Pelagian. Since a similar charge of Pelagianism has also been brought against Chrysostom and Theodore, this points to a major tenet of the Antiochene tradition: the safeguarding of the human will in Christ as well as its role in the divine economy of salvation. Nemesius, however, was no more a Pelagian than Chrysostom and Theodore.[47] First of all, Nemesius wrote at a time when Pelagianism had not yet erupted into a bitter, full-blown theological controversy. Even if he were aware of the issue, it would be expecting far too much to demand that Nemesius deal with the Christian doctrine of grace in an apologetic treatise directed primarily to non-Christians (422–23). But above all, his concern, like that of the other Antiochenes, was aimed at defending the will as being not evil, *in se*, but good, and on maintaining its pivotal role in attaining the future life planned by God. How far the will can actually do good without the aid of grace was not a question that troubled him. His interest was solely to show that "badness is not in the faculties, but in our habits, and our habits are as we choose; and surely it is by our choice that we become evil. We are not so by nature" (421).

While the relationship of free will to grace was not an issue for those in the Antiochene tradition, Nemesius does show that he was sensitive to human weakness and its effect upon a person's will-power. He states this when discussing the after-effects of Adam's disobedience: "But, in so doing, (Adam) sacrificed his own advance towards perfection, and became

47. For a treatment of this question, see Telfer 420–21.

the slave of bodily needs" (239). Since Adam's fall has meant that all his descendants have been born with a mortal body and a mutable soul, it follows that Nemesius would also likely hold that they too will be, like their forefather Adam, subject to personal enslavement. Moreover, by stating in passing that redemption entails a change from mortality and mutability to a future state of immortality and immutability, Nemesius would seem to require the intervention of divine grace not only to move to a new immortal and immutable life but also to do what is required to achieve this.

Nemesius's theory of morality combines what he understood to be the psychology of Aristotle (as found in his *Nicomachean Ethics* or more likely a commentary on this) with that of Galen.[48] He moved from a consideration of voluntary acts in general to their value in a moral sense. As a Christian, he realized the critical roles that the practical reason and free will exercise in an individual's moral life, for if a person's individual actions are to be judged fairly by God, this presumes an awareness of what is good and evil and a freedom to determine what one wants to do.[49] In commenting on Nemesius's treatment of the relationship between human freedom and mutability, Telfer faults Nemesius for not fulfilling what he promised to do: to demonstrate that "rational creatures, despite their creaturehood, should come, through continual exercise of right choice and contemplation of God himself, to share the divine immutability" (420). It is a theme, however, that Theodore set at the heart of his own approach to Christology and Soteriology.

One final point needs to be made. Nemesius was critical of what he understood to be Aristotle's viewpoint regarding providence. He chided Aristotle for not going far enough in his teaching about the role and extent of providence. Though Nemesius believed that he had found in Aristotle's sixth book of the *Nicomachean Ethics* "a hint . . . that it is Nature that manages the details of our lives" (436), he granted that Aristotle restricted the guidance of providence over particulars. Telfer comments upon this, pointing out that Aristotle was an agnostic who could not permit God in

---

48. Ibid., 350. Nemesius is dependent especially upon the opening chapters of the third book and the sixth book of the *Nicomachean Ethics*. See Telfer, 413.

49. For a discussion of this point, see Richard A. Norris, Jr., *Manhood and Christ* (Oxford: Clarendon, 1963), 49.

his system to exercise any moral sway that could be rightly termed "divine providence" over the world, for it would undermine a human being's real freedom of choice.

Nemesius's Eclecticism

Even a mere perusal of Nemesius's text and Telfer's commentary and notes makes it patently evident that Nemesius was familiar with the thought of the leading Greek philosophers. Telfer points out that citing opinions of famous thinkers on a particular subject and then coming to one's own conclusions by an analysis and criticism of their positions was customary in philosophical treatises of Late Antiquity (224–26). While it may be academic whether Nemesius had acquired his knowledge directly or, as Telfer has demonstrated in convincing fashion, mediately from Neoplatonic commentaries or doxographies, Telfer appears correct in his assessment that Nemesius appealed to classical Greek philosophers primarily to bolster his own Christian arguments among his educated non-Christian readers. For it would afford his own personal synthesis concerning the many fundamental problems about human nature raised by philosophers a more rationally persuasive and compelling respectability and thus would render it harder for his pagan readers to reject out of hand.

What stands out as a recurring theme throughout Telfer's notes and commentaries is Nemesius's ceaseless dependence upon Neoplatonic commentaries and doxographies. Since Neoplatonism was the foremost philosophical system championed in Late Antiquity, this is hardly surprising. But in asserting this, we need once again to keep in mind that Nemesius was not simply restating Neoplatonic ideas with minor changes. He treated their opinions in the same eclectic way that the leading Neoplatonists assimilated the best of other philosophical outlooks, especially Aristotle's. He used them when they were in agreement with what the Scriptures and the Antiochene tradition had to say concerning human nature. He rejected them or adapted them when they were in opposition.

In general, Nemesius tried to balance the idealism of Plato with the Stoic world-view and with the Aristotelian ideas regarding the substantial union of soul and body, the nature and role of free will, and methodology. He agreed with Plato's emphases upon a real intelligible world that exists beyond the present changing world of matter, but he felt that the later Neo-platonists paid only very fleeting attention to the material world in which humans actually lived, rendering it almost irrelevant to everyday life.[50] He also agreed with the Neoplatonists that a human person is more than a physical being since the human soul is immortal, incorporeal, and self-subsisting (224–5, 269). But he rejected the Neoplatonic division of a human being into the three entities of a body, a soul, and a mind or *nous* which is detached from the soul's irrational faculties.[51]

In his notes and commentaries on Nemesius's text, Telfer cites examples where Nemesius has woven the Neoplatonist's and Galen's views into Aristotelian psychology. For instance, to Aristotle's opinion that human nature is a substantial union of body and soul, Nemesius has added the Neoplatonic opinion of Ammonius Saccas that the soul is an intelligble being, capable of union with the body but remaining unconfused and im-perishable in its immortal nature (295). This is a viewpoint that later be-came the standard Antiochene response explaining how, in the union of the divine and the human natures in Christ, the Word can complement, complete, and transform the human nature, while keeping intact His own divine nature (301). In his notes, Telfer points out how Nemesius has intro-duced Galen's arguments that are supportive of the Neoplatonic opinion that all souls are immortal and incorporeal (293).

In addition, Nemesius approved of the Platonic teaching regarding how divine providence exercises a particular as well as a general sway over the created universe (432–33). He cited this Platonic teaching as an author-ity against those, especially Aristotle, who maintained that providence does not rule over particular events and circumstances (435–38). For this, he lauded Plato, yet he also sees a fatal weakness in the Platonic view. He re-jects the Platonic opinion that providence can be discerned in the motions of the heavenly bodies. He was also in whole-hearted agreement with the criticism of Plato by Aristotle—with which the Neoplatonists also con-curred—that a universal form cannot exist in the present world apart from and independent of the material world in which particulars exist (442).

---

50. Telfer, 227. In his Enneads 4:4.18, Plotinus argues that, while the body is a stranger to the soul, it is the soul alone that constitutes the real human person.

51. Nemesius probably misconstrued the thought of Plotinus and Apollinaris when he accused them of maintaining a trichotomy of body, soul, and mind. Certainly, both laid emphasis upon the differences between the soul in its higher rational contemplative activities and in its lower sense activities. See Telfer, 226–27 and 294.

Aristotelian Influence

Since Aristotle's philosophical views have come down through what seems to be a reworking by his editors and commentators, it is important to remember that Nemesius's knowledge of Aristotle may be a mediated one. This can be seen in Nemesius's criticism of Aristotle or rather what was a popular secularistic view of his thought in the late fourth century. But while taking into account that Nemesius's knowledge of Aristotelianism has been most likely filtered through Neoplatonic lenses, we can nevertheless discern clear traces of Aristotelianism when Nemesius used its opinions to explain and support his own Christian understanding of human nature. For instance, a clear indication of this can be detected in Nemesius's insistence that human nature is a substantial composite of soul and body (225, 227). He used this idea to reject the opinion of those holding for a three-tiered division of human nature where the mind is thought to be separated from the irrational soul as well as from the body. He maintained with Aristotle that the mind is an essential part of the soul. When Nemesius cited Apollinaris as espousing this trichotomy (224, 284, 286, 316), he revealed that he was sensitive to the christological ramifications involved here. For if Christ's rational soul or mind has been replaced by the Word, then Christ also lacks a human mind capable of deliberation and independent action. This would indicate that Christ's humanity would not be truly and fully human and would not have fulfilled its role in God's redemptive plan. Nor would it have served as an exemplar of what other humans must freely do to attain salvation.

Nemesius agreed too with Aristotle that the body should not be considered merely an instrument that the soul can use in the same way that a person puts on and takes off a coat. Yet he dismissed Aristotle's opinion that the soul is simply and solely the "entelechy" (Telfer translates this as "fundamental energy") of the body, for it would then be merely a by-product of the union.[52] He rejected this because he believed that the soul

---

52. Ibid., 259. In a note on 275–76, Telfer also suggests that "entelechy" can also be rendered as "self-fulfilment" or "completion." He offers an important caution that must be heeded if one is to understand Aristotle's thought about "entelechy": "To do Aristotle justice we must recognize that he does not say that the soul is nothing but entelechy. He only says that the concept of entelechy covers much of what can be scientifically apprehended about the soul of a living creature."

is "life . . . [which] pertains to the nature of soul, while it belongs to body only by participation" (278). In other words, while the soul may be the life-giving form of the body, it can continue to exist apart from the body. Telfer observes that Nemesius's criticism of Aristotle's understanding of the soul indicates that he most likely did not read Aristotle's work *On the Soul* in the original but a commentary, perhaps by the pseudo-Plutarch or another Neoplatonist philosopher who badly misrepresented Aristotle's thought on this point (259).

Nemesius also resorted to Aristotle's theory of knowledge to describe how the soul and the Word can be united to the body and to the human nature of Christ without suffering any transformation or alteration. Just as the mind can, by its inherent power, detect what is intelligible in a sensible "object" without any change in either the mind or the object (295), the same can be affirmed of the other two relationships. Nemesius, however, qualified Aristotle's opinion by insisting with the Neoplatonists that the intelligible world is the true home of the mind (296). He reverted back, however, to Aristotle when he refuted the Neoplatonic opinion that the soul is impassible. This is significant not only because it deals with how Nemesius understood the relation between feelings and the soul, but for the larger question of whether and how the Word can suffer together with Christ's humanity—that is, out of sympathy.

In regard to Nemesius's treatment of Plato's and Aristotle's views on pleasure, Telfer observes that Nemesius was not presenting Plato's actual position but the one developed in Neoplatonism. He points out how Nemesius has brought "the Aristotelian battery to bear upon the Neoplatonist distinction, giving us a further instance of an eclecticism diverging from Neoplatonism on the Aristotelian side"(356). Nemesius also looked to Aristotelianism and possibly even Stoicism as providing the criterion for judging to what extent a pleasure is good. Telfer states it thus:

> The achievement, in finding a criterion [for what constitutes the good involved in pleasure], is not remarkable, but the firmness with which Nemesius clings to "what is natural" as an essential part of the criterion, is remarkable. It reflects his belief that "the nature of man" is not only a subject of question, but involves an ideal to be actualized. (359)

For Nemesius, therefore, pleasure is deemed to be good, provided it coheres with and promotes the goals of human nature.

Stoic Influence

From his study into the Stoic influence upon Nemesius, Telfer regards Posidonius[53] to be the primary source of those Stoic ideas Nemesius incorporated into his anthropological synthesis. First of all, he appears to be influenced by the two Stoic views that the visible creation has evolved in such a way that the higher orders of being share in the attributes of the lower and that human beings act as the link between the intelligible and phenomenal worlds.[54] He appears to have employed these to support the Genesis account that portrays humans as being the final creatures fashioned by God. From these, he draws the conclusion that all other creatures have been created to serve human needs. In commenting upon this point, Telfer observes that, while Nemesius is indebted much more to Scripture than to Stoicism for this outlook, he employed Posidonius's argument to affirm "deductively that man is the crown of the natural order, because the lower grades of being, directly, and the celestial bodies, indirectly, serve his needs."[55]

Nemesius combines the Stoic view that all created beings are called to serve human needs with their outlook that human beings are both the pinnacle of visible creation and the bond linking the spiritual and the material worlds of creation. Telfer notes that this union of the two is something we do not discover in any other extant work of the time, except, as has been ascertained above, in a modified form in Theodore. He also believes that Nemesius did not derive his idea on humankind being the crown of the universe directly from a lost work of Posidonius. He speculates that the source is, in reality, Origen's *Commentary on Genesis* (also no longer extant). So if Origen is the primary source for Nemesius's "Posidonian theme in the Platonized and Christianized form in which he reproduces it"(231), this provides us with one more striking example of how eclectic was the age in which Nemesius lived and wrote.

53. Posidonius lived in the first century B.C.E. He was a pupil of the Stoic Panaetius and the mentor of Cicero. Though his writings have not survived, his influence upon Nemesius is clearly pointed out by Telfer in his notes.

54. Telfer (231) maintains that Nemesius alone has united the views that the higher orders of visible creation share the attributes of lower beings and that humans function as the bond linking the spiritual and material worlds.

55. Ibid., 251. Telfer believes that the Posidonian doctrine was received through the work of Origen's *Commentary on Genesis* which in turn seems to be dependent upon Philo's *On the Creation of the World*.

Two other points deserve some comment. Nemesius is indebted to the Stoic tenet that there exists a true parallelism between human nature and nature itself. The unity present in the visible universe reflects a similar unity within human beings. For everything moves along a road of cause and effect towards a pre-designated ultimate goal, because of the guiding activity of a single rational world-soul. This parallelism means that the orderly arrangement detected in the cosmos can also serve as a moral standard for regulating and ordering human conduct. While praising the Stoics for being "the wisest of the Greeks" (403) because of their insight here, Nemesius was led by his Christian understanding of providence to reject both the determinism and materialism of the Stoics (426). He realized, moreover, that, even though the world-soul or the "seminal principle" can be proclaimed as Zeus, it can also be regarded as an impersonal force present in nature (399).

The Neo-Pythagorean Influence

Although Neo-Pythagoreanism has had the least impact upon Nemesius of all the philosophical schools we have examined, it may have added one key idea to Nemesius's understanding of how humans function as the link binding the opposite elements of creation in a unified universe. The Neo-Pythagoreans held that whenever and wherever the harmony is dissolved, everything suffers, for the universe is a holistic whole in which everything is interrelated. Though Nemesius does not state that Adam's sin has disrupted each and every level of the universe, from the personal, to the social, to the cosmic, it is inherent in his thought. The same can be said of his conviction that the risen Christ has enabled other humans to achieve, as he has, an immortal and immutable state in heaven. By so doing, he has restored once again, at least in principle, the original harmony established at creation between the spiritual and the material worlds. Christ is now functioning as the true bond linking the human, spiritual, and material worlds to one another and to God.

Conclusion

This chapter has sought to establish the background necessary for understanding what the Antiochenes meant by the terms they used to affirm their belief in Christ as fully human and truly God. This is important, for the questions to which they had to respond, especially those raised by the Arians and the Apollinarians, were framed in then-contemporary terms suggestive, if not evocative, of philosophical opinions. It was inevitable that these issues would be raised, for the Scriptures are, for the most part, descriptive of how Christ had functioned in human and divine ways and have not elaborated on what sense "the Word became man." Theologians (and others) not only began to argue how this could be but also expressed and explained their positions in abstract language according to their speculative and metaphysical bent.

Because of their conviction that the Arian and Apollinarian doctrinal statements were undermining what both Scripture and traditional Christian literature had revealed about the Word's relationships with His Father and Christ's humanity, the Antiochenes were forced out of their scriptural framework to clarify their own understanding of the principal terms being bandied about in the trinitarian and christological controversies. The present chapter has considered the three background influences that might have played a major role in affecting their thinking: their educational training, the various possible meanings of the words used by the councils for defining the Trinity and union of natures in Christ, and Nemesius's classic work *On Human Nature,* which may reflect what kind of metaphysical ideas were current at Antioch at the beginning of the fifth century.

From the little that has survived about what was taught at the schools of Libanius and Diodore, we can only speculate about how much formal metaphysics they received and whether they were taught to understand basic philosophical terms in a certain way. It would seem that their metaphysical training was, at the most, minimal. When we add to this the Antiochene full absorption in explaining and preaching the Scriptural message and their negative attitude toward Greek philosophers, it appears more likely than not that they used the terms ὑπόστασις, πρόσωπον, οὐσία, and φύσις in the ordinary ways they were understood in the documents of the Councils of Nicea and Constantinople I. As will be shown in the following chapters, the Antiochenes interpreted the wording of these councils by looking upon πρόσωπον and ὑπόστασις as equivalent, in the sense that a πρόσωπον is the external visible manifestation of a human ὑπόστασις and that ὑπόστασις indicates an existing οὐσία inseparable from its complete φύσις.

While it is probable that at least John Chrysostom, Theodore, and Nestorius had little or no formal philosophical training other than in logic and the virtues, they do manifest a familiarity with, and preference for, particular Stoic, Aristotelian, and Platonic viewpoints.[56] This raises questions as to whether and to what extent they were committed in general to any one philosophical school's outlook on human nature, especially Aristotle's. Because of his close association with the Antiochene tradition, Nemesius's work *On Human Nature* provides us with some reasonable grounds for judging whether the Antiochenes were as eclectic as Nemesius was in the ways that he wove together different Greek philosophical opinions (most likely drawn wholly from Neoplatonic commentaries and the doxographies of his day) to form his own synthesis.

Nemesius's work is significant too for its focus and purpose. He introduced metaphysical insights into his work insofar as they were favorably disposed for explaining and reinforcing the then traditional Christian outlook at Antioch towards human nature. The point that he sought to make was that the best of Greek philosophy cohered with and substantiated what the Christian Scriptures affirmed. This is evident from those passages where he offered the Christian responses to questions that Greek philosophy was unable to answer. In other words, the content of Nemesius's work may have been philosophical, but his motivation and criteria for judging what was to be incorporated into his synthesis were Christian. We find the same mentality present in the surviving writings of the Antiochenes. If they appear to be using metaphysical terms and opinions, they should be thought to have introduced them not for philosophical reasons but because they fitted in with, supported, and explained their own traditional Christian orientation and emphases.

While the question is still open as to how much Nemesius actually influenced Theodore and the other Antiochene Fathers, it is evident that, at least on a number of points, Nemesius shared a common scriptural and theological substratum with them. From what we have seen about Theodore's

56. Of all the metaphysical viewpoints that the Antiochenes have assimilated, the one that influenced them the most was their idea that God's wholly transcendent nature excludes any immediate and direct contact with created beings. While they probably came to this conclusion from their exegesis of the Scriptures, it is a viewpoint to which they would willingly agree as corroborating their fundamental principle regarding the impossibility of any substantial union between God and His creatures, even Christ's human nature.

views regarding humans as the "image of God," we can liken them to Nemesius's ideas, especially on how humans are the bond of the universe whom other creatures are obliged to serve, how Christ's divine nature functions in its union with his humanity, and why Christ must possess a truly free human will. With all this as a background, we can proceed now to determine the meaning of those christological terms that the Antiochenes, especially Theodore and Nestorius, employed in their writings. If we are to interpret rightly Theodore's thought on how Christ serves as God's image in a unitive way, such clarity is of primary importance.

4

THE ANTIOCHENE TERMS FOR HUMAN NATURE

AND THE UNION OF NATURES IN CHRIST

A SSESSING THE METAPHYSICAL OUTLOOK that prevailed at the School of Antioch in the late fourth and early fifth centuries is like trying to explain the significance of a complicated musical score. There are simply far too many parts needing to be taken into account. For, once again, there are five disparate personalities to be dealt with, three of whose works have been substantially lost—namely Diodore, Theodore, and Nestorius. While it is true that a staggering number of John Chrysostom's works have survived, they deal principally with his scriptural, homiletical, pastoral, and spiritual interests—with little philosophical content. Moreover from the few—mainly negative—comments that Chrysostom has made about the Greek philosophers,[1] one can only speculate as to his background and outlook regarding philosophy. Finally, Theodoret's surviving works contain considerable philosophical material, but his own metaphysical opinions have to be extracted chiefly from his christological writings and, to some extent, from his surviving work that deals with his assessment of pagan thought.

1. See for example John Chrysostom's *Homily 4 on 1 Corinthians 1:18–20*, NPNF, First Series, ed. Philip Schaff and Henry Wace (1889; reprint, Peabody, Mass.: Hendrickson, 1994), 9:16–22.

Since so few of Diodore's writings are now available and his philosophical outlook appears to be similar to Theodore's, there is little profit in determining whether his theological and scriptural outlook have a specific philosophical component.[2] We will proceed immediately to offer a few tentative comments about Chrysostom's philosophical orientation or, rather, lack of it. Afterwards there will be examined the same or similar viewpoints regarding human nature that are detectable in Theodore, Nestorius, and Theodoret. The primary concern here is to explore the affinities that exist between them and Nemesius in three major areas: how humans are the bond of the universe, what kind of union and mutual activity exists between the soul and the body in a human being, and what are the roles that free-will and mortality play in the divine economy. After discussing these points, we will then consider what meaning Theodore and Nestorius attached in general to their christological terms. The understanding acquired here will be used in the next chapter as a means to delve into how Theodore and Nestorius understood Christ's unitive role as the image of God.

John Chrysostom

To what extent Chrysostom received philosophical training as a student at the school of Libanius is shrouded in uncertainty. The historian Sozomen informs us that Chrysostom "learned rhetoric from Libanius, and philosophy from Andragathius,"[3] but without expanding upon what

2. For a relatively recent attempt at explaining Diodore's thought, see Rowan A. Greer, "Antiochene Christology of Diodore of Tarsus," *Journal of Theological Studies* 17 (1966): 327–41. His purpose is to dispute Aloys Grillmeier's (*Christ in Christian Tradition: From the Apostolic Age to Chalcedon [451]*, trans. J. S. Bowden [Atlanta: John Knox, 1975], 352–60) treatment of Diodore as one who holds a 'Logos-sarx' instead of the Antiochene 'Logos-man' framework. But in so doing, he clearly shows how Diodore and Theodore's christological outlooks are similar to each other. For a fine summary of Greer's position, with English translations of several of Diodore's most relevant christological fragments, see D. S. Wallace-Hadrill, *Christian Antioch: A Study of Early Christian Thought in the East* (Cambridge: Cambridge UP, 1982), 119–22. Here, Wallace-Hadrill concludes that "the fragments of Diodore's work . . . give us little basis for understanding his mind and little idea of the power that he undoubtedly possessed" (121).

3. Sozomen, *Historia Ecclesiastica*, trans. Chester D. Hartranft, NPNF, Second Series, ed. Philip Schaff and Henry Wace (1890; reprint, Peabody, Mass.: Hendrickson, 1994), 2:399. For a discussion of how much philosophy had an influence upon Chrysostom, see Chrysostomus Baur, *John Chrysostom and His Time*, 2 vols., trans. M. Gonzaga (Westminster, Md.: Newman, 1959–60), 1:306–12.

kind of philosophy this was. He does, however, contrast the philosophy that Chrysostom received from Andragathius with that practiced "according to the law of the Church." Since the sophist education included a study of the moral virtues, this suggests that Sozomen may be alluding to the different ways that Greek philosophy and Christian asceticism instruct a person on how best to live out one's moral and spiritual lives. It may also not be too much off the proverbial mark to presume that Andragathius would have exposed his students to the eclectic philosophical thought contained in one or other of the doxographical collections of the day.[4]

Whatever philosophy Chrysostom learned from Andragathius, the few tidbits of metaphysical opinions that can be gleaned from the vast outpouring of Chrysostom's literary works point to a minimal practical impact upon him. Chrysostomus Baur speculates that the main reasons for this may have been "that he possessed no special gift for real philosophy, and also, that he seems to have prematurely given up his education with the sophists . . . [and that] there were no first rate philosophers to be found in the fourth century in Antioch nor even in the whole Roman empire."[5] Chrysostom, however, does show—as one would expect from a student who had excelled at the Sophist school of Libanius—a rich appreciation of all the subtle insights, elegant and polished expressions, and rhetorical power present in Greek literature.[6] Chrysostom also displays in his references to the human body that he was familiar with the Greek anthropological views regarding anatomy and physiology—a knowledge he most likely obtained directly from the medical treatises of Galen.[7]

But while Chrysostom treasured the literary power of the Greek language and applauds Plato for his sublime thought, he railed, in general, against Greek philosophers for their immoral lives, their pagan superstitions, and their empty, artificial rhetoric.[8] He saw very little real value too

---

4. See Baur, 1:23. He also mentions on 306 that Chrysostom cites Zeno, Plato, Socrates, Diagoras, Pythagoras, and Aristotle.

5. Ibid., 1:310.

6. Chrysostom's appreciation of Greek literature did not extend to their philosophical works, as Baur observes: "not only the pagan *content* of the works of the philosophers and rhetoricians repelled him; the artificial and unnatural *form* of the rhetoric was no less offensive to him" (1:311).

7. William Telfer, ed. and trans., *Cyril of Jerusalem and Nemesius of Emesa*, Library of Christian Classics 4 (Philadelphia: Westminster, 1955), 275.

8. See Baur, 1:307 and 310.

in their high-minded speculations. For him, "it is no art to philosophize with words. Show me your wisdom in your deeds and in practical life; that is the best method of teaching."⁹ Moreover even when he extoled Plato for being the finest of the Greek philosophers, he belittled his wisdom as inferior to that proclaimed in the writings of Saint Paul.¹⁰ For him, Christian Scriptures and faith convictions—and not meaningless philosophical speculations—contain the answers needed for life.

Yet despite his negative comments about philosophy, Chrysostom does offer some glimpses into his metaphysical point of view when he professes his belief in the Trinity. His terminology reflects an intermediate period between the final decline of Arianism and the growing christological controversies regarding the union of the two natures in Christ. He distinguishes the terms for substance (οὐσία) and nature (φύσις) from the word used in Greek to express the idea of a person (πρόσωπον).¹¹ While he generally employs πρόσωπον in its most common non-technical meanings as signifying a face, an outward appearance, a mask, a dramatic part, he refers to the three πρόσωπα present in the Trinity, reflecting the declaration of the Council of Constantinople I and indicating thereby that he regarded the term as signifying something more than an external demeanor. As one would expect from a theologian committed to the dogmas asserted at the Councils of Nicea and Constantinople, he rejected the Arian contention that the Son is inferior to the Father. He even utilized the code-word of the day, ὁμοούσιος, to express how the two share the same nature.¹² But he preferred to describe the Son as "equal to the Father," or as "one in all things with the Father," or, in a more nuanced way, as being also "of the same nature" with the Father, but with a "personhood" distinct from his Father's.¹³

Except for voicing his opposition to Arianism, Chrysostom rarely entered into speculative dogmatic questions.¹⁴ His interests and strengths lay in his extraordinary ability to expound in his sermons and writings the

9. I am indebted to Baur, 1:311, for this quotation.

10. Chrysostom, PG 48:6.

11. For a brief summary of Chysostom's dogmatic terminology, see Baur, 1:356–60.

12. For the location of these citations and a treatment of their significance, see Baur, 1:356–57.

13. See ibid., 1:356.

14. For a treatment of Chrysostom's Christology, see Grillmeier, 418–21, where he acknowledges his debt to C. Hay, "St. John Chrysostom and the Integrity of the Human Nature of Christ," *Franciscan Studies* 19 (1959): 298–317. Both Grillmeier and Hay argue that

meaning of Scripture for daily life. He is first and foremost a pastor entrusted with the task of instructing, edifying, and challenging his flock to cultivate their faith lives. In brief, he was, because of his background, situation, and personal temperament, a brilliant rhetorician who appealed to a sound common sense and a practical scripturally-based wisdom rather than to any reasoned insights flowing from what he considered to be speculative and shallow philosophical systems.

Theodore

Theodore emerged from a background that was very similar to Chrysostom's. Yet while it would be a stretch of the imagination to designate him a philosopher, his dogmatic speculations allow us to conjecture about his outlook toward human nature more easily than is possible with Chrysostom.[15] For as we will soon see, Theodore appears to have been more disposed than Chrysostom to utilize the then-current metaphysical terms used to express human nature, if these fit in with and further advanced his own theological synthesis of how the whole cosmos is to be saved through Christ. Two concerns interest us here: how Theodore understood human nature in general and the Greek terms οὐσία, ὑπό-στασις, πρόσωπον, and φύσις, in particular; and, with these as a background, how Theodore and Nestorius understood the union of natures in Christ and both Christ and Adam's roles as God's image and the bond linking the spiritual and the material worlds to God.

One can only hazard a guess at how much philosophy Theodore received as a young student. If Sozomen's remark can be accepted that "Theodore was well conversant with the sacred books and with the rest of the discipline of rhetoricians and philosophers,"[16] it seems that Theodore

---

Chrysostom is closer in his Christology to the younger Cyril of Alexandria and Athanasius than to his friend Theodore. Since Chrysostom is predominantly involved in pastoral issues, it is difficult to assess his doctrinal views regarding Christ. His Christology impresses me as being a scripturally functional one with the emphasis upon Christ's divinity.

15. For a critical evaluation of the positive and negative aspects of Theodore's Christology, see Grillmeier, 421–39; and for a study into how Theodore provides an understanding of Antiochene theology, see Ulrich Wickert, *Studien zu den Pauluskommentaren Theodors von Mopsuestia: Als Beitrag zum Verständnis der Antiochenischen Theologie* (Berlin: Töpelmann, 1962).

16. Sozomen, 399.

was exposed to at least a rudimentary education in philosophy (perhaps like Chrysostom under Andragathius?) while studying at the school run by Libanius.[17] His philosophical courses there were likely directed toward sharpening his ability to reason in a logical, discursive, argumentative, and systematic manner and to be aware of moral values. But as Norris has concluded after his in-depth study into the possible philosophical influences shaping Theodore's viewpoint on human nature, it was Christian revelation, not philosophy, that had the greatest impact upon his thought: "the connexion between Theodore's doctrine of man and his christology must be sought in what we have labeled the 'biblical' strain in his anthropology."[18]

It would have been during his years at the school of Diodore that Theodore acquired his mastery of Scripture and his familiarity with the traditional Antiochene defense of Christ's full humanity. As he read and responded to the arguments raised by the Arians and the Apollinarians and, above all, as he evolved his own theological synthesis, he would doubtless have been forced to think out and be continually consistent with the metaphysical presuppositions that underlay his terms. It is also quite likely that Theodore would be familiar with Nemesius's work *On Human Nature*, for not only did it quickly become a classic presentation of how Christians understood human nature but it contained a rejection, albeit stated in a very deferential way, of what Theodore taught regarding "a union of good pleasure" between the Word and the humanity of Jesus. Theodore was, from all indications, a well-read scholar who would be familiar with what his critics wrote, even if we do not have any evidence of this in his few surviving commentaries.[19]

Because Nemesius and Theodore are contemporaries who lived in or around Antioch at the beginning of the fifth century, they offer a handy framework for comparing and contrasting their opinions on human

17. See Joanne McWilliam Dewart, *The Theology of Grace of Theodore of Mopsuestia*, Catholic University of America Studies in Christian Antiquity 16 (Washington: Catholic University of America Press, 1971), 6.

18. Richard A. Norris, Jr., *Manhood and Christ* (Oxford: Clarendon, 1963), 233.

19. See J.-M. Vosté, ed., *Theodori Mopsuesteni Commentarius in Evangelium Johannis Apostoli*, CSCO 115–116 / Syr. 62– 63 (Louvain: Officina Orientali, 1940), 2. When speaking on the duty of a commentator, Theodore professes that it is his duty "to not only expound (upon his text) with authority but also refute an opinion which goes contrary to his own words."

nature, especially as they relate to an understanding of the union of natures in Christ. In so doing, the purpose here is not to resolve whether or not Theodore was in fact dependent upon Nemesius—although this is a distinct probability. Rather it is to indicate that they both shared a similar outlook, if not a common tradition, that is both eclectic in the way they regard philosophical opinions and are similar in their general outlook toward human nature and in their perspectives regarding redemption. For Nemesius's systematic treatise provides us with a rich source for comparing those points where Theodore's thought overlaps with his, specifically regarding human nature in general, its role as the bond linking the invisible and visible worlds with both one another and God, the significance of mortality within the divine economy, the habitual ways the soul acts towards its body as indicative of the Word's relationship with the humanity of Christ, and his stress upon the central role free will plays in the drama of salvation.

Human Nature as a Composite of Soul and Body

In a fragment that has survived in a Latin translation of his treatise against Apollinaris, Theodore affirmed: "according to us a human being (*homo*) is said to be composed of a soul and body, and indeed we say that these two natures, the soul and the body, to be truly one human being (*homo*) comprised of both."[20] Like Nemesius, he rejected a division of human nature into three entities of soul, mind, and body. His adamant opposition stemmed from his dogmatic recognition of how Apollinaris's opinion that the Word had replaced Christ's human mind undermined the full integrity of Christ's human nature.[21] In his homily *On Baptism*, he

20. *Theodori Episcopi Mopsuesteni in Epistolas B. Pauli Commentarii*, ed. H. B. Swete, 2 vols. (Cambridge: Cambridge UP, 1880 and 1882), 2:318. The fragments of Theodore's treatises against Apollinaris are published in Swete, 2:312–22. Here and in the following citations from the surviving Greek, Latin, and Syriac works of Theodore, the translations are my own.

21. See Nabil el-Khoury, "Der Mensch als gleichnis Gottes: Eine Untersuchung zur Anthropologie des Theodor von Mopsuestia," *Oriens Christianus* 74 (1990): 62–71, for his explanation of how Theodore's understanding of "image" impacts on his views toward the union of an immortal soul and a mortal body and its ramifications for binding the universe. See Grillmeier, 426–27, for a critique of Theodore's views in regard to Christ's human soul.

refers to Apollinaris, in a lengthy list of heretics, as a dedicated disciple of Satan "who, under the pretense of an orthodoxy which would render our salvation incomplete, categorically asserted that our mind was not assumed and did not participate like the body in the assumption of grace."[22] Theodore clearly grasped the soteriological implications of Apollinaris's position, for if it were true that the Word did not assume the whole of Christ's human nature, then not only Christ's mind but all human minds would be excluded from any sharing in salvation. Theodore is expressing here what has become known as the Athanasian principle that "what is not assumed is not saved."

Theodore shared the same outlook as Nemesius regarding how the human composite of soul and body functions at the heart of creation as the bond linking together the spiritual and the material worlds. Two quotations express this. In his *Commentary on Romans*, Theodore stated his conviction that the cosmos is an organic body: "God made the entire creation one body; because of this, the sum total of everything, whether visible or invisible, is called the cosmos."[23] In his *Commentary on Genesis*, he expanded upon his vision of how the visible and invisible worlds are linked together with human beings. The context of his remarks indicates that Theodore is indebted here more to what the Genesis account of creation reveals about the role of humans in the cosmos and possibly to Nemesius than to what the Stoics have said about it. He explained it thus:

For (God) fashioned Adam with an invisible, rational, and immortal soul and a visible and mortal body. By the former, he is like unto invisible natures; and by the latter, he is akin to visible beings. For God willed to gather the whole of creation into one, so that, although constituted of diverse natures, it might be joined together by one bond.[24]

While it is debatable whether Theodore is directly dependent upon Nemesius for his understanding of the role that humans play as the bond of the universe—for they both may be reflecting a common tradition at

22. *Commentary of Theodore of Mopsuestia on the Lord's Prayer and on the Sacraments of Baptism and the Eucharist*, ed. and trans. A. Mingana, WS 6 (Cambridge: Heffer, 1933), 40.

23. Theodore, PG 66:824.

24. Edward Sachau, ed., *Theodori Mopsuesteni Fragmenta Syriaca* (Leipzig: G. Engelmann, 1869), 7 in the Syriac and 15 in the Latin. See also Theodore's commentary on Eph. 1:10 (Swete, 1:128–29) and the Greek fragment on Rom. 8 which is reproduced in Swete, 1:128.

Antioch—Theodore appears to use it as a confirmation of the Genesis account of creation and perhaps also of the Pauline idea of Christ's recapitulation of the universe at the end of time and/or that expressed in Ephesians 1:22–23: "He has put all things beneath his feet and gave him as head over all things to the church, which is his body, the fullness of the one who fills all things in every way." Theodore would have connected this functional role of Christ as the archetypical image to a comparable role that he believed Adam must have been called to play in a typical fashion at creation. His position on this question may be a clear example of how Theodore alluded to, if not incorporated, a Stoic view that supports his own theological synthesis. Theodore stated it thus:

> Therefore all things, those which are in heaven as well as those on earth, he renewed (or rather, recapitulated) in Christ, making, as it were, a certain vast renovation and reintegration of every creature through him. For by making the body incorrupt and impassible by means of his resurrection and joining it again to the immortal soul . . . he is seen to have returned the bond of friendship upon the entire creation.[25]

As the following quotation indicates, Theodore also combined together, as Nemesius did, the two views about humans as the bond linking the spiritual and the material worlds and their role at the "apex" of material creation. But he expanded upon Nemesius by also making humans to be created "in God's image" and by having spiritual as well as material beings expressing their love and glory for God by caring for the needs of human beings:

> Then [Moses] wrote thus: "He created him in the image of God," to indicate that what is exceptional in his fashioning is the fact that all creatures are bonded together in him, so that by means of his image they might draw near to God. When they fulfill the laws whereby they are obliged to minister unto him, they are pleasing to the Legislator by caring for him. For since God needs nothing and is invisible, they offer the glory that is due Him by being useful to that one who is needy and visible to all.[26]

---

25. Swete, 1:130.

26. Sachau, TFS, 24–25 in the Syriac and 15 in the Latin. Theodore also compares God's conferring the role of image upon Adam to a king who has constructed a magnificent city and set his image in its center, so that the inhabitants would know the city's founder and be able to honor him by venerating his image. See Françoise Petit, ed. and trans., "L'homme créé 'à l'image' de Dieu: quelques fragments grecs inédits de Théodore de Mopsueste," Le Muséon 100 (1987): 275–77.

Salvation in Terms of a Passage from Mortality to Immortality

Like Nemesius, Theodore expressed salvation in terms, not of divinization, but of a transformation from a mortal to an immortal state.[27] It appears, however, that they differ over whether Adam was originally created immortal or mortal. While this is a minor point, seeing that they agree that Adam was mortal after the Fall and look upon salvation as the attainment of an immortal and immutable state in the next life, it has generated some controversy as to what Theodore held.[28] While Theodore may have evolved in his own thinking, it seems that he held as his definitive position an original mortality because it fit more coherently into his theory of the two "ages" or states in life—a present life of mortality and a future destiny of immortality. For if Adam were initially created in an immortal state, this would necessitate a threefold state: one that is originally immortal, then mortal, and finally immortal.

27. While the mystical allegorizing of the Alexandrians and Cappadocians greatly favored the development of a doctrine of divinization, the moral and literal emphases of the Antiochenes were obstacles to this, for they were dedicated to the concrete, mostly functional language of Scripture and leery of what they considered to be speculative abstractions. When such an attitude is added to both Theodore and Nestorius's understanding of God's totally transcendent nature, it is difficult to grant Gross's belief that the principal elements of divinization are implicitly found in the writings of Chrysostom and especially Theodore. See Jules Gross, *La divinisation de chrétien d'apres les pères grecs* (Paris: Gabalda, 1938): 253, 262, and 270. In his article, "Being Transformed: Chrysostom's Exegesis of the Epistle to the Romans" (*Greek Orthodox Theological Review* 36.3–4 [1991]: 211–29), Demetrios Trakatellis discusses the radical transformation that he finds in Chrysostom's homilies on Romans. I do not interpret this to be the same as what others mean by divinization. I believe that the Antiochene viewpoint has precluded even the possibility of human divinization in the sense of a direct, immediate sharing in God's divine life. They would understand this as meaning that one's human nature has been transformed into the divine. The most they could admit to in this life was that humans can share potentially in an immortal, immutable, and incorruptible future life that will later become actualized in heaven.

28. For a statement of Nemesius's position, see Telfer, 239, where Nemesius opts for an original state where Adam was poised between immortality and mortality. Theodore's stand appears to have been similarly ambivalent. In his *Commentary on Galatians*, he contends that: "If at his creation the first man had remained immortal, there would not be, to be sure, the present life. . . . But because he has been made mortal through sin, the present life is called the current life in comparison with that future life which we expect to occur at the end time" (Swete, 1:26, 29, and 31). In his *Commentary on Genesis* Theodore maintained the opposite: "For if, as it happened, (God) had made us

Whatever may have been Adam's original state, his sin had dire reper-
cussions for him, for all humans, and for the whole cosmos—indeed, for
all creation. It resulted in his dignity as God's image becoming tarnished
and in his human nature remaining (or becoming) mortal. This entailed
the entrance of death into human life and thus the total breakdown of the
organic unity established in the universe; in Theodore's words: "Death
was introduced [into this world-order] by our sinning. From this there has
resulted a separation of both [orders of creation]. For the soul was separated from the body; and the separated body sustained total dissolution.
On account of this, the bonding of creation was therefore dissolved."[29] In
other words, death causes a rendering of the whole cosmic order as well
as the bond between the soul and body. It severed both human nature and
the bond uniting the spiritual and the material worlds to human beings, to
one another, and to God. As Nemesius did, Theodore turned to Scripture
to explain why humans are mortal and weak by nature. Such an outlook,
of course, can be judged similar to what the Stoics and Neo-Pythagoreans
held.

The Reason for Mortality

Theodore speculated on why God was so willing to permit a mortal
Adam and Eve to sin and thus bring a tragedy upon the human race and
the whole of creation. He agreed with Nemesius that the present age of
mortality is a preparatory, pedagogical period of testing in which humans
have to learn the truth about their nature and to practice the kind of virtuous life that leads to salvation.[30] It is a time during which a Redeemer
was to be expected, sin condemned, virtues acquired, death overcome,

immortal and immutable to begin with, we would not be differentiated in any way from
irrational creatures. For we would have no knowledge of our own proper good" (PG
66:633). To untangle this confusion, a number of possible explanations have been proposed. Norris (*Manhood*, 184) suggests that the answer is to be found in God's fore-
knowledge of what Adam would freely do in Eden. Because God foreknew that Adam
would sin, He created Adam in a mortal state. It is his mortal nature—and not his sin—
that Adam subsequently passed on to his descendants. It is a nature subject to not
merely to death but temptations that entice a person to sin.

29. Swete, 1:129–30.

30. Telfer, 239. For a fuller statement of Theodore's views about this, see Kevin
McNamara, "Theodore of Mopsuestia and the Nestorian Heresy I," *Irish Theological
Quarterly*, July 1952: 262–65.

and the present mortal state of the body readied for its transformation into one that is immortal.[31] It is a period during which mutable human beings must freely determine whether they want to journey on the virtuous path God has set as the right way to proceed toward salvation and, if one has turned to sin, to repent and return once again to God's predetermined path. It is a time, too, when created beings need an image or exemplar to show them how to live their lives rightly. It is Christ who fulfills this role.

Although Theodore wrote of Adam's sin as the reason humans have inherited a mortal and mutable nature liable to personal sins,[32] he did not believe that a mortal, mutable nature necessitates a human to sin. For he clearly attributed sin, Adam's as well as all humans', to an individual's own decision. He expressed his attitude when he asserted that "it is evident that the inclination to sin begins in the spiritual will."[33] In other words, Theodore regarded the soul's mutable nature, despite its ability to sin, to be not evil *in se* but rather an inherent condition of its being a creature that is in union with a mortal body. The soul's mutability, however, makes it possible for the passions (which Theodore seems to locate, as Nemesius did, in the body's mortal nature) to tempt one to sin. The passions can arouse the soul because the soul is *sympathetic* to what is going on in its body.[34]

The Soul's Immortal Nature

Although Theodore insisted that the soul forms a unique composite with a mortal body, he granted that it can exist independently of its partner at death, for its nature is immortal. Theodore expressed this when he distinguished between a human and an animal soul: for an animal soul

31. In discussing this, Rowan A. Greer (*Theodore of Mopsuestia: Exegete and Theologian* [Westminster: Faith, 1961], 22–23) suggests that Theodore may be influenced by Theophilus of Antioch and Irenaeus's viewpoint that compares Adam to a child who needs to be trained on how to attain incorruptibility and the vision of God. Whatever may have been its origins, it became a hallmark of the Antiochene tradition.

32. For a discussion of this point, see Norris, *Manhood*, 181.

33. Raymond Tonneau with Robert Devreese, trans., *Les Homélies Catéchétiques de Théodore de Mopsueste* (Vatican City: Vaticana, 1949), 115.

34. For various meanings that "passion" can have, see the distinctions that Nemesius makes in Telfer, 347–49. In regard to Theodore's understanding of the role that human passions plays, Norris (*Manhood*, 133–34) is of the opinion that "Theodore offers no consistent or thought-out statement on the question of passion and its seat . . . And the reason for this seems to be simply that the question is not an important one for him."

"does not have its own ὑπόστασις [a substantial nature capable of independent existence] . . . (whereas a human) soul exists in its own ὑπόστασις and is elevated far above the body . . . and as it leaves [at death] it
remains indestructible, but continues forever in its ὑπόστασις because it
is immortal."[35] Although the soul is able to subsist apart from its body at
death, it needs, nevertheless, to be reunited with its body, if it is to attain
its sought-for immutability in the next life. Theodore implied this whenever he discussed how the soul will become forever immutable as soon as
it is rejoined in the future age with its then-transformed, immortal body;
to cite but one example, "our Lord Jesus Christ, who was assumed from
us and for us died . . . and through His resurrection became immortal, incorruptible and for ever immutable, and as such ascended into heaven, as
by His union with our nature, he became for us an earnest of our own
participation in the event."[36] The immortal soul's need for the body is insinuated too in Theodore's insistence that the whole composite of soul
and body is what constitutes a person: "Yet the two (the soul and the flesh)
are one human being; and neither of them is ever absolutely and properly
said to be a human being by itself."[37]

While Nemesius and Theodore agree that salvation will consist of the
attainment of an immutable soul and an immortal body, Nemesius only
briefly alluded to this when he mentioned in passing that the age-to-come
will be one of "immortality which, by favour of the Creator, he [a human
being] is to recover at the last."[38] This is understandable because Nemesius
was writing a work of philosophical, not theological, anthropology.
Theodore, however, has made the theme of mortality and immortality
the centerpiece of his theological synthesis, for, as he conceived God's

35. Tonneau, THC, 121. See also Sachau, TFS, 1; and Swete, 2:318, where Theodore
declares in a fragment from his lost work against Apollinaris that the human soul is "indeed immortal and rational." Theodore denies that the human soul pre-exists in any
way before it has been united to its body. On this point, he has parted company with
Nemesius who holds that God created all souls at the beginning of the world and later
joined each to its proper body at the appointed time. See Telfer, 282–83. For a treatment
of Theodore's view on the nature of the soul, see Norris, *Manhood*, 125–48.

36. Mingana, WS 6:19–20.

37. Swete, 2:319. The term translated by "human being" is "man" in its generic
sense.

38. Telfer, 240. Since Nemesius's aim was to establish an acceptable philosophical
explanation of how Christians understand human nature, his reticence about a future
life was certainly in keeping with his focus.

plan for redemption, human beings will enter into communion with God when they too achieve the same state of immortality and immutability that Christ's humanity acquired at the time of his resurrection. He used the image of being an adopted son and daughter of God as analgous to achieving a state of immortality: "Thus the Apostle says the filial adoption to be the resurrection because we will then be immortal. For we are said to attain filial adoption at baptism in that we receive the first fruits at baptism by undergoing a form of death and also of resurrection."[39] He expanded upon this when discussing God's plan for salvation.

This was what indeed pleased God: to divide creation into two states: the one which presently is, in which He made everything mutable; and the other, the one which is going to be, when after renewing everything He will transform it to an immutable state. He shows us the basis for this is in what happened to the Lord Christ, whom He raised from the dead as one like us and made immutable in body and soul. He demonstrated thereby what is to going to come to be for all creation.[40]

Why he chose to express redemption in terms of immortality is open to speculation. The most likely reason is that this is what he found to be Paul's way of portraying it.[41] Perhaps too it was because he looked upon divinization (as he understood the term) as an impossibility.[42]

The Union Between the Soul and the Body

Before there can be a discussion of Theodore's understanding of the union between the body and the soul and between the two natures in Christ, there is a prior need to sort out his metaphysical understandings of the terms for οὐσία, ὑπόστασις, πρόσωπον, and φύσις as well as of the kinds of union that are possible.[43] First of all, as the previous chapter has highlighted, these terms were in such a fluid, evolving state at the

39. Swete, 1:56.
40. Theodore, PG 66:633–34.
41. We see this expressed in 1 Cor. 15:53–54.
42. Grillmeier treats Theodore's attempt to explain how a creature can participate in God's divine life in 422–25. He is of the opinion that "'Theodore is searching for a new interpretation of the participation of man in God and the conjunction of God and man in Christ, so as to be able to achieve a synthesis between the immanence and the transcendence of God in us and in Christ in the face of the Arians and Apollinarians" (424).
43. For a treatment of these terms, see also Kevin McNamara, "Theodore of Mopsuestia and the Nestorian Heresy II," *The Irish Theological Quarterly*, April 1953: 181–86.

beginning of the fifth century that they were often used interchangeably with one another. We see examples of this in the ways that Nemesius and Theodore have employed abstract and concrete terms as synonyms; e.g. "human nature" as a synonym for "Jesus the Man," and "divine nature" for the "Word" or the "Son of God" or simply "God." This demonstrates that they understood a φύσις to be not an abstract term, but one that always connoted a concrete, existing entity. As Norris observes, this usage of "nature" for something specific and concrete was not uncommon in the late fourth century. He points out in passing that Theodore's "'errors' in using this language were in fact the common habits of his time, which was quite accustomed to references to the 'Man' in Christ."[44]

Cyril of Alexandria, however, seems to have understood "nature" in a different way, conceiving it more in a Platonic sense as having an abstract reality. Taken in this generalized sense, a "human being" can be imagined as being a distinct nature that exists apart from the particular in which it is embodied. Theodore could not envision how this was possible. For him, everything that exists is a particular, existential being, not a universal. It is a view that is very Semitic, as indicated by Graham Warne in his work on Hebrew perspective of the human person:

> . . . the Hebrews used one single term to express both a concrete, observable reality (to which they could readily relate), and a non-concrete, or figurative meaning. . . . That which was concrete and observable provided the means whereby the non-concrete could be perceived. The human person, therefore, was characterized by function, rather than by metaphysical abstraction.[45]

Aristotle has a somewhat similar outlook. Though he distinguished between concrete and abstract nature, he insisted against Plato that an existing nature was a concrete individual. While one can argue that Theodore's way of speaking about nature substantiates the opinion that he is

---

44. Norris, *Manhood*, 209. The constant interchange between the concrete and the abstract on the part of the Antiochenes may be an indication of their dependence more upon the classical Hebrew way of understanding the human being than upon Aristotle's distinction between an abstract and a concrete nature.

45. Graham J. Warne, *Hebrew Perspectives on the Human Person in the Hellenistic Era: Philo and Paul* (Lewiston, N.Y.: Mellen, 1995), 59–60. The same view of a person as a psychosomatic whole is also expressed in the New Testament, especially in Paul; see Bruce J. Malina and Jerome H. Neyrey, *Portraits of Paul: An Archeology of Ancient Personality* (Louisville: Knox, 1996).

an Aristotelian, this should be understood in the same general, eclectic sense that Nemesius was affirmed above to be such.

Whatever may be the source of Theodore's understanding of the divine and human natures as being concrete entities, this had ramifications for how Theodore could speak about these, for it meant that he had to look upon each of these concrete natures as the agents of their own individual free actions. This in turn affected how he could properly speak of each nature, for this meant that only divine attributes can be directly predicated of the Word and human attributes of the Man Jesus because their natures are the source of these attributes. For example, Theodore could not assert that Mary was truly the "Mother of God" without any qualification: "When they ask whether Mary was the mother of the man or of God, let us reply that she was "both;" the first by nature and the second by the Word's relationship to the assumed humanity."[46] But shortly afterwards, he confessed that "It is indeed madness to say that God was born of a virgin. For this is equivalent to saying that He was born from the seed of David of the substance of the virgin."[47] So, too, when he contended that Christ's humanity can be said to share in the Word's Sonship and power, one can always expect—not surprisingly—to discover lingering nearby the distinction that the "assumed man" possesses such divine honors only by grace, not by nature.[48]

As regards how φύσις is related to the terms ὑπόστασις and πρόσω-πον,[49] there fortunately exists a fragment attributed to Theodore that employs the three terms in a christological context: "For when we distinguish the natures, we say that the nature of God the Word is complete, and that [his] πρόσωπον is complete (for it is not correct to speak of an ὑπόστασις without a πρόσωπον and also that the nature of the man is complete and likewise [his] πρόσωπον. But when we look to their union, then we affirm

---

46. Theodore, PG 66:992. For an English translation of the whole passage from which this quotation has been taken, see Richard A. Norris, Jr., trans. and ed., *The Christological Controversy*, Sources of Early Christian Thought (Philadelphia: Fortress, 1980), 121–22.

47. Theodore, PG 66:993.

48. Grillmeier notes that Theodore's use of this kind of language "should not simply be measured by the yardstick of the 'communicatio idiomatum' without it being said at the same time that in his time it had to be demonstrated afresh that the 'communicatio idiomatum' was, in fact, a valid standard" (436).

49. For an overview of how the Latin word *persona* evolved, see Grillmeier, 123–29.

one πρόσωπον."⁵⁰ This passage—if it is authentic⁵¹—indicates that Theodore looked upon an ὑπόστασις as denoting a complete, specific nature capable of independent existence and activity. He understood φύσις as synonymous with it in the sense that a part can be taken for the whole. The nuance between the two terms appears to be that φύσις denotes the sumtotal of all that a person has been born with and has acquired through growth, whereas ὑπόστασις refers more to the real, individual, substantial elements of a nature. As we indicated in the previous chapter, this was then an acceptable understanding of the terms and cohered with the Nicea and Constantinople's usage of ὑπόστασις, οὐσία and φύσις.

Thus it is readily understandable why Theodore believed that a hypostatic union meant that Christ's human nature had been so absorbed into the divine that there is presently only one existing nature. But this runs wholly counter to Theodore's conviction that the divine and the human natures in Christ must remain unaltered and individually operational in the Incarnation. It explains too why Theodore explained the meaning of "factum est" in John's Prologue as he did: "But he did not say 'factum est,' as though [the Word] was changed, but because it was believed to be so by his appearance."⁵² In other words, Theodore holds that the Word's nature remains wholly unchanged, even though His presence appeared altered because Christ's human body is now what is visible to others.

While it is not clear what Theodore meant by asserting that each of Christ's natures has its own complete πρόσωπον⁵³ and that the two to-

50. Swete, 2:299. Grillmeier quotes this passage even while questioning its authenticity. He tends towards the view that "in the genuine works of Theodore there is no teaching of two prosopa and a third common one" (432 n. 49). It seems to me, however, to be consistent with Theodore's thought. He held that each nature has its own πρόσωπον in the sense that each concrete nature has at least the potential for revealing itself in a functional way in and through its πρόσωπον.

51. For a discussion of this point, see Grillmeier, 432–39, especially 438 n. 61 where he concludes: "But the new fragment of the 18th book against Eunomius quoted above now shows quite clearly that Theodore does not speak of one *hypostasis* in Christ."

52. Vosté, TJA, 23.

53. The word was a term widely current in the late fourth century. It is also found in the Septuagint and the writings of Paul, such as in 2 Cor. 2:10: "for indeed what I have forgiven, if I have forgiven anything, [is done] for your sakes in the πρόσωπον of Christ." See also 2 Corinthians 3:7, 5:12, 19:1, 11:20, and Galatians 1:22, 2:6. Theologians employed it too in reference to the Persons within the Trinity. For a study into the various meanings πρόσωπον can have, see Hodgson, NES, 402–10 and Grillmeier, 123–31, 337–40, 365–66, 372–77, and especially 431–37.

gether constitute a single πρόσωπον, it seems that he was using the term πρόσωπον in different nuanced ways. The common πρόσωπον would be Christ as he had visibly appeared to others throughout his earthly life. The two individual πρόσωπα would be the Word and Jesus' natures that are each able to function in free, self-determining, and visible ways in and through the πρόσωπον common to both.[54] In other words, their common πρόσωπον would be underscoring Christ's external appearance but implying some real relationship to his two underlying natures in such a way that their natural attributes can be said to be shared with each other. For Theodore, this meant that the Word can reveal His power and glory through His visible humanity and Christ's humanity can also share in the Word's prerogatives as Son. It may be likened to the way that an individual's qualities can be surmised from his or her external manner of acting and to the unique ways that an individual can express these in an outward, visible manner. It is the same "reality" viewed from two different perspectives. In this exchange, Christ's natures would remain, of course, unaltered.

Further corroboration of the above interpretation can be found in the way that Theodore understood ὑπόστασις and πρόσωπον in reference to the Trinity. In his *Commentary on Haggai*, he wrote: "At that time, the men of the Old Testament did not understand the ὑπόστασις of the Holy Spirit to be distinguished by his πρόσωπον from God . . . the Father has his own πρόσωπον, the Son his own, and the Holy Spirit his own; and we believe that each of them equally belong to the divine, eternal οὐσία."[55] In other words, while the term οὐσία expresses the unity of divine nature, ὑπόστασις and πρόσωπον both connote something about each person of the Trinity. Because the Hebrews of the Old Testament were not aware of the Spirit's πρόσωπον, Theodore believed, they were

54. In his treatment (504–19) of how Nestorius has used the phrase "a natural *prosōpon*," Grillmeier explains it thus: "The 'natural *prosōpon*' has its reality from the reality of the nature whose mode of appearance it is. But without the natural *prosōpon* the natures are incomplete, unrecognizable and indistinguishable. Thus the natural *prosōpon* is the complex of the properties, the differences and the characteristics by which a nature is differentiated, limited and finally determined. If two natures no longer preserve their *prosōpon naturale*, in their union they are no longer differentiated but mingled. Thus 'nature' in its 'natural *prosōpon*' is the 'hypostasis.' In fact, *hypostasis* coincides with *natura completa*, but formally it describes the completeness of the *natura completa*" (507).

55. Theodore, PG 66:484–85.

not able to distinguish the Spirit as an individual "person" separate from the Father and the Son. A revelation was necessary for them to know that the Spirit existed with and apart from the Father and the Son in the Trinity. The sense seems to be that a ὑπόστασις denotes a person's existing individual nature, whereas the term πρόσωπον expresses what makes such a ὑπόστασις visibly recognizable as such.

The next chapter will relate how Theodore connects his "union of good pleasure" or "divine favor" with πρόσωπον. The point needing to be stressed here is why he was so adamantly opposed to a hypostatic or substantial union of Christ's natures according to his own conceptual understanding. He maintained: "to say that God dwells within another in a substantial way is most unfitting. For this necessitates that he be substantially contained only in that which he is said to indwell and be external to everything else—which is an absurd thing to say about an infinite nature that is everywhere and circumscribed nowhere."[56] For Theodore, to assert that the Word's divine nature is hypostatically united to Jesus' human nature is equivalent to saying that it has now limited itself to one location. In his *Catechetical Homily on the Nicene Creed*, Theodore insists: "It is well known that the one who is eternal and the one whose existence has a beginning are greatly separated from each other, and the gulf found between them is unbridgeable. . . . It is not possible to limit and define the chasm that exists between the one who is from eternity and the one who began to exist at a time when he was not."[57] With this as his fundamental premise, Theodore logically accepted whatever conclusions to which this led him concerning the union of natures in Christ and human divinization.

What complicates the whole issue today concerning Theodore's view of the difference between a hypostatic and a prosopic union is that, when ὑπόστασις was chosen in the mid-fifth century to be the correct word for affirming a "person," it may have been initially understood by the Fathers at the Council of Chalcedon as being more a descriptive rather a metaphysical term.[58] It seems that they looked upon it as an elaboration of

56. Ibid., 66:972.
57. *Commentary of Theodore of Mopsuestia on the Nicene Creed*, ed. and trans. A. Mingana, WS 5 (Cambridge: Heffer, 1932), 45.
58. See Grillmeier, 549–50. He points out that the Council of Chalcedon was not seeking to provide a metaphysical explanation of *hypostasis*. As the previous chapter has indicated, this term has to be understood against the background of Scripture and the whole patristic tradition.

the creed of the Council of Nicea which simply affirms the Word to be the subject of all that is said of Christ's humanity. They would, therefore, have been using the term ὑπόστασις in point of fact in a metaphysical way as denoting a person's unified center.[59] Such an understanding runs counter to today's general conception of the term "person" as signifying or better describing the conscious state in which an individual or a subject is able to act as a rational, free, and responsible agent.[60] This wholly descriptive and functional way of referring to a "person" is a view that Theodore seems to have shared at least in part. He would have added the notion that a πρόσωπον is known through the visible revelation of one's inner self to others.

The Relationship Between Spiritual and Material Entities

When Nemesius discussed the union between the soul and the body, he invoked the Word-Man union in Christ as an example of how the soul and the body are related to each other.[61] He explained both unions in light of Ammonius Saccas's observation of how the spiritual members of the unions remain unchanged in their natures, while providing vitality and energy to their bodily co-partners.[62] When Theodore's thought is examined in the next chapter, a similar outlook will appear. For the present, the point here is how Nemesius considered the soul-body and the Word-Man unions to be grounded in nature and in a clear aside directed against

59. For a discussion of this position, see Richard A. Norris, Jr., "Toward a Contemporary Interpretation of the Chalcedonian Definition," *Lux in Lumine: Essays for W. N. Pittenger* (New York: Seabury, 1966), 62–79.

60. I have become aware only at the end of my present work of a recently completed dissertation that studied Gregory of Nyssa's understanding of πρόσωπον. It argues Gregory utilized the term at times also in a psychological way. See David L. Stramara, "Unmasking the Meaning of ΠΡΟΣΩΠΟΝ: as Person in the Works of Gregory of Nyssa" (Ph.D. diss., St. Louis U, 1996).

61. Norris (*Manhood*, 217) asserts that Theodore's "christological theory differs markedly from that of Nemesius of Emesa, who explicitly employs the Neo-Platonic doctrine of body-soul 'mixture' as a model for his account of the union of Deity and humanity in Christ."

62. See Telfer, 295–96 and 297–98. For a study regarding the influence of the Neoplatonic theory upon Theodore and Nestorius, see also R. Arnou, S.J., "Nestorianisme et Neoplatonisme: L'unité du Christ et l'union des 'Intelligibles,'" *Gregorianum* 17 (1936): 116–31.

Theodore and his followers: "The manner of union is, therefore, not by divine favour, as is the opinion of certain men of note, but is grounded in nature . . . the unconfused union is a proper work of the divine nature, and not of divine favour, alone."[63]

While it is true that Theodore emphasized the union of natures in Christ as one of "divine favor," it should be understood in terms of his efforts to explain by a scriptural phrase how the Word acts in concert with the humanity that He has assumed. This is affirmed in the following distinction that he made between Christ's human power to act and its source arising out of the union with the Word: "(the assumed one) showed [in the curing of the leper] that there existed one will [and] one operation, one according to one and the same power, produced not by reason of nature but of good pleasure, through which he is united to God the Word . . . who had an inherent affection for him from the womb."[64] When Norris comments on this passage, he concludes that Theodore held that there is "a single source (though not a single subject) of all that Christ is and does, and that this source is the divine Word who indwells the Man."[65]

Telfer provides us with further insight into what Theodore meant when he spoke about the union of natures in Christ, when he observes in a note that Nemesius's understanding of how the soul dwells by habit within its body is like Theodore's viewpoint on how "God indwells in the righteous, not by omnipresence, but by his good favor ($\epsilon\mathring{\upsilon}\delta o\kappa\acute{\iota}\alpha$)."[66] His observation here is perceptive because Nemesius has repudiated a union of divine "good pleasure" in favor of one grounded in nature.[67] Yet as Telfer points out, Nemesius's "habitual" relationship and Theodore's union of "good pleasure" are both describing in different words how the Word acts upon Jesus' humanity. They both affirm that, while the Word is not directly altered by His contact with Jesus' human nature, He is continually disposed to act sympathetically on his behalf, as a lover would toward his or her beloved.[68]

---

63. Telfer, 303.
65. Norris, *Manhood*, 228.
64. Theodore, PG 66:1003.
66. Telfer, 299 n. 8.
67. Nemesius seems to be using "nature" in its vital, dynamic sense. If so, he is affirming how the substantial union of the two natures in Christ comes about in a dynamic and active way. In other words, Christ is one because he is a living unity of Word and man. Nemesius may have interpreted the creedal statements of the Councils of Nicea and Constantinople I in light of his knowledge of Greek metaphysics.
68. For a critique of this, see Grillmeier, 390–91 and 434.

We see, therefore, at this point that Theodore has shifted from a metaphysical rejection of a possible substantial union of natures in Christ to a functional and a psychological explanation of how the two can act as one. He believed that, when the Word was pleased to assume Christ's humanity at the moment of his conception, He then became the single source of all that is done by the humanity. But this activity does not entail any alteration or even modification within the Word's divine nature. Nor does it violate Christ's human freedom of action. For Theodore wanted to safeguard two truths about the union: Christ's human ability to be the agent of his own activity, while his will is at the same time in a harmonious but subordinated union with that of the Word. Theodore is so insistent upon Christ's human integrity that he expressed it in terms that suggested that the Word and the "assumed man" were two separate individuals, although one in their unique union of natures and wills.

For Theodore, therefore, protecting the reality of Christ's human free will was a central concern, for he realized the pivotal role that it was called to play in God's economy for salvation. Since Theodore excluded a substantial union between God and creatures, he had to seek the union on two levels, that of grace and that of a harmony of wills. While Christ's case is unique because only his human nature has been assumed and been graced to live a sinless life, he too had to commit himself freely in a human way, as all other humans must do, to God's will. On this point, one can detect a difference with Nemesius, who acknowledged tangentially the mind's ability to contemplate and enter into a mystical communion with God.[69] Theodore could not conceive of a union on this level. For him, it had to be a relationship with God that comes about because of a sharing in a common nature with Christ and a commitment to live a life dedicated to following, with divine grace, God's will.

Because of his emphasis upon preserving the critical role that human free-will is meant to play in salvation history, Theodore has been labeled a Pelagian. A close, careful reading, however, of his works reveals that he was sensitive to the need for divine grace both for inspiration and for the strength a person needs to act in accord with God's moral law.[70] For instance, he asserted that even the "assumed man" required divine cooper-

69. This may indicate his direct or indirect dependence upon the Neoplatonic understanding of how an inferior being can become united with its source.

70. For a detailed examination of Theodore's views on grace, see Dewart.

ation so as to be able always to fulfill God's will: "When the divine Word united him to Himself at the first moment of his conception, He cooperated with him by offering greater assistance in the right performance of what was needful."[71] Theodore also looked upon salvation as being a gift—and thus a grace—from God that enables a person to move from a mortal, mutable state to an immortal and immutable one. This changeover is not something that anyone could achieve by one's own natural powers. He wrote: "To acquire justification by one's own efforts was most difficult, indeed, I would say, impossible. . . . For it is altogether impossible for existing man not to sin. This is overcome through grace alone."[72]

Other examples can be cited particularly when Theodore discusses the role and importance of prayer. In his catechetical instruction *On the Lord's Prayer*, Theodore urges his readers: "In this world we ought to persevere as much as possible in the will of God and not to will or do things that are against Him . . . [for] it behooves us not to do now the smallest act which by our will or our thought would contradict that will."[73] But he has realized that this is "impossible for men who are mortal and changeable by nature" and therefore we must pray since "we are not able to do anything without the help of God."[74] The same need for divine assistance is clearly alluded to in Theodore's *Commentary on Galatians*: "Nor are we able ourselves sometimes to perform works of virtue by ourselves, just as we cannot obtain the fruits of the earth, even if we labor much, if God has not deigned to give them."[75]

In summation, the extant writings of Theodore reflect at least a similarity in outlook with several classical philosophical opinions, above all with Nemesius' eclectic synthesis. Theodore shared the Platonic outlook regarding the existence of two worlds: a material, visible world as well as a spiritual, invisible world. He expressed the same world-view as the Stoics who station human beings at the heart of the cosmos where they link together the intelligible and material worlds to one another, so that all form one organic body. He can moreover be thought to possess an

71. Swete, 2:298.
72. Ibid., 2:77.
73. Mingana, WS 6:9–10. I altered Mingana's translation slightly to bring out more clearly the meaning of the Syriac text.
74. Ibid., WS 6:10–11. I have again slightly changed the text so that the translation may conform more closely to the Syriac text.
75. Swete, 1:101.

Aristotelian philosophical perspective on life because of his emphases upon God's totally transcendent nature, the impossibility of a substance being the form of another substance to which it can be united without either nature being altered, and the role of free-will and use of one's critical reason to substantiate one's statements. But, as was true with Nemesius, he cannot be presumed to be an adherent of or even a product of any particular school of philosophical thought. He simply appears to be replicating the intellectual commonplaces of the diffused Neoplatonic eclecticism current in his day, with a partiality for Aristotelian and Stoic philosophical viewpoints, but since the philosophers of his day were defenders of paganism, it is easy to understand why Theodore was so negative and biting in his assessment of "those Greek philosophers who, intending to destroy all the doctrines and religions received among human beings, have striven to say of the sun that it in no way gives light."[76]

The most formative influence upon Theodore was definitely the kind of education that he received as a young man at the School of Diodore. While his temperament and rhetorical training at Libanius's school also played important roles in shaping his outlook, still it was his immersion in a literal, rational, and historical scriptural exegesis that had the greatest intellectual bearing upon his way of thinking regarding human nature and the meaning of life. As he drew upon scriptural arguments to refute such adversaries as the Arians and Apollinarians who denied or undermined an autonomous human nature in Christ and those who espoused a theory of "divinization" that minimized, if not excluded, the role of the body within the economy of salvation, Theodore was doubtless forced to reflect on and clarify the underlying metaphysical presuppositions and principles arising out of his biblical perspective and the Antiochene tradition. Whether he was aware of this metaphysical dimension is, of course, another question.

When all the defining factors are taken into account, it is Scripture and the creedal statements of Nicea and Constantinople I, not pagan philosophy, that determined Theodore's anthropological viewpoint. He employed metaphysical opinions, terms, and arguments, so it seems, if they accorded with his overall synthesis of biblical revelation.[77] For instance, he

---

76. Vosté, TJA, 7.

77. Grillmeier (424) asserts that Theodore's "speculative theology is therefore subsidiary, and not an aim in itself. His philosophy stands even further in the background." See Norris, *Manhood*, 125, for the same conclusion.

believed in the existence of a spiritual world and a final destiny in heaven, not from Neoplatonic teaching, but from his Christian faith. His view of an organic world where humans are the bonds uniting the spiritual and corporeal worlds flows less from Stoic teaching than from the Genesis recounting of creation and the Pauline teaching that the risen Christ is the head of the body which is the church and the *plērōma* who is going to recapitulate all at the end of the world.[78] And his emphasis upon the pivotal role that free-will has been called to play in life arises primarily out of his own systematic explanation of salvation rather than upon any reliance on Aristotelian categories.

One final factor that is independent of Theodore's educational and cultural backgrounds deserves some elaboration. When we consider how Theodore's style and approach to theological issues differ from those of Chrysostom, who came out of the very same background, the question arises as to why this is so. While much of this can be explained by the dissimilar audiences to whom each was writing and speaking and by the different purposes each had in mind, one must confront the role that Theodore's temperament played in all this. Admittedly his theological approach was shaped by his training, but, as his writings frequently reveal, Theodore was basically a realist willing to proceed wherever his reason led him in his explanation and defense of revelation, even to the point of turning to classical metaphysical speculations when they fit his own theological synthesis. He even spoke out in opposition to widely-held positions, whenever he believed they were not well founded upon rational as well as scriptural arguments. In all of this, one can recognize how Theodore's own bent of mind shaped his understanding of God's plan for salvation.

Nestorius

Our present sources for understanding Nestorius's philosophical viewpoint are *The Bazaar of Heracleides* (the lengthy apologetic defense that he wrote in banishment shortly before his death) and the brief fragments that have survived from his letters, homilies, and other miscellaneous works.[79]

78. This, of course, prescinds from the question of how much Stoic ideas have been incorporated into late Jewish scriptural thought and then into the New Testament.
79. This work survived in a Syriac version. The translator, unfortunately, misinterpreted the original title. He translated the Greek word *pragmateia* as "bazaar," which can

His theological education most likely involved, as it did for Chrysostom and Theodore, a thorough grounding in Scripture and in the Antiochene commitment to defending the complete integrity of Christ's human nature against the followers of Paul of Samosata, Arius, and Apollinaris. Like them, his formal philosophical training was likely minimal; and the outlook that he did acquire was shaped mainly by the cultural eclecticism prevalent at Antioch and by the apologetic need to be able to reply intelligently with well reasoned arguments against those who were attacking his and Theodore's explanation of the union of Christ's natures in one πρόσωπον.

Like his predecessors at the School of Antioch, Nestorius came out of a tradition committed to a reasoned literal exegesis of the Scriptures and one conditioned by almost a century of theological battles over the divinity of the Word and the full integrity of Christ's humanity. He was a product, too, of a cultural milieu and a religious tradition that had a profound effect on how he understood the terms for human nature and the kinds of union that were possible. When these factors are combined with his pressing needs to counter a charge that he was a heretic and to repulse Cyril of Alexandria's efforts to define the union of the natures in Christ as a hypostatic union, he was impelled by necessity to move beyond the scriptural moorings to which Diodore, Chrysostom, and Theodore had bound Antiochene theology. Though not a metaphysician in any sense of the term, Nestorius was drawn into an anthropological discussion of what he meant by a voluntary union of the divine and the human natures in Christ's one πρόσωπον. His many appeals to Scripture, the Council of Nicea, and the orthodox teaching of the Fathers were utilized to buttress his rational arguments. It is in these arguments one discovers his metaphysical way of thinking.

---

be a possible meaning. It actually means here a "treatise." By comparing the extant Greek fragments of Nestorius, scholars today are firmly convinced that this nineteenth-century Syriac manuscript is a copy of a work or works written by Nestorius himself under the pseudonym Heracleides. After some controversy, they also believe that the text is genuine. For an extended discussion of the controversy, see Grillmeier, 559–68 and 501–19 for his theological critique of Nestorius's Christology. For a close and profound study into Nestorius's thought, see also Anthony Daly, "Nestorius in the *Bazaar of Heracleides*: A Christology Compatible with the Third Letter and Anathemas of Cyril of Alexandria" (Ph.D. diss., University of Southern California, 1983).

Nestorius's Metaphysical Understanding of Terms

To understand Nestorius's viewpoint, one needs a clear, accurate understanding of what he intended by his terms for human nature, that is, for οὐσία, ὑπόστασις, πρόσωπον, and φύσις. The whole issue is clouded over because he has not explicitly defined these words in his extant works. Three scholarly studies that have explored these at length are those by Godfrey Driver and Leonard Hodgson in their chapter on "The Metaphysic of Nestorius," in their edition of Nestorius's *Bazaar of Heracleides*;[80] Anthony Daly in his unpublished thesis;[81] and Aloys Grillmeier in his classic work on *Christ in Christian Tradition*.[82] First of all, Hodgson favors a distinction a Professor Webb made regarding Aristotle's explanation for the term ὑπόστασις: it signifies a specific individual with "two notes of real being, its intelligible character and its concrete independence, [ὑπόστασις] emphasizing the latter, as οὐσία [substance] emphasized the former."[83] Hodgson maintains that Cyril also understood ὑπόστασις in this specialized sense, but as the following sentence clearly indicates, Nestorius has taken it to be equivalent to οὐσία: "It is not indeed that one *ousia* without *hypostasis* should be conceived."[84] This is the same outlook we have seen expressed in the creed of the Council of Nicea where ὑπόστασις and οὐσία are affirmed to be equivalents.

Hodgson also comments on how Nestorius understood ὑπόστασις as connoting an essential relationship with φύσις and πρόσωπον. This is seen in the praise of Athanasius for "not making the human nature nor the divine without *prosōpon* and without *hypostasis*."[85] Yet there are occasions when he does show at least an awareness of how the three terms, ὑπόστασις, οὐσία, and φύσις are each distinguished in the

80. Nestorius, *The Bazaar of Heracleides*, ed. and trans. Godfrey R. Driver and Leonard Hodgson (Oxford: Clarendon, 1925), 411–20.
81. Daly, 11–37.
82. Grillmeier (506 n. 62) notes that Nestorius's understanding of these terms appears close to that of Basil and Gregory of Nyssa. See also his treatment on 372–76 and Edwin Hatch's *The Influence of Greek Ideas and Usages upon the Christian Church*, ed. A. M. Fairbairn, 5th ed. (1895; reprint, Peabody, Mass.: Hendrickson, 1995), 273–79.
83. NES, 218–19, esp. n 3. Grillmeier (506–7) explains the relationships thus: "The *hypostasis* is thus the *ousia* in so far as it is determined by the whole complex of properties. Nestorius calls this complex of properties the *prosōpon*."
84. NES, 218–19, especially n. 3. See also 163, and Daly 33.
85. Ibid., 216.

Trinity: "Dost thou [Cyril] wish to regard a *hypostasis* as a *prosōpon* as we speak of one *ousia* of the divinity and three *hypostases* and understand *prosōpa* by *hypostases?*"[86]

In a note on how the term ὑπόστασις evolved in meaning during the early church, Hodgson traces how over time it took on different shades of meaning from οὐσία. The Cappadocians understood ὑπόστασις as signifying the real center of a person's being—a meaning that the Latin word *persona* often conveys. It then came to connote something objectively existing and, in theological circles, restricted to only human beings. This is how both Cyril of Alexandria and the Council of Chalcedon understood the term when speaking of the "hypostatic union" in Christ. But it is to be noted here that such an outlook (which is more biblically than metaphysically founded) leaves open and unresolved the questions of whether, psychologically speaking, Christ also possessed a human will, a human consciousness, and a human personality. Since the term "person" is understood today in the sense of a human being who is self-conscious, rational, free, and endowed with a unique personality, one must be sensitive to whether something is being affirmed on the metaphysical or descriptive levels and not confuse both of these with operational psychological questions—which seems to have occurred in the controversy between Nestorius and Cyril.

Daly provides us with greater clarity as to what Nestorius meant by the terms οὐσία, ὑπόστασις, φύσις, and πρόσωπον, and a new word that clarifies the meaning of πρόσωπον, σχῆμα, which we will examine shortly. While he acknowledges that Nestorius used these in different, nuanced ways, he shows through an example that Nestorius himself employed the most precise denotations of these terms. Nestorius refers to a king who dresses as a common soldier.[87] Since the king's human οὐσία is the same as that of every other human being, there is the need for a term that will qualify and limit it to the particular human being that the king is. Nestorius uses the term φύσις to signify this. While the king's οὐσία can be said to differ from his φύσις in the same way a genus does in regard to one of its species, both terms have the same basic meaning: they indicate that the king is a human being.[88]

---

86. Ibid., 156. See also 172 and 228.

87. Ibid., 20–23 and 55.

88. Grillmeier (504) describes φύσις "as a purely factual, qualitative expression of being" and as "simply equivalent to reality as opposed to the 'phantasmagorical, illusory, unreal'" (505).

Daly points out how the term ὑπόστασις in Nestorius' writings connotes that an existing nature is complete and, as such, includes an individual's οὐσία and φύσις.[89] To speak, therefore, about the king's ὑπόστασις is to affirm everything that makes him to be essentially what he is personally as a man and as this king. However, when the term is applied to the Trinity and to Christ, Nestorius does not use it to signify a distinct person in a metaphysical sense, as Cyril does when he refers to the three divine ὑπόστασεις in the Trinity and to Christ's one ὑπόστασις. Rather for him, it means a complete, concrete, existing nature that functions as the subject of its own actions. From several of his remarks, Nestorius seems to have sensed that Cyril was using ὑπόστασις in a similar sense to the way he understood πρόσωπον,[90] but he apparently dismissed the possibility that they both were in agreement, probably because he felt that Cyril's overall teaching belied what he occasionally remarked about the unity of the two unconfused natures in Christ.

Daly also elaborates on another important word that Nestorius used in his christological vocabulary—that of a person's σχῆμα. He explains its meaning by noting how water can be found in a liquid and a frozen state. Liquidity and solidity are the two different σχήματα or forms under which water can appear. Nestorius used this to explain how the Word can assume flesh without His divine nature being altered. In other words, σχῆμα is the specific form under which something or someone is presently recognized.[91] One's σχῆμα may change outwardly, but there remains an underlying concrete, substantial nature. Thus the king who has assumed the σχῆμα of a common soldier is still kingly by his own nature, no matter how he may appear to the contrary. It is, however, possible that one's σχῆμα, or appearance, may be deceptive, seeming to be what it is really not. In this sense, the appearance is falsely manifesting what ought to be its true ὑπόστασις with its proper οὐσία and φύσις .

Following L. I. Scipioni's[92] understanding of what these three terms

89. Daly 17–18. See also NES, 208, esp. note 2.

90. NES, 37– 43, 163– 64, 178–79, and 181–82.

91. Daly, 16–18, 19, and 27–28. He interprets the *schēma* as being ultimately "the form or mode of appearance of a being manifested by the *prosōpon*."

92. L. I. Scipioni, *Richerche sulla cristologia del 'Libro di Eraclide' di Nestorio. La formulazione teologica e il suo contesto filosofico*, Paradosis 11 (Freiburg: Universitarie, 1956). Scipioni believes that the way to elucidate Nestorius's thought is through an understanding of Stoic terms.

meant for Nestorius, Grillmeier affirms the same but with more emphasis upon the role that an individual's properties serve in their interplay.[93] Nature is thought to be "complete" when it includes those real properties, differences, and characteristics that make a nature recognizable and distinguishable from another nature; such as for human beings, their reason, free will, birth, growth, and development. Taken in this sense, "substance" (οὐσία) refers to the real essential content of a nature which, when determined by its properties, is to be designated as its ὑπόστασις. As we will now see, the term πρόσωπον signifies how this ὑπόστασις reveals or can reveal itself to others.

Nestorius's Understanding of ΠΡΟΣΩΠΟΝ

The final and most difficult word to understand is Nestorius' use of πρόσωπον. In his Appendix on this topic, Hodgson first details how the term can run a gamut of meanings in Scripture and patristic literature: from face, mask, dramatic part, and actor, to the outward appearance and the inner spiritual personality of an individual.[94] As the term is open to such a wide spectrum of meanings, it is important to know exactly what Nestorius meant by the term. From his analysis, Hodgson believes that it "means the appearance of a thing . . . not as opposed to the thing's reality, but considered as an objectively real element in its being."[95] In other words, it says something objectively real within a person, yet distinguishable from this. Hodgson explains it thus: "But *prosōpon*, whatever it is, must be a permanent element in the being of a thing, without which, or if it were other than it is, the thing would not be what it is. Might it be that the *prosōpon* is the unity of the successive *schēmata* of a thing?"[96] Hodgson then cautions that in judging Nestorius's position on πρόσωπον, one

93. Grillmeier, 506–10.

94. While it is true that Nestorius had no term to express the idea of a personality, he would certainly want to include self-consciousness, personal reflection, and free will within Christ's human nature. While I believe Nestorius's understanding of *prosōpon* overlaps with our contemporary viewpoint regarding person, it has a wider application than today's outlook.

95. NES, 415.

96. Ibid., 15 n. 2. See also 416 where Hodgson concludes that *prosōpon* is the "permanent element in the being of a thing, without which, or if it were other than it is, the thing would not be what it is."

ought also to be mindful not to apply too rigidly our modern distinction between what something is "in itself" and what it "outwardly appears to be," for they are not mutually exclusive.

In his treatment of Nestorius's metaphysics, Hodgson explores the reason why there is a need for a term such as πρόσωπον. He expresses it thus:

> In the first place, an analysis of reality into *ousia* and *physis* almost demands such a completion. If the invisible *ousia* is that in which the various elements of the *physis* are united, a word [*prosōpon*] is needed to describe the external undivided appearance of the whole. And secondly, the common conception of the Godhead as invisible but revealed in Christ who is the *eikon tou aoratou patros* [the image of the unseen Father] is a conception akin to that which we are considering.[97]

The term πρόσωπον, therefore, affirms a need that an inner invisible reality has for a prosopic form to express what it is in a visible way to those unable to see it. As Hodgson notes, Christ's πρόσωπον is an image or, as has been pointed out in the previous chapter, a symbol or an icon (as understood in their theological senses) of the Divinity.

Daly also treats of Nestorius's understanding of πρόσωπον. Two quotations express his viewpoint regarding first its relationship to ὑπόστασις and then to the other terms that have just been examined: "Mechanistically speaking, it is the *prosōpon* which, by supplying concrete reality, actualizes the *ousia* and *physis* of a being so that it becomes an *hypostasis*"[98] and:

> All of these metaphysical principles, *ousia*, *physis*, *prosōpon*, *schēma*, and *hypostasis* were real for Nestorius; real in the sense that they exist objectively in actual beings and not merely in the mind of the philosopher. These, then, are the metaphysical building blocks Nestorius used to construct his technical account of the union of God and man in Christ: the *ousia* and *physis* which together determine the qualitative structure of a being, the *prosōpon* which accounts for its concrete individuality and its insertion into the world of beings, the *schēma* or mode of appearance manifested by the *prosōpon*, and the *hypostasis* which includes all of these principles and designates the complete and concrete nature.[99]

When Daly explains how πρόσωπον and ὑπόστασις are applicable to the example of the king who dresses as a common soldier, he sees the word πρόσωπον adding to the king's specific substantial nature the notion

97. Ibid., 415.
99. Daly, 18–19.

98. Daly, 18.

that the king is a concrete existing being; that is that the king manifests his actual presence and role in the world that goes beyond his general essence and his specific nature. It includes, for example, everything that contributes to how others perceive and describe him as a particular king who can act in authoritative ways and is acted upon in certain outward and inward ways. While all these aspects contained in the notions of the king's πρόσωπον manifest what defining characteristics are present in his οὐσία and φύσις, they are distinct from these two in the sense that they express an individual's actual existence and specific role in the world.[100] This immediately leads to a consideration of how Nestorius understood the role that the prosopic union played in the relationship between Christ's human and divine wills and their common and individual actions.

Christ's Human Will

Like Theodore, Nestorius believed that both the Word and Jesus possess their own free will and that their unity of wills presumes an already existing union between their natures. He affirms this in the following passage: "And because also the *prosōpon* of the one is the other's and that of the other the one's, and the one [comes] from the other and the other from the one, the will belongs to each one of them. When he speaks as from his own *prosōpon*, [he does so] by one *prosōpon* which appertains to the union of the natures and not to one *hypostasis* or [one] nature."[101] A prosopic union, therefore, allows that each of Christ's two wills can function independently according to their own hypostatic natures and yet be combined so that they both appear as one.[102]

Nestorius explains the union of Christ's natures in one πρόσωπον in

100. For a further discussion of this, see Daly, 13–15 and also Grillmeier (460) who suggests *prosōpon* means "the mode of appearance of a concrete nature" and sums it up as "a collective term for all that pertains to the characteristics of a nature, inwardly and outwardly" (461). He also believes that Nestorius's analogy which relates the union of Christ's natures to the common *prosōpon* to that of the Persons in the Trinity with their one Nature is "an incontrovertible proof that he is concerned with a substantial unity in Christ. Just as in the Holy Trinity the three *prosōpa* are joined through the one *ousia* and thus penetrate each other in essence, so in Christ the two *ousiai* penetrate each other without confusion to form the unity of one *prosōpon*" (516).

101. NES, 163. See also 59.

102. The issue of Christ's two wills festered in Orthodox circles until the Sixth Council of Constantinople (681) when the existence of both was solemnly affirmed.

terms of a "voluntary union."[103] By a "voluntary union," Nestorius meant much more than a union of wills wherein Jesus would subordinate his in an obedient way to the Word's.[104] For him, a "voluntary union" stands as the contrary of a "natural" and therefore "necessary union." It connotes primarily the Word's free appropriation of the humanity in the Incarnation as well as a kind of unity wherein the Word and Jesus each freely act as a single existing being. This distinguishes it from the "natural" kind of union where the soul and the body are bound by God to form a human being. This kind of union does not require the free consent of the soul for it to be effected, but rather is necessitated by God's decision to create the soul and the body as constituting the essential elements of a human nature. In other words, a voluntary kind of union ought not to be interpreted as denoting a moral agreement of two wills in opposition to a true personal union, but rather in the sense discussed above where there was treated Theodore's understanding of how the Word supplies the power that the humanity needs to act, but leaving the humanity to be the free responsible agent of his own human acts.

Nestorius was pressed to go beyond the position that Theodore had staked out in affirming the union between Christ's two natures, while he manifested the same perspective as Theodore regarding the meaning of the terms. He was forced to progress beyond Theodore, as will shortly be seen, by defending πρόσωπον as a metaphysical term rather than declaring it to be a descriptive word that seeks to affirm how Christ has functioned in the Gospels in divine and human ways. While one can argue that his intent was to maintain a true personal unity in Christ, he lacked the language required to be able to express this because of his understanding of what is involved in a natural, substantial union. In other words, his weakness is more linguistic and metaphysical than creedal.[105]

Theodoret

Theodoret adds little new to our understanding of the School of Antioch's outlook towards the terms used in the christological controversy.

103. For a treatment of this, see Grillmeier, 514–15.

104. For the teaching of Nestorius regarding the agreement of the divine and human wills in Christ, see NES, 22, 87–88, 108–10, 113, and 147–52.

105. See Grillmeier, 517–19 for an elaboration of this view.

Like his three predecessors, he manifests a thorough training in and a grasp of Scripture that he used in his dogmatic works as his primary means for refuting those who were attacking the traditional Antiochene position regarding the complete integrity of Christ's human nature. He did, however, show that he was familiar with pagan philosophical positions and could summarize their opinions in a fair, accurate way. But as Wallace-Hadrill has rightly observed, "Theodoret is not a philosopher at all, and there is no attempt in his work . . . to grapple with the major issues argued by the philosophers."[106] While this is true, his personal involvement in the theological controversies raging over Nestorius and Eutyches had a metaphysical impact upon him, for he too had to carefully think out how he could honestly reconcile and defend the most basic Antiochene views on Christ in a way acceptable to Orthodox thinking.[107] Moreover, with the ascendency of the Eutychian form of Monophysitism, he was fortunate to be able to go on the attack in the 440s against the opinions of those maintaining that only the divine nature remained once the Incarnation occurred. It was easier to assail their position rather than to explain and justify in a metaphysical way the Antiochene formulation on how Christ's natures were united in one πρόσωπον.

Since Theodoret's approach to both the trinitarian and christological questions of his day is predominantly scriptural, we must turn to the few passing statements he made in his dogmatic works, especially the *Eranistes* or *Dialogues*, to obtain some inkling of the metaphysical meanings lurking in the terms he employed regarding human nature. His educational background appears to be similar to that of Theodore and Nestorius. Likewise, his theological outlook regarding terms is similar to what was already seen present in their writings, but with some interesting differences. First, in his work *Eranistes*, Theodoret pointed out how the Fathers have distinguished the terms for οὐσία and ὑπόστασις from the philosophical ways that they are understood. It is a viewpoint similar to that of Theodore and Nestorius.

106. Wallace-Hadrill, 102. See also his endnote 79 where he cites R. Walzer's opinion that the eastern Church as a whole abandoned philosophy during the fourth and fifth centuries.

107. For a treatment of how Theodoret has evolved in his thought, see Grillmeier, 488–95. Grillmeier believes that: "Only at the Council of Chalcedon does the word ὑπόστασις acquire a positive significance for the christology of the Bishop of Cyrus" (490).

In extra Christian philosophy, there is not [any difference], for οὐσία signifies *to ōn*, that which is, and ὑπόστασις that which subsists. But according to the doctrine of the Fathers there is the same difference between οὐσία and ὑπόστασις as between the common and the particular, and the species and the individual."[108]

When referring here to the Fathers, Theodoret is speaking about their formulations of the Trinity. Theodoret expresses it in this way: "we understand the divine οὐσία to indicate the Holy Trinity, but the ὑπόστασις denotes any person; for following the definitions of the Holy Fathers, we say that ὑπόστασις and individuality mean the same thing."[109] Because Theodoret understands ὑπόστασις as signifying an individual within its own natural species, it is understandable why he is reluctant to speak of the Incarnation as a hypostatic union. It would denote to him a union of two distinct individuals with the same nature rather than a union in which two different natures are now personally united as one.

Like Theodore and Nestorius, Theodoret regards the union of the divine and the human natures in Christ according to φυσική or καθ' ὑπόστασιν as obliterating the distinction between the two. For him, this kind of language is asserting that Christ's human nature has been transformed into the divine or vice versa or that a new tertium quid has been formed. Like his predecessors, he feared that a natural union καθ' ὑπόστασιν could be interpreted in the sense that God was really metamorphosed into a man or that the Word of God would be made subject to passions, human sufferings, and even death. He argued in the third part of *Eranistes* that the Word being God has to be impassible. What is detected here is the fundamental focal point of the Antiochene christological outlook: the need to preserve the vast chasm separating the nature of the Creator from that of his creatures, including also the humanity of Christ.

Theodoret manifests the same insistence upon the immutability of God's transcendence as did Theodore and Nestorius. He reasoned as they did that this means that the Word cannot be substantially united with the humanity of Christ in a "natural" union, for this would require an alteration on the part of one or both of the natures: "If therefore you assert that the Divine Word underwent the change in the flesh, why do you call Him God and not flesh? For change of name fits in with the alteration of

108. Theodoret, *Eranistes*, trans. Gerald H. Ettlinger (New York: Oxford UP, 1975), 161.
109. Ibid., 162.

nature."[110] In other words, Theodoret understands the naming of a reality to be an assertion of its concrete existence. So to change its name is equivalent to affirming that its specific nature has also been altered. Then, as regards the make-up of human nature, Theodoret maintained that it is composed of soul and body against the belief "that man is composed of three parts, of a body, a vital soul, and further of a reasonable soul, which he terms mind. Holy Scripture on the contrary knows only one, not two souls."[111] He saw that those maintaining that Jesus possessed only an irrational soul and body undermined the integrity of Christ's human nature in its union with the Word.

Summation

What stands out from this analysis of the Antiochenes is that they did not adhere to any school of philosophy. Because they mirrored almost the same anthropological view of human nature as that contained in Nemesius's Christian synthesis of Neoplatonic, Stoic, and Aristotelian ideas, they can be said to share a very similar eclectic cultural outlook regarding human nature but with an emphasis upon the Aristotelian and Stoic perspectives. Their writings reveal them to be first and foremost Scripture scholars. From the rare passing remarks they have made about philosophers, they appear to have been opposed to Greek philosophy as such but were prepared to employ its terms and rational arguments, if doing so substantiated or elucidated their own explanations of Christian revelation.[112] But all their ideas about human nature appear ultimately to have originated out of their literal, historical, and rationalistic approach to the Christian Scriptures, tradition, and their culturally-influenced understanding of what the basic terms for human nature meant, as well as, so it seems, out of an inherited Semitic outlook regarding divine transcendency and the human person.

The Antiochenes differ in one major respect from Nemesius. While Nemesius admitted that Christ's human nature can be united "substan-

110. Ibid., 163.   111. Ibid., 183.

112. Though dated, H. S. Nash's article, "The Exegesis of the School of Antioch: A Criticism of the Hypothesis that Aristotelianism was the Main Cause of its Genesis" *Journal of Biblical Literature* 11 (1892): 22–37, was the first article to point out that the Antiochenes could be said at the most to be influenced by Aristotle's teaching on logic and rhetoric (36).

tially" with the divine, it is not a position that the Antiochenes found to be intellectually possible.[113] They were influenced, so it appears, by a Jewish and metaphysical outlook regarding divine transcendence. This conditioned them to maintain as a bedrock principle that the infinite gulf between the Deity and all creatures precluded their natures from being combined in any substantial, hypostatic way. The Antiochenes, at least Theodore, Nestorius, and Theodoret, believed that the only way to express how Christ is both divine and human and yet one is to use a word for "person" that portrays Jesus in the same way he is depicted by the evangelists—as functioning as God's unique Son and the Lord of the universe.[114]

Another area of difference between some of the Antiochenes and Nemesius appears over his view that humans serve as the bonds linking together the spiritual and material worlds. While Theodore highlights this in his writings, Chrysostom and Theodoret give no indication that this influenced their own thought. (We do not have sufficient works of Diodore and Nestorius to judge whether this also applies to them.) As seen earlier, Theodore has combined this teaching on humans as the bonding element within the cosmos with his outlook on the image of God and Christ's role in salvation. It is a major point of divergence with the view that Diodore, Chrysostom, and Theodoret take toward image. It also exemplifies how Theodore was an independently-minded synthesizer who did not walk lockstep with other Antiochenes in his presentation of theology. While the Antiochenes agreed on a common front regarding their commitment to a literal, historical kind of exegesis and to a defense of Christ's full humanity, there did exist a variety of views under this umbrella.

With this kind of general understanding of how the Antiochenes viewed the philosophical thought of their day, we turn now to probe more deeply into how they understood the kind of metaphysical union between Christ's human and divine natures. Although their meanings have been derived from the way they were understood in the culture of the day and within conciliar statement, they are, nevertheless, terms with

---

113. It is not clear what John Chrysostom's position on this was. He stoutly maintained a personal union between the divine and the human natures in Christ. But he did not enter into the dispute of what kind of terms best expressed this.

114. Grillmeier also sees an influence upon Nestorius from the Cappadocians. He believes that Nestorius's "concept of *prosōpon* is largely determined by the Bible and then, above all, by the approach made by the Cappadocians in distinguishing nature from *hypostasis* in trinitarian theology" (460).

metaphysical undertones that need to be expressed whenever one is pressed to say what meanings they have for him or her. Rowan A. Greer, however, sums up well the Antiochene outlook, when he remarks about Theodore: "Theodore is striving to express the union in as careful and philosophic a way as possible. Yet throughout his terms are Biblical and ethical in their import."[115]

115. Greer, *Theodore of Mopsuestia*, 57. See also 65.

5

THE UNITIVE FUNCTION OF IMAGE

Y EQUATING THE NOTION of human beings as the image of God to that of their role as the bond of the universe, Theodore has interpreted the scriptural phrase "image of God" primarily as describing the functions that Adam and Christ play as the unifiers and the recapitulators of the universe. As seen in our treatment of Theodore's understanding of image, Christ is the perfect mediator who sums up creation and unites all beings to God by means of his bodily and spiritual natures and by the union of his human nature with that of the Word. For by means of his human nature, he is consubstantial with all human beings, all spiritual powers, and the entire non-rational world of matter. He is like the apex of a triangle where the lateral sides of the triangle converge upon him. So the question arises: how does Christ link the created universe to God or, to state this in a different way, what kind of communion does Christ mediate between all creation and its Creator? Since only Theodore associates image with the human role as the link uniting the entire universe as one, the emphasis as we examine his christological thought will be on how Christ's human and divine natures are united in a "personal" way.[1]

Since Nestorius has linked the idea of "image" to that of πρόσωπον,

1. As regards Theodore's dependence upon Diodore, see Rowan A. Greer, "Antiochene Christology of Diodore of Tarsus," *Journal of Theological Studies* 17 (1966): 327–41. And for a relatively brief but unmatched summary of the christological disputes

we will also include his views. Although he makes no explicit mention of the unitive function of image in his extant writings, he was most probably reflecting Theodore's ideas when he spoke of image's revelatory function and the need for all humans to live in a responsible voluntary way as God's image, in order to be in a true communion with Christ and God. Finally we will also discuss Theodoret's view on the union of natures in Christ, for he has reconciled the Antiochene defense of Christ's integral human nature with what the Chalcedonian formula has affirmed regarding the union of Christ's human nature with the Word's. He demonstrates that the two can be bridged, if the reality underlying the terms is agreed upon.

In regard to Chrysostom's position on the union of the divine and human natures in Christ, he has left no developed theological statements about the specific metaphysical kind of union that he held this to be. This is understandable, seeing that the dogmatic implications of this had not yet become a full-blown dispute in his own day.[2] He professed a unity between the divine and the human in Christ, but he never asserted in wholly unambiguous terms that there are two natures in one "person."[3] The closest that he came to this was a statement that the Council of Chalcedon cited, in which he expressed his belief in the reality of the union and the limit to which one can speak about it: "Through union, God the Word and the Flesh are one, without the occurrence of a mingling, without the disappearance of the natures, but [one] because of an ineffable, indefinable union. How this union took place, ask not: God alone knoweth."[4] By

---

in the early church, see the introduction in Richard A. Norris, Jr., *The Christological Controversy*, Sources of Christian Thought (Philadelphia: Fortress, 1980).

2. See Jean-Marie Leroux's article on "Theodor" in *Theologische Realenzyklopädie*, ed. G. Krause and G. Müller (Berlin: de Gruyter, 1981), 17:122–23.

3. Except in the case of the Trinity where there are three divine persons with one nature, Chrysostom understood φύσις in the same way as did all the other Antiochenes as a concrete, existent ὑπόστασις or "person." This, of course, affected how he was able to think about and express the Incarnation. For a treatment of Chrysostom's theological thought, see Aloys Grillmeier, *Christ in Christian Tradition: From the Apostolic Age to Chalcedon* (451), 2d ed. (Atlanta: John Knox, 1975), 418–21. Grillmeier comes to the conclusion: "The whole way in which Chrysostom's picture of Christ is drawn accords with this: everything is conceived of in the light of the Logos and of the unconditional predominance of the divine nature. The typically Antiochene difficulties in the interpretation of the unity in Christ do not exist for Chrysostom" (421).

4. I am indebted to Chrysostomus Baur (*John Chrysostom and His Time*, trans. M. Gonzaga, 2 vols. [Westminster, Md.: Newman, 1959–60], 1:358) for this quotation.

staying close to what Scripture has affirmed about Christ, Chrysostom has evaded all controversy regarding his Christology. This was not the case with his friend Theodore, whose systematic, rational bent of mind led him to seek a deeper explanation of what Scripture says about who Christ was, is, and will be.

Theodore

Because so much of Theodore's writings regarding the union of the two natures in Christ have been destroyed, the reconstruction of his thought must depend primarily on those fragments that have survived and those quotations that have been referred to as heretical by his opponents at the Council of Constantinople in 553.[5] Since these latter were taken out of context, it is difficult to reconstitute Theodore's thought, particularly as there are texts justifying the positions of those attacking and those maintaining his orthodoxy.[6] In the last chapter we saw that one principal reason for this ambiguity was the fluidity in meaning attached in his day to the most basic terms employed to express human nature, specifically those for οὐσία, ὑπόστασις, πρόσωπον and φύσις as well as the terms for various kinds of union that were affirmed about Christ's two natures, namely "substantial," "accidental," and "prosopic" kinds of union.

Since the issue of Christ's union of natures is so complex, in fact ultimately a mystery, our treatment begins by presupposing the meaning of the terms from the last chapter and noting the opinions about Christ that Theodore repudiated as false. This will establish the general context of his thought. Then Theodore's understanding of his description of the union as one of "good pleasure in one πρόσωπον" will be discussed. After this, the roles he allowed for grace and for, what is a critical issue for him, the

5. For a clear and fair statement of the issues involved in the condemnation of Theodore at the Council, see Richard A. Norris, Jr., *Manhood and Christ* (Oxford: Clarendon, 1963), 239–45. For a contemporary English translation of the fragments that have survived of Theodore's work *On the Incarnation*, see Norris, *The Christological Controversy*, 113–22.

6. For a discussion of this, see R. Devreese, *Essai sur Théodore de Mopsueste*, Studi e Testi 141 (Vatican City: Biblioteca Apostolica Vaticana, 1948), 169–93 and 259–72; and for two critical evaluations of this question, Kevin McNamara, "Theodore of Mopsuestia and the Nestorian Heresy," *The Irish Theological Quarterly*, July 1952: 254–59; and Grillmeier, 421–39.

preservation of Christ's human free will within the union will be probed. This section on Theodore will conclude by delving into the kind of communion that Christ mediates with God, especially by those receiving baptism and the eucharist. This is central to understanding how Christ fulfills his unitive role as God's image for other human beings.

The General Parameters of Theodore's Christological Thought

The general outlines of Theodore's Christology can be obtained by considering the various opinions he has repudiated as heretical. He condemned Paul of Samosata as an angel of Satan for teaching "that Christ our Lord was a simple man."[7] He assailed Apollinaris for his belief that the Word had supplanted Christ's rational soul, as this would undermine a central Antiochene tenet, which held that Christ truly possessed an integral human nature. His rejection of these two positions reveal that Theodore regarded Christ as being fully human and yet more than human because his humanity has been assumed by the Word. But when Theodore came to explain how the "assumed man" is more than human, he was faced with a fundamental outlook that will bedevil his Christology: his firm conviction that "to say that God dwells within another in a substantial way is most unfitting."[8] At the same time he asserted this, he also denied that God is united to Christ in the same way that He is usually present in the world; that is, by means of His power and providence, for "the same can be said of [His ordinary ways of] operating."[9]

Theodore, therefore, believed that the Word's nature is united to Christ's full humanity in some kind of a unique, graced way that would

7. Commentary of Theodore of Mopsuestia on the Lord's Prayer and on the Sacraments of Baptism and the Eucharist, ed. and trans. A. Mingana, WS6 (Cambridge: Heffer, 1933), 40. Theodore also expressed his belief in Christ's divinity in the preface of his Commentary on John's Gospel where he affirmed that some of the faithful in Asia brought John the works of the evangelists for comment. After he praised their works, John supposedly pointed out that certain miracles and almost all dogmatic reflection were missing. Theodore then remarked "that, when they discussed the coming of Christ in the flesh, his divinity should not have been passed over in silence . . ." (Commentarius in Evangelium Joannis Apostoli, ed. J.-M. Vosté, CSCO 115–116/Syr. 62–63 [Louvain: Officina Orientali, 1940], 3:3–4.)

8. Theodore, PG 66:972. All translations in this section are my own.

9. Ibid. For a translation of the whole fragment, see Norris, The Christological Controversy, 114–15.

not be a substantial union but yet more than His ordinary presence within creation. Theodore's adversaries have interpreted this to mean that he is actually holding, despite his protestations to the contrary,[10] for an accidental kind of union that is simply moral or voluntary. They have found this to be verified in the way he has described the union of Christ's natures as being one of "good pleasure in one πρόσωπον" and in his reluctance to speak forthrightly of Mary as the mother of God without distinguishing between the Word and the "assumed man's" separate natures. As a way to determine whether his references to the Word and the "assumed man" indicate that he actually looked upon these natures as independent and separate individuals, an answer will be sought in his opinion of how Christ fulfills his role as the image who unites creation to God.[11]

A Union of Good Pleasure

When Theodore came to state what kind of union united Christ's human and divine natures, he explained it in terms of God's "good pleasure" or benevolence:

Therefore one can say that it is neither by substance nor by activity that the Divine has made a dwelling. What then is left? What reason will we use that will clearly affirm what is peculiar to these matters? It is clear, therefore, that it is fitting to say that the indwelling has come about by good pleasure. Good pleasure is said to be the highest and most sublime act of God's will which He will exhibit when pleased with those who have been devoted and are still devoted in their dedication to Him, since this [saying] "about being well and sublimely pleased with them" has been generally received and found in Scripture.[12]

Three points need to be stressed here. First, Theodore's reference to "good pleasure" (εὐδοκία) is alluding here to Matthew 3:17, Mark 1:11, Luke 3:22,

10. For example, McNamara (189) believes: "What is beyond all doubt, however—and, let us stress it again, it is the essential point—is that for Theodore the problem of Christ's unity was the problem of the unity of two subsisting natures, and with this premiss it was inevitable that he should set up what was in fact nothing more than an accidental union."

11. For summaries of Theodore's Christology, see the third chapter of Rowan A. Greer's *Theodore of Mopsuestia: Exegete and Theologian* (Westminster: Faith, 1961), 48–65; Norris, *Manhood*, 211–34; and Luise Abramowski, "Zur Theologie Theodors von Mopsuestia," *Zeitschrift für Kirchengeschichte* 72 (1961): 263–93.

12. Theodore, PG 66:973. All translations in this chapter are my own.

and Colossians 1:19. While εὐδοκία makes sense in English when translated "to be well pleased," it becomes somewhat perplexing when rendered by the nominal phrase "good pleasure." It is better translated here as "benevolence," the Latin root of which means "to wish one well." In the present context, it refers to the benevolence God manifested towards Christ's humanity by choosing it to be what the Word would assume. Secondly, by stating here that God has expressed His delight in those dedicated to His will by doing something for their betterment, Theodore was emphasizing that God has freely chosen to act generously toward those committed to His will. While this statement needs to be further nuanced because of Theodore's insistence that God takes into account the human will's role in salvation, the point is that God was in no way compelled to bestow His blessing in a particular way, even by His foreknowledge of how an individual will respond to the graces that he or she receives. And thirdly, it is important to note that Theodore turns to Scripture—not philosophy—for such words as "indwelling" and "benevolence" to describe the Word's union with Jesus' humanity.

The question, however, has to be faced: does God's showering of His benevolence upon Jesus differ from the ways He bestows His graces on those who have fully and zealously committed their whole lives to Him, especially the saints. And, if so, how so? Theodore answered these questions in his work *On the Incarnation* where he maintained that there exists a radical difference in the ways God manifested His good pleasure toward Christ and His saints: "When, then, (God) may be said to dwell either in the apostles or generally in the just . . . we do not say that the indwelling [of the Word] happened thus in his case—for we would not rave in such a way—but as [He dwells] in [His] Son (ὡς ἐν Ὑιῷ)."[13] Theodore then clarifies what he means by this last phrase.

What is meant by "as in [His] Son?" It means that by His indwelling He united the one who was assumed wholly to Himself and made him share in all the honor in which He who indwells as Son by nature participates so as to be accounted one person (πρόσωπον) in accordance with his union with him, and to share with him all his dominion and thus to work all things in him.[14]

13. *Theodori Episcopi Mopsuesteni in Epistolas B. Pauli Commentarii*, ed. H. B. Swete, 2 vols. (Cambridge: Cambridge UP, 1880 and 1882), 2:295–96. In the phrase, "as in [His] Son," the word "Son" does not have an article. Rather than interpreting this in a generic sense, I believe that the context indicates that "Son" is to be understood as a proper name and should be capitalized.

14. Swete, 2:295–96. Theodore appears to be dependent here upon Romans 8:28–30.

The main difference, therefore, between God's union with the saints and with Christ is that the Word who is God's Son by nature was pleased to assume Christ's humanity and to share all His honors and powers with the one in whom He dwells in a prosopic way. This union explains why the "assumed man" has become God's Son in a graced manner far transcending the sonship and daughtership of all others. This is corroborated in the following: "the Apostle clearly numbers the 'assumed man' with the rest [of humanity] in respect to sonship, even though he does not share sonship in the same way as the others, but to the extent that he assumed sonship through grace."[15] It is, in other words, the "assumed one's" graced union with the Word that has enabled his human nature to participate in a truly unique—but yet qualified—sense in the Word's Sonship and power. The Word is Son "by nature," while the "assumed man" is Son by a special grace. This clearly reveals how Theodore understood God's active benevolence as being equivalent to a singularly unique grace.

In commenting on John 3:35, Theodore spells out in more detail how the graces Jesus' human nature received because of his unique sharing in the Word's Sonship differed from the rest of humankind. Besides being assumed by the Word at the moment of his conception and sharing in His universal dominion over all creation, Christ alone has received the fullness of grace.

For [God], he says, did not bestow a meager part of the grace of the Spirit upon him, as upon the rest of human beings, but the total plenitude, because He loved him; and on that account He also granted him universal domination. For it is clear that these pertain to that human nature which, because of its union with God the Word, received universal domination over all things.[16]

In commenting upon how Jesus' Sonship differs from that of all other human beings, H. B. Swete observes that it is only through Jesus' mediatorship that all others can become God's sons and daughters: "In Jesus alone, God dwelt 'as in the Son'. . . . [Whereas] In the members of Christ the Divine 'indwelling' is effected through their union with the *homo susceptus*."[17] Theodore expands upon this, when he writes: "For through [his singular] union with God the Word, he has been made, through the

15. Theodore, PG 66:985.
16. Vosté, TJA, 59. The same idea is expressed in Theodore's work *On The Incarnation* (Norris, *The Christological Controversy*, 120).
17. Swete, 1:142.

mediation of the Spirit, a partaker of the true sonship. From his spiritual grace, we receive a part and are made, through the same grace, participants together in adopted sonship, although we are far removed from that dignity."[18] In other words, Jesus became God's Son because of his immediate graced union with the Word. Other humans have become sons and daughters only in a mediate way because of their participation in the same grace that Jesus has received in its fullness. Human beings can, therefore, enter into a partial and mediate kind of union with God similar to what Christ enjoys as God's unitive image.

Theodore thus regarded Christ's role as the universal mediator between God and creation as coalescing with his role as the Lord of the universe. But in addition to possessing the *plērōma* of power and grace, Christ has also been entrusted with the twofold task or role of re-creating and then recapitulating all things in himself, as has been seen in the treatment of how Christ will fulfill Adam's role as the bond uniting spiritual powers and material beings. Adam failed because of his sin to live up to his responsibility as God's bonding image; Christ, as the *plērōma*, will restore all of creation to the original harmony that existed between human nature and the rest of creation and between humans and God. On this point, Swete remarks that among patristic exegetes Theodore is the only Father to interpret the *plērōma* mentioned in Colossians 1:19–20 in this way.[19]

Christ's Union of Natures

Theodore was insistent that the Word and the "assumed man" are to be thought of as indissolubly linked as one. He expressed this by his constant references to the Word and the "assumed man" being *one* Son and *one* Lord. To confirm this, he argued that to be counted as two sons and two lords, they would have to have the same nature, but because their natures are different, one can rightly maintain that there is only one Son.[20]

Likewise in the present case, if each of them was by nature Son and Lord, one could say two sons and two lords in the order of persons (πρόσωπα).[21] But since

18. Vosté, TJA, 26.

19. Swete, 1:286.

20. For a summary of Theodore's thought, see D. S. Wallace-Hadrill, *Christian Antioch: A Study of Early Christian Thought in the East* (Cambridge: Cambridge UP, 1982), 122–26.

21. *Parṣope* is the Syriac equivalent for the Greek πρόσωπα.

one is Son and Lord by nature, while the other is neither Son nor Lord naturally speaking, we believe that it is due to his close union with the Only-Begotten, God the Word, that he has received these (titles). We confess that the Son is unique. . . . But we add to this (title) in our way of thinking also the former, [namely] the "temple" whom He indwells at all times and from whom he is not separated by reason of the indissoluble union that he has with him. And it is for this reason that we believe that he is Son and Lord.[22]

When Theodore observes that one can speak of the Word and the "assumed man" as two persons only if they have the same nature, he is arguing, of course, in a specious way. While it is true that we do not say "two" apples or oranges when we have one of each, still the two are said to be separate and different pieces of fruit. So to assert that the Word and Jesus constitute one Son by nature and grace is a play on words. It can be interpreted without further elaboration that Theodore is maintaining, in reality, the existence of two sons who are different—one Son by nature and another son by grace. But at the same time, one must not overlook Theodore's intent in stating this argument: that there is a true unity between the Word's Sonship by nature and the Sonship enjoyed by Christ's humanity because they exist and function harmoniously and flawlessly as one in their same common πρόσωπον because of God's benevolence.

A Prosopic Union of the Natures in Christ

Theodore believed that the union of Christ's two natures was best expressed by a term that has generated heated discussion as to what exactly he meant by it—namely a prosopic union.[23] For as shown in the previous chapter, πρόσωπον can denote the external appearance of an individual, with some connotation of or a connection to a person's innermost being. In the case of Christ, this means a relation to his human and divine natures. Cyril and his followers, however, rejected this as being an inadequate expression of what the Christian faith believes to be true—that Christ is one and the same subject as the Word. So to understand what

22. Raymond Tonneau with Robert Devreese, trans., *Les Homélies Catéchétiques de Théodore de Mopsueste* (Vatican City: Vaticana, 1949), 209.
23. For a contemporary study that indicates the difficulties involved in trying to understand the meaning of "person" in Late Antiquity, see Bruce J. Malina and Jerome H. Neyrey, *Portraits of Paul: An Archeology of Ancient Personality* (Louisville: Knox, 1996).

Theodore intended when he stated "that both natures are unified and that there is one resulting *persona* formed from the unification [of the two],"[24] we need to attend carefully to the specific point he was seeking to make when he proposed three analogies[25] for clarifying his thought on the union.

First, Theodore contrasts the Word's dwelling within Christ to God's presence in the Temple, with the difference that his humanity is "a temple from which it will never be separated, as it possesses an ineffable union with the one who is dwelling in it."[26] Christ's πρόσωπον, therefore, is like a "temple" wherein one can forever encounter and permanently worship God because the Word dwells within Christ. This suggests the ancient practice of showing worship to the king as the image of God. This interpretation of the analogy, however, does not provide us with any illumination as to what the ineffable union is but rather how long Christ's two natures have functioned and will continue to function together in a cultic fashion.

In his next analogy, Theodore compares the relationship of the Word and Christ's humanity to that between a husband and a wife.[27] He is exemplifying here, however, not how two persons combine to become another reality, but how two distinct personalities can be said to be one flesh. While Norris is correct in cautioning us that it is not evident whether Theodore wanted to highlight some sort of volitional union between the two,[28] the chief point of his analogy seems to be how two persons can join together in a way that can be universally affirmed as being truly one. They are each a separate being but form a unique relationship where both give of themselves fully to the well-being of the other. It is another example of a functional union.

The third analogy, which became highly disputed, compares the linking of the soul's union with the body to that of the divine nature with the human nature of Christ. It is an analogy that Nemesius made, but in the

24. Swete, 2:308. The fragment has survived in Latin. Though the word translated as "person" is *persona*, it is without doubt a translation for the Greek πρόσωπον.

25. I find it to be significant that the Antiochenes tried to explain the unity in Christ on the basis not of philosophical theories but of a reliance upon Scripture aided by similes and analogies.

26. Mingana, WS 6:86.

27. Theodore, PG 66:981. See also Norris, *The Christological Controversy*, 120.

28. Norris, *Manhood*, 153.

reverse order, when he cited the union between Christ's natures as illustrative of that between the soul and the body. As will be shortly discussed, Nestorius rejected this analogy of the soul-body relationship to that between Christ's natures. Since Theodore only alludes to the analogy in his extant writings,[29] it would appear to have had minimal interest for him. For this reason, it is difficult to draw any conclusion directly from it. However, it may be possible to glean Theodore's thought from an explanation Narsai has provided, especially as it expresses overtones of Theodore's own phrasing, if not thought.

We call the created one, "the temple" whom the Word fashioned for His dwelling; and the Creator, the Only-Begotten who was pleased to dwell within his handiwork. (They are) like the soul and the body that are co-partners and called one *parṣope* [Syriac for πρόσωπον]. The soul has a vital nature, and the body, a mortal nature. And we call the two that are distinct from one another one *parṣope*. The Word is the Nature of the Divine Essence; and the body, the nature of humanity. One is the creature; and the other, the Creator: they are one in [their] unity. . . . The soul does not suffer in the body, when its limbs are scourged; and the Divinity did not suffer in the sufferings of the body in which It dwelt. And if the soul does not suffer, seeing that it is something created like the body, how does the Divine Essence suffer, whose Nature is exalted above passions? The soul suffers with the body in love and not in its nature; and the sufferings of the body are predicated of the soul in a metaphorical sense.[30]

This passage is significant for a number of reasons. First, it shows once again how in the Antiochene tradition the term "Word" is used interchangeably with "divine nature," and the "body" with the "humanity." It signifies that the term "nature" should be understood in a concrete, existential sense similar to the ancient Hebrew usage. *Parṣope*, on the other hand, is used to signify the union of the Word with Jesus' humanity in such a way that the Word's nature is not directly altered or affected by what Jesus in his humanity experiences. This highlights for us how the appeal to the soul-body analogy seeks to emphasize how the Word and Jesus

29. See Vosté, TJA, 119. Theodore may be alluding to Paul's comparison of the union between God and His church with that of a husband with his wife.

30. This quotation from Narsai is found in the Vatican Syriac Collection #594, fol. 69v., in the Vatican Library. The Syriac text for the quotation can be found in *Narsai's Metrical Homilies on the Nativity, Epiphany, Passion, Resurrection and Ascension*, ed. and trans. Frederick G. McLeod, PO 40, Fasc. 1 (Turnhout: Brepols, 1979), 27. The Syriac word that has been translated "metaphorically" is š'ýl' yt.

function as one in a true, intimately bound union where the spiritual entities can be said to suffer only in an applied or a metaphorical sense, out
of love for their bodies. This kind of relationship reflects what was elaborated upon in the discussion above about Nemesius's understanding of
the habitual way that a spiritual nature can function with a material body.
The soul is said to supply the power that the body needs to act but without its spiritual nature being in any way altered.

Theodore's use of the analogies of the Word dwelling in the Temple,
and the unions of a husband and wife, and of the soul and body do not define, therefore, the specific type of union between the two natures in
Christ. They are illustrative of how two radically different natures in a permanent partnership can each function according to its own nature but in
such a harmonious way that the spiritual is not altered when it acts on behalf of the corporeal by supplying the power and the graces that it requires. In light of Nemesius's opinion of how the soul will act habitually
in a loving way on behalf of its bodily co-partner, these analogies should
be understood as exemplifying how Theodore conceived of the way that
Christ's two natures can function as one in a prosopic union.

Richard A. Norris sums up Theodore's understanding of the term
πρόσωπον as "the outward manifestation by which one or more concrete
natures are recognized as an hypostatic, historical, functional, or generic
'unit,'"[31] He observes, however, that πρόσωπον does not strictly define a
kind of union and concludes that Theodore used it as a word indicating
Christ as he is presented in the Gospels as a single concrete object of recognition.[32] In other words, Theodore's intent was not to employ πρόσωπον as a metaphysical term. Rather he chose it to describe what the evangelists and Paul in his epistles portray as the constant way Jesus and the
Word act together in a permanent "personal" way that safeguards the
transcendent character of the Word's divinity and the exercise of the "assumed man's" human free-will. This is, however, a functional Christology
that still leaves unanswered the question of its underlying metaphysical
reality.[33]

31. Norris, *Manhood*, 230.

32. It is here that we can see the difference between the Antiochenes and their theological adversaries who maintain that the Word is the common subject of Christ's say-
ings and actions.

33. For two theological analyses of Theodore's understanding of πρόσωπον that
discuss its metaphysical inadequacies, see Kevin McNamara, "Theodore of Mopsuestia

By understanding πρόσωπον as a term describing how the natures in Christ function as one in a visible manner, Theodore, therefore, could easily equate πρόσωπον with Christ's role as the image of God. His union of "good pleasure in one πρόσωπον" could have just as readily been stated as a union in which God shows His graced benevolence by making Christ's human nature to be the true image of the Word. Because Christ is a fully human being in whom the Word dwells, his body serves as the visible way for God to manifest Himself and His power within creation. He is also the authentic way for all other creatures to manifest their love and worship to God in the manner God wants. In fact, for Theodore, Christ in his human nature can receive the adoration due to God. "This one has been assumed by Him (the Word) in grace and [it is] because of [having received this] grace he is adored by all of creation."[34] Yet while asserting that worship is to be extended to Christ as a visible being, Theodore does not intend it to be offered to Christ *qua* man but to Christ insofar as he enjoys a prosopic union with the Word. Norris sums up well how the major functional roles of πρόσωπον can merge with that of image when he writes: "Because of the union between the Word and the assumed Man, the Lord presents himself to the world and to the believer as a single object of knowledge and faith and a single agent of reconciliation with God."[35]

Christ's Union of Wills

Besides being uniquely graced at conception by his being assumed by the Word, Christ's humanity also had to be endowed with the special graces he needed to unite continuously his will and his activity entirely with the Word's: "[The assumed one] was joined in the womb to God the Word according to a kind of benevolence. Since being born of a virgin, he has remained an undivided temple, having in all that he does the same will and the same operation with Him. It is not possible to have a closer union

---

and the Nestorian Heresy," *Irish Theological Quarterly* July 1952: 254–78; April 1953: 172–91; and Francis A. Sullivan, *The Christology of Theodore of Mopsuestia*, Analecta Gregoriana 82 (Rome: Gregorianae, 1956).

34. Edward Sachau, ed., *Theodori Mopsuesteni Fragmenta Syriaca* (Leipzig: G. Engelmann, 1869), 47.

35. Norris, *Manhood*, 231.

than this."[36] Thus there also exist, in addition to a union of two natures in Christ, other unions on the moral and the psychological levels or orders— between the human and the divine wills and their activities. These kinds of unions are constitutive, not of their basic union, but of that process whereby Christ's humanity grew and became the perfect instrument for revealing God and His will in a visible way and for dispensing His graces to the rest of creation. One may indeed argue that these lifelong graces uniting Jesus' will to that of the Word indicates a moral union. But this misses, in my opinion, Theodore's insistence that the unions of Christ's two wills and operations are based upon the union of natures that occurred at the moment that Christ was humanly conceived in grace—long before he could exercise his human free will.

Because of his commitment to the School of Antioch's defense of Christ's full, integral human nature within its union with the Word, Theodore was aware of the role that Christ's human free will had to play in God's plan of salvation. While he granted that the Word was the source of the energy power that the humanity needed to act, he opposed those who looked upon the Word as also being the subject of Christ's human actions, for he believed that this would sever the nexus between Jesus' free and perfect observance of his Father's will and affect his bodily resurrection in heaven. This is implied in his homily *On Baptism* where he depicted the "assumed man" as achieving a forensic victory over Satan and death, "because he was found to be exempt from all sin . . . [and] from a sentence of death."[37] It is because the "assumed man" had not sinned that Satan's imposition of death was unjust and that God bestowed a new immortal and immutable life upon him.

---

36. Theodore, *Epistle to Domnus*, PG 66:1013. In her brief analysis of the notion of "person" within Theodore's Christology ("The Notion of 'Person' Underlying the Christology of Theodore of Mopsuestia," *Studia Patristica* 12 [1975]:199–207), Joanne McWilliam Dewart speaks of Theodore as "working within a stoic framework where will and activity constitute what we call personality" (207). While one can speak of a union of personalities on the levels of will and activity and call it a substantial union, the question can be raised whether this is sufficient to explain from a psychological and philosophical point of view a true personal union which seems to be on a deeper level than will and activity. Moreover it is difficult to conceive how the latter union would be present at the moment of conception when Jesus' humanity was assumed by the Word. Nevertheless the point is well taken that this is how the Stoics and Theodore conceived of a substantial union which others regard as a functional union of wills and activity.

37. Tonneau, THC, 335.

Theodore's understanding of the way that Christ's humanity has sur-passed that of all others is close to the distinction that the Scholastics make between sanctifying and actual graces—between a grace that ele-vates one's nature and one that assists its human operations to be commit-ted to God's will throughout his earthly existence. As noted previously, the bestowal of these latter graces is associated with the initial grace Christ's humanity received when it was assumed by the Word. Graces were offered chronologically after the union, so that the assumed man's will could cooperate with the Word's.[38] Theodore, in fact, argued that Christ's human ability to cooperate fully with the Word was indeed proof that the union took place at the moment of his conception and that it was the Word who has accomplished everything that Christ has achieved in a human way: "Thus after he had showed himself by his resurrection and reception into heaven to have also been through his own will-effort worthy of the union which had been established before this at the time of his conception by the good pleasure of his Master, he has given proof of the union, seeing that no act on his part was separated from God the Word, and, because of his union with Him, that God the Word was the one who has done all things in him."[39]

In his seventh book *On the Incarnation*, Theodore speculates that God had conferred unique graces on Christ's humanity because of His fore-knowledge of how the "assumed man" would use these graces: "So it is evident that he was more strictly and with greater ease capable of virtue than the rest of humanity, to this extent that by foreknowing what kind of *persona*[40] he would be, God the Word united him to himself at the begin-ning of his conception."[41] The sequence is noteworthy. God may have foreknown how the assumed man would actually take advantage of the graces afforded him in his life, yet chronologically speaking, the Word manifested His benevolence by joining Himself to Jesus at the very mo-ment that his human nature was conceived—a time when no free will cooperation was possible. In so doing, Theodore has preserved two truths: God's freedom to act as He intended and God's desire to have all humans play a role in the attainment of their salvation. His view is that

---

38. For an extended discussion of this, see Norris, *Manhood*, 222.
39. Swete, 2:297.
40. The Latin word *persona* is doubtless used here for the Greek word πρόσωπον.
41. Swete, 2:298.

God is the one who ultimately actually saves, but He will not do so without human cooperation, including Christ's assumed humanity.[42]

Theodore was adamant in maintaining a role for Christ's human will in a prosopic union because he realized the need to underscore the voluntary role that God intends for the human will to play in redemption.[43] But while he emphasized human effort, this should not be interpreted as any disregard for the role grace is meant to play in living out a spiritual and moral life. Rather he has taken this for granted, for his concern was primarily centered on protecting free will's critical role in God's plan for salvation. He may also have been reacting against those explaining Christ's union in such a way that there appeared to be only one will, that of the Word, or against those granting that Christ possessed a human will but never exercised it in an active way. Or finally he may have simply been sensitive to the danger inherent in the position of those who were so stressing a contemplative and mystical union with God that they were fostering the opinion that ordinary human activities were of little or secondary value for those seeking to be in communion with God.

Christ's Mediating and Unitive Role as God's Image

From this exposure to Theodore's christological thought, one is now able to reflect on how he would understand Christ's unitive role as God's image. Besides mediating God's graces to others, Christ also provides the necessary means for others to enter into communion or a relationship with him and through him to God. It is here that one observes a significant difference between Theodore and those Fathers who espouse a mystical union with God. Because of his adherence to his understanding both of God's transcendence and of a hypostatic union, Theodore had to look upon "eternal life" as being an entrance into a future immortal and immutable state where a individual could forever know and love God through Christ as His perfect image. He appears to have understood John's words, "Now this is eternal life, that they should know you, the

42. For a discussion of the role that will is called to play in Theodore's thought, see Norris, *Manhood*, 145–46.

43. Those Fathers who were influenced by Neoplatonic thought concerning the rational soul's ability to contemplate the One saw this as a way that humans could be divinized or united mystically with God. They were, of course, primarily influenced by what they were able to discover in the Scriptures and from their own prayer experiences.

only true God, and the one whom you sent, Jesus Christ" (17:3), as signifying that one comes to know God only through the humanity of Christ. He rejected the idea of eternal life as a graced experiential knowledge of God enabling one to participate in God's divine life, as such. Rather eternal life is experiencing in oneself the new resurrected life Christ has won through his victory over sin and death and knowing God through the visible image that Christ's human nature provides.

This is a wholly different theological perspective on salvation, of course, than what most Greek Fathers in Late Antiquity have promoted in their writings regarding how a person's spiritual nature can become united with God's. This latter idea was appealing in an intellectual milieu wherever was accepted the Neoplatonic opinion that there can be a real loving participation in the divine life without any diminution of one's personal identity. This was possible—provided one has first undergone a moral and spiritual purification. Inspired by this view, most Greek Fathers realized its deeper relevance for understanding the mystical dimension enunciated in the scriptural writings of John and Paul. They interpreted the indwelling of the Trinity as a transforming presence whereby God has united Himself with human beings in a union so close that human nature can participate in the divine life of the Trinity in an immediate way, in the case of Christ, and, for others, in a mediate way through Christ—without human beings being absorbed into the Godhead in a pantheistic way.

To probe more perceptively into how Theodore understood the kind of communion with God that Christ provides, we turn now to his opinion on the effects baptism and the eucharist exercise on those who receive these sacraments.[44] In his lengthy commentaries on baptism, Theodore has probed how the baptized person will undergo a complete transformation in the sense that they have received the potency to become, as Christ now is, immortal and immutable. For him it is a potency waiting to be actualized.

After (a person) has been baptized and has received a divine and spiritual grace, he will undoubtedly undergo a complete change: he will be fashioned from a mortal into an immortal nature, from one that is corruptible into an incorruptible one, and from a mutable into an immutable nature; and he will be changed completely into a new man according to the power of the One who fashions him. And inasmuch

44. For a study into Theodore's thought on the sacraments, see Greer, *Theodore*, 66–85.

as the one who is born of a woman has potentially within himself the faculties of speaking, hearing, walking and working with his hands, but is very weak to perform all these acts in reality till the time in which God has decreed for him to perform them, so also is the case here in regard to the one born at baptism. This one possesses within himself potentially all the faculties of an immortal and incorruptible nature, but is not now in a position to make use of them and put them into a complete, perfect actuation of incorruptibility, immortality, impassibility and immutability. The one who receives through baptism the potential ability to attain all these actuations will receive the power of performing them in reality at the time when he is no more a natural but a spiritual being.[45]

Theodore describes the kind of potentiality present in this "faculty" when he speaks of the spiritual rebirth that the Spirit provides through Christ in terms of a "pledge," an "anticipation," a "type," and the "first-fruits" of a future life.[46] While baptism dispenses a forgiveness of sins, it is, however, only an initial, fundamental step toward a future life of immortality, for though death's power has been broken, it is still necessary for a person to die before he or she can attain a new life of immortality. So while the future age has begun potentially in this life, the life baptism promises will be actualized and attained only later in eschatological times. Until that comes to pass, it is imperative to adopt here and now a mindset that regards the present world as a type of what is to be eternal and then to live out one's present life in communion with Christ who now represents the actualization of what others possess potentially.

By rejecting the possibility that human nature can be changed by grace so that it becomes divine, Theodore had no option but to repeat in different ways that all those living out their lives in accord with God's will and participating in the sacramental life of the Church do now possess a future immortal life—but it is only in a well-founded hope of achieving after death a resurrected life like that of Christ. While saying this, Theodore did not believe that baptism and the eucharist have no transforming effect. He stated it thus: "so likewise for us now, because we are in a mortal nature, we must receive this renewal by baptism. But when we are molded again by baptism and receive the grace of the Holy Spirit who will strengthen us more than any fire, we will no longer need a second renewal."[47] For Theodore, a baptized person is like a clay vase that remains

45. Mingana, WS 6:55–56.
46. See Tonneau, THC, 356, 414, 448, 576–78, and 553.
47. Ibid., 429.

malleable, until it is baked. Though initially shaped in a certain way, it can still be altered until the clay becomes hardened under fire. So in a similar way, human nature has been fashioned in such a way that it cannot be re-fashioned without becoming different, but it is not yet formed in a perma-nent way. Human nature must still await its appearance in heaven before it can attain its immortal state. In the meantime, one has been strength-ened to both maintain and develop his or her present potentiality, much like a seed needs to be cultivated if it is to reach its full sprouting.

Besides having a basic unrepeatable effect, baptism assures a person that he or she will some day share in Christ's resurrection: "It is because of this that we [now] expect to move with these [earthly] possessions to that awe-inspiring birth, namely of the resurrection. For this assures us of what we have sacramentally by faith in types and in signs; for it assures us [of passing] from one to the other."[48] What Theodore means by this is ex-plained more clearly in the following quotation where he likens the new life a person receives at baptism to a male's semen: "Just as a [husband's] semen enters into his wife's womb without life and without a soul and without knowledge, but when formed by the divine hand, it comes forth as a living human being endowed with a soul and knowledge and a nature capable of taking on every human activity, so likewise here the one bap-tized descends into a womb-like water."[49]

For Theodore, therefore, baptism is an unrepeatable action that now entitles a person to share inchoatively and potentially in the benefits of the resurrection. But as the last quotation has affirmed, it is a strange kind of potentiality; it is lifeless. The new life it promises does not begin until God intervenes to bestow immortality to those who have cared for the seed im-planted at baptism. In the meantime, a person has to care properly for his or her seed by nurturing its potentiality by faithfully remaining in com-munion with Christ. For Christ is the head of all those who constitute his body through [their] reception of the eucharist: "We have been thus joined in communion to these holy mysteries and we have been in-structed about this by our head, Christ our Lord whose body we believe we are and from whom we have communion with the divine nature."[50]

One last passage will suffice to reveal Theodore's thought on the kind of transformation he envisions taking place in baptism and at the euchar-

48. Ibid., 459. See also 409.
49. Ibid., 421.
50. Ibid., 555.

ist. In the section above, Theodore seems to allude to a eucharistic epicle-
sis. If so, he would be affirming the Spirit's active role in transforming the
bread and the wine into Christ's body and blood. The question then
arises: does this also suggest that a person receiving communion is being
transformed in some mystical way? However granted Theodore's overall
theological viewpoint, this is an interpretation that he would passionately
oppose, for this is equivalent to saying that the reception of the eucharist
transforms human nature into one that is divine. The most that Theodore
would be open to at baptism is the transformation of a human nature into
a superior one: "the one who descends there is formed anew by the grace
of the Holy Spirit and born anew into another *superior human* nature."[51]

In brief, the union that the eucharist nurtures between the one par-
taking of it and Christ should be regarded as a type of what will come
to pass in the future state.[52] It promises those receiving communion
that they will share in the immortality and immutability that Christ
presently enjoys. But as noted in our treatment of how types are related
to their archetypes, Theodore would consider that the situation and the
relationship delineated by the type are real, historical ones and that they
provide insight as to what will be the eschatological fulfillment in a future age. The point he is making is that a person's communion with
Christ does not result in either a present or even a future participation
in God's nature as such. Rather, it promises a future radical transformation where one's humanity will be changed from being mortal and mutable to immortal and immutable. It results in a true communion with
Christ, the Man-God, who points to and guarantees the fulfillment that
God has promised to bestow on those who will have journeyed on the

51. Ibid., 424. The italics are my own.
52. In his insightful article on "Eucharist and Christology in the Nestorian Controversy," *Journal of Theological Studies* New Series 2 (1951): 145– 64, H. Chadwick points out
that Cyril held that there existed a hypostatic union between the spiritual and physical
elements in a consecrated host. This highlights a fundamental difference existing between Cyril and Theodore over what kind of union actually takes place between Christ
and those receiving the eucharist. While Theodore has acknowledged that the consecrated bread and the wine are actually transformed into the body and blood of Christ
and confer graces upon those who receive them, this enables the recipients to become
superior human beings. Moreover, at that moment one can only share in a potential way
the future immortality and immutability that Christ now shares in actuality. The actual
sharing of immortality and immutability must await the coming of the future age. For
a discussion of this, see Wallace-Hadrill, 160– 62.

path He has initiated. Such a hope can be compared to a person possessing a long-term treasury bond the government has guaranteed but which cannot be cashed until its maturity date has been reached. Like the seed in the example mentioned above, one must await the moment that God has appointed to intervene with His power in order to actuate its potential.

Nestorius's View of the Union

Nestorius's *Bazaar of Heracleides* is a difficult work to read, let alone comprehend, for it is frequently rambling and repetitive. As was true with Theodore, the parameters of Nestorius's christological thought can be determined by attending to the theological positions he rejected. He began his treatise with a brief spurning of what he considered the principal errors of the pagans, Jews, Manichaeans, Paulinians, Arians, and Cyril of Alexandria. In response to the charge that he was teaching two separate individuals in Christ, he strongly denied that he was advocating a merely voluntary union,[53] such as that between God and His saints.[54] He was firmly convinced of the orthodoxy of his formulation of how the Word and the full humanity of Christ are united. He insisted strenuously that his christological views were fully consistent with Scripture,[55] the faith proclaimed at the Council of Nicea,[56] and the teaching of other Fathers.[57]

A Prosopic Union of One, Not Two Sons

Nestorius explained the unity of Christ's natures in a number of ways. He referred to them positively as being not two but "one." He expressed this by categorically denying that he was making the title, "Christ," a catchword concealing the fact he was actually affirming two separate sons

53. See Nestorius, *The Bazaar of Heracleides*, ed. and trans. Godfrey R. Driver and Leonard Hodgson (Oxford: Clarendon, 1925), NES 47–49 and 179–82. All the translations are from this work.

54. Nestorius expresses this clearly and forcefully in his *First Sermon Against the* θεοτόκος: "But Christ is not a mere man, O slanderer! No, he is at once God and man" (Norris, *The Christological Controversy*, 129).

55. NES, 59–70. 56. Ibid., 144–45.
57. Ibid., 191–203.

and two lords. He asserted this again and again in *The Bazaar*, such as in the following: "But add what thou has accepted and confessed, that there has been a union of two natures and that for this reason we confess one Christ, one Son, one Lord."[58] To support his contention that his maintaining of two concrete, existing natures in Christ did not signify the existence of two persons, he appealed to Gregory of Nazianzus's statement that the divine and human natures in Jesus Christ should not be referred to as masculine—ἄλλος καὶ ἄλλος—for this would signify the presence of two separate persons. Rather the endings should be neuter—ἄλλο καὶ ἄλλο,—indicating two separate natures.[59] But when he was later pressured to state clearly what kind of unity he was actually holding, he turned to the term favored by Theodore—that of a πρόσωπον.

Since Nestorius began with a fundamental presupposition that Christ's divine and human natures must always be maintained as two separate and wholly different entities, he had logically to reject any mixture of natures that would result in a natural composition of the two: "for there has not been confusion nor has there been mixture nor again a change of *ousiai* resulting in one nature of the *ousia* nor again also a natural composition resulting in a composite nature."[60] This same idea is expressed too in Nestorius's opposition to the soul's union with its body as a true analogy of the union between the two natures in Christ. While it is true that the different natures of the soul and the body can be combined to form a substantial nature, that is of a human being, these are incomplete and created entities needing each other to become one substantial nature.[61] But this does not apply to the union between the Word and the "assumed man," for these natures are specific, concrete, complete natures that cannot be united to form a substantial nature without either the Word or the assumed man being changed from what each is or without some hybrid being created.

Nestorius also offered a second cogent argument for rejecting the analogy, for it would imply that Christ's two natures have been joined

58. Ibid., 295. For other instances, see the references in the Index in Driver's edition under the heading "Two Sons."

59. NES, 220.

60. Ibid., 216.

61. Nestorius (Ibid., 304) expresses it thus: "For in a natural composition it seems that neither of those natures whereof it is [formed] is complete but they need one another that they may be and subsist. Even as the body has need of the soul that it may live, for it lives not of itself, and the soul has need of the body that it may perceive."

together by an outside force. The natural union between the soul and the body requires the intervention of an external power, namely God's, that can combine them together. This would mean that the Father would have had to impose the Incarnation upon the Word. If true, this would signify that the Word did not freely choose to enter the union but rather had been necessitated to do this, ". . . since [those things] which are united in one nature are not united voluntarily but by the power of the Creator, who combines them and brings them to a fusion."[62] In a third argument comparable to this, Nestorius pointed out the ramification that a natural union between Christ's two natures would imply for the theological meaning of the eucharist. He reasoned that, if Christ's two natures had been joined together in a natural union as that between the body and the soul, Christ's human nature would have to be transformed into the divine. This would shatter the belief that the reception of the eucharist is, in fact, a real participation in Christ's victory over death. But if a believer is to share in Christ's bodily resurrection by reception of the eucharist, Christ's body has to be human: "For if we are not of one, we are naturally not called his brothers nor his sons, nor are we any more his bread and his bodily frame; but, if all these belong truly to Christ, we are his body and consubstantial with him, in that we are that which is also the *ousia* of his body."[63]

According to Nestorius's way of conceiving the union of natures in Christ, each nature possesses its own ὑπόστασις and πρόσωπον. So when he heard Cyril defending a "hypostatic union" between the natures, he interpreted it in an Antiochene framework as affirming that Christ's natures have been united to comprise one nature. For Nestorius, an ὑπόστασις signifies a complete existing nature. He believed that his understanding was borne out by Cyril's statements that made the Word the subject of the humanity's action. So when Cyril wrote that the Word has suffered, Nestorius construed this as literally meaning that the Word has suffered in His Nature—which he dismissed as a patent absurdity. Instead of a hypostatic union, he proposed the presence of a common πρόσωπον that enables each nature to *function* together as one by sharing in one another's properties within the union.[64] He argued that only this kind of a union

62. Ibid., 37. See also the extended footnote on the bottom of 8–9.
63. Ibid., 33.
64. See ibid., 49–64 and 156–68.

provided a fully satisfactory rationale for explaining how the natures could remain integral and could fit in with the role that God intends the sacraments to play in His redemptive plan for salvation.[65]

Nestorius believed that only a "voluntary union" can explain in an adequate way how Christ's natures can be "self-sustaining."[66] This does not in any way contradict Nestorius's statements about how the Word is the "final source" of activity in Christ. Instead it implies that each nature must be such that, if the Incarnation had not taken place, the human could exist on its own. For although the human nature has never existed independently of the Word, it has always possessed all the elements essential to its specific human nature, having its own proper qualities, passions, and activities, especially its ability to act in a free, self-determining way. The same can also be said of the Word, for although the Word's nature existed in His own personal manner within the Trinity before the Incarnation took place, it should not be thought afterwards as being different from what it was beforehand.

Nestorius's Communicatio Idiomatum

When Nestorius employed the term πρόσωπον as the unifier of the natures in Christ, he never conceived of it as an abstraction. Rather he understood Christ's πρόσωπον to be a living existential being that enables the divine and the human natures to function as one. Though Christ's πρόσωπον is not coequal to these natures, it nevertheless reflects their presences in such a way that the attributes of each can be mutually exchanged. Three citations can exemplify to what extent Nestorius permitted this reciprocation. He first conceded that both the Word and Jesus can share in each other's πρόσωπον because they are united in one common πρόσωπον: "For in respect to the natural *prosōpon* on the one, the other also makes use of the same on account of the union; and thus (there is) one *prosōpon* of the two natures. The *prosōpon* of the one οὐσία makes use of the *prosōpon* of the other οὐσία in the same (way)."[67]

Nestorius expressed to what extent each nature's predicates can be exchanged, in the following, rather awkward, translation:

65. See ibid., 212–14 and 254–56.   66. See ibid., 38, 300–301, and 313–14.
67. Ibid., 218–19.

For the divinity makes use of the *prosōpon* of the humanity and the humanity of that of the divinity; and thus we say one *prosōpon* in both of them. Thus God appears whole, since his nature is not damaged in aught owing to the union; and thus too man [is] whole, falling short of naught of the activity and of the sufferings of his own nature owing to the union. For he who refers to the one *prosōpon* of God the Word the [properties] of God the Word and those of the humanity and gives not in return the *prosōpon* of God the Word to the humanity steals away the union of the orthodox and likens it to that of the heretics. For you have learnt of the orthodox in the testimonies which they have written, that they give in compensation the [properties] of the humanity to the divinity and those of the divinity to the humanity, and that this is said of the one and that of the other, as concerning natures whole and united, united indeed without confusion and making use of the *prosōpa* of one another.[68]

Nestorius specifies further what he means by this ability of the natures to share their prosopic properties with one another when he writes: "the flesh, which is flesh by nature, is also the Son by the union and the adoption of the [Word's] *prosōpon*; although he (Christ) exists in both of them, yet he is called one Son and one flesh."[69]

While Nestorius had no problem in speaking of how Jesus shares in the Word's Sonship and dominion and also how the Word inhabits Jesus' flesh—for these are stated in Scripture—he ran into a predicament, as Theodore did, when someone wished to honor Mary as the Mother of God. Because of his adamant refusal to apply the term θεοτόκος (mother of God) directly to Mary, Nestorius has been universally castigated as an heresiarch by the "Orthodox" and "Monophysite" Christians. The term θεοτόκος, in fact, soon became a catchword used to distinguish the so-called "Nestorians" from those who are considered orthodox. But as has been observed earlier in Nestorius's rejection of the opinion that Christ was a mere man and his insistence upon maintaining a true union between the divinity and the humanity in Christ that is different from the way God is united to His saints, Nestorius is not a "Nestorian" in the popular sense of how this term is understand by most today. For Nestorius insinuated that he was willing—but doubtless very reluctantly—to accept the term θεοτόκος provided that it was not understood to mean that Mary was actually the mother of the Divinity. In reply to a report that he had acceded to the use of the term θεοτόκος, Nestorius stated

68. Ibid., 240–41. See also 70.
69. Ibid., 53.

his position: "the other [John of Antioch] has confessed that I have accepted quite simply [the name] 'Mother of God.' There is then need to state the meaning, according to which both the hypostatic and the natural union of God and the natural birth from a woman is excluded. . . . For we decline not the term 'birth' but the 'hypostatic union of God the Word.' For this reason we have caused it to be excluded."[70]

What Kind of Union?

Despite the fact that Nestorius admitted Christ's human nature shares with the Word in His titles and reality of Son and Lord, the question can be properly raised, as it was with Theodore, whether there really exists a unity whereby the Word and the humanity not only can be said to be one in point of fact but are truly one in a metaphysical sense. For first of all, it is hard to comprehend what specific kind of unity Nestorius is actually promoting when he asserts that the πρόσωπα of the divinity and the humanity were voluntarily united in one πρόσωπον. Daly is right when he observes that Nestorius is in fact presenting his common πρόσωπον as a metaphysical subject that is distinct from the natures.[71] This means that he is actually arguing for a true union of natures that is more than a merely moral or accidental unity, yet something in a different order than that of a substantial natural union, as he understood these words.

There is some value in Hodgson's statement that "*prosōpon* is no *mere* appearance . . . [but] a real element in the being of a thing, without which, or if it were other than it is, the thing would not be what it

70. Ibid., 294. See also 99–100. Nestorius repeated the same viewpoint in a fragment published in *Nestoriana: Die Fragmente des Nestorius*, ed. Friedrich Loofs with S. A. Cook and G. Kampfmeyer (Halle: Neimeyer, 1905): "I have often said that if any simple person among you or anyone else delight in the title, I do not object to it. But do not let such a one make the virgin into a goddess" (353). For Nestorius's reason for objecting to the title, see Norris, *The Christological Controversy*, 124–25.

71. Anthony Daly ("Nestorius in the Bazaar of Heracleides: A Christology Compatible with the Third Letter and Anathemas of Cyril of Alexandria," [Ph.D. diss., University of Southern California, 1983], 29) remarks that: "if Christ were lacking personal unity the common *prosōpon* could not fulfill its function of manifesting him and rendering him actual as one independent being." See also 31: ". . . it is the *prosōpon* of the union which accounts for the actual existence of Christ as one independent being and which at one and the same time manifests both his personal unity and the diversity of the divine and human natures united in him."

is."[72] But Nestorius never really explains how the two natures with their individual πρόσωπα are, metaphysically speaking, related to the common πρόσωπον called the Christ. What he appears to have done is to specify in general how the two separate natures operate together in a unified way whereby the Word can be said to have "become man" and that Christ's humanity participated in the Word's Sonship, His power, and even the adoration due Him as God.[73] Such a view may safeguard the integrity of both natures and may warrant designating each nature as the subject of its own actions. But such a functional explanation leaves unanswered the deeper metaphysical reality underlying this ability of the common πρόσωπον to act as a subject in a twofold way, especially as Nestorius has rejected the possibility of a hypostatic union, at least in the sense that he understood it.[74]

Not only has Nestorius used an ambivalent term to explain the union of Christ's natures, but he has defended it in a way that has opened him to the charge that he is self-contradictory. For if each of Christ's natures possesses its own πρόσωπον with some relationship to an objectively real element within its nature, it would, therefore, seem to follow that the obverse ought also to be true: namely that Christ's overall πρόσωπον ought to have its own underlying nature, and not natures. While the objection can be partially answered by stating that πρόσωπον is a word describing how Christ's natures can coordinate their "natural" properties and activities together in a functional way so that they both appear outwardly as one, the question must again be raised: what kind of metaphysical union underlies this? Perhaps the answer lies, as Daly concludes, in that Nestorius is struggling to express the same kind of union Cyril was actually expressing by his "hypostatic union."[75] Grillmeier states it more emphatically: "This (Nestorius's analogy of a mutual compenetration) is an incontrovertable proof that he is concerned with a substantial unity in Christ."[76]

What lies at the very heart of Nestorius's understanding of the union is the same one held by Theodore: their unbending adherence to the principle that the divine transcendence clearly prevents a substantial union between God and His created handiwork, for they believed that this would entail a limitation being placed upon the Divine nature. To his

72. NES, 416.
74. See Daly, 24–25.
76. Grillmeier, 516.

73. Ibid., 221.
75. See ibid., 64–68.

credit, Cyril of Alexandria realized—whether or not he was fully cognizant of what he was doing is another question—what the Fathers at Nicea
were presupposing when they solemnly defined as an orthodox belief that
God has directly created everything in the universe. He rightly concluded
that God could have directly created a real union that is substantial and
immediate between Christ's divinity and his humanity, so that one can
rightly assert that the Word became man, suffered, died, and was raised
on the third day. Hodgson sums this up well, when he writes:

> It is the heretics, Apollinaris, Nestorius, and Eutyches, who are the logically con-
> sistent upholders of this outworn conception of the relation between godhead and
> manhood. Cyril's teaching, no doubt, without his realizing the fact, *was* inconsis-
> tent, for he had not consciously abandoned this ante-Nicene position, with the re-
> sult that his positive teaching on the Incarnation, while consistent with the Nicene
> doctrine of Creation, demanded a revision of his conception of godhead and man-
> hood, a fact which he does not seem to have realized. But, as has happened so often
> in the history of thought, the inconsistency of a thinker great enough to recognize
> truth at the cost of his system won for his thought a place in posterity far above that
> of the barren coherence of his rival.[77]

Cyril may have been able to come to the conclusion he did because of
his exposure to the Neoplatonic view that human souls originally existed
in a direct, immediate contemplative union with the divine *nous* and can
re-establish this union through a program of moral and intellectual purification, while remaining individuals. Or it may have flown from his belief
in the Word's real presence in the eucharist.[78] Whatever may have been
the source, it is a view that provided a metaphysical justification for those
like Cyril who saw its ramification for substantiating how Christ is both divine and human and, as such, the true mediator between God and His
creatures. It is an insight that Nemesius also had when he rejected the
opinion of those proclaiming "a union by divine favor." There is perhaps
no better statement of what Nemesius meant by this than what Telfer has
pithily declared when commenting on this passage: "But Nemesius sees
that Theodore's argument [and the same can be said of Nestorius'] is

---

77. NES, xxxv. See also 419 where Hodgson affirms why he believes that Nestorius's
metaphysical explanation has to falter: "Nestorius is throughout perfectly consistent,
and his theory a brilliant attempt to solve the problem on the basis of a principle which
renders all solution impossible."

78. Chadwick, "Eucharist and Christology," 145–64.

based upon a negation, namely, that God is such as could not unite himself with man. Nemesius retorts that it is because of what God is, that is because of God's nature, that the paradox of incarnation is credible."[79]

Theodoret

Because Theodoret follows Diodore and Chrysostom's opinion of image as referring to men sharing in God's power to rule over the material world, our interest here is to have some understanding of Theodoret's view on the union of Christ's natures. Theodoret was the one selected by John of Antioch to defend the Antiochene tradition after Nestorius's condemnation and was later personally willing to reconcile this with the formulation agreed upon at the Council of Chalcedon. He provides us, therefore, with a perspective to discern what is positive in Theodore and Nestorius's wording of the union natures and what, if any, significance it can have for our concern to clarify the unitive function that Christ plays as God's primary image.

To understand Theodoret's viewpoint,[80] one must reflect on a remark that he made concerning what properties can be predicated of the πρόσωπον of Christ after the Incarnation. He applied πρόσωπον to Christ as the "person" within whom the Word's and Jesus' natures are united in an unconfused way and to whom the attributes that are proper to each are to be assigned.[81] What is significant here is Theodoret's insistence on the need to preserve Christ's two natures separate in the union, howsoever one may want to express this. He writes:

Just in this way should we speak of the Christ, and, when arguing about His natures, give to each its own, and recognize some as belonging to the Godhead, and some as to the manhood. But when we are discussing the πρόσωπον we must then make what is proper to the natures common, and apply both sets of qualities to the Saviour, and call the same Being both God and Man, both Son of God and Son of

79. Nemesius of Emesa, *Cyril of Jerusalem and Nemesius of Emesa*, ed. and trans. William Telfer, Library of Christian Classics 4 (Philadelphia: Westminster, 1955), 303.

80. For a study on how Theodoret's exegesis influenced his dogmatic outlook, see Silke-Pera Bergjan, "Die dogmatische Funktionalisierung der Exegese nach Theodret von Cyril," *Christliche Exegese*, J. Oort and U. Wickert (Kampen: Koh Pharos, 1992), as well as Grillmeier's general critique on 488–95.

81. Theodoret, PG 75:1456. The translations from Migne in this section are my own.

Man. . . . to me it is alike an unhallowed thought to split the one Son in two and to gainsay the duality of the natures.[82]

Theodoret's thought about predication is expressed clearly when he discusses in a letter to a Bishop Irenaeus his view on the title of Mary as the Mother of God. His concern centered not on the words but the reality that underlies these terms.

What does it matter whether we style the holy Virgin at the same time mother of Man and mother of God, or call her mother and servant of her offspring, with the addition that she is mother of our Lord Jesus Christ as man, but His servant as God, and so at once avoid the term which is the pretext of calumny, and express the same opinion by another phrase? And besides this it must also be borne in mind that the former of these titles is of general use, and the latter peculiar to the Virgin; and that it is about this that all the controversy has arisen, which would [to] God had never been.[83]

When pressed by the Patriarch Dioscorus to clarify his view about the term θεοτόκος, Theodoret affirmed his acceptance of the term while reiterating the Antiochene denials that Jesus Christ is a mere man or that the Word and Jesus are two sons: "If any one refuses to confess the holy Virgin to be 'θεοτόκος,' or calls our Lord Jesus Christ bare man, or divides into two sons Him who is one only begotten and first born of every creature, I pray that he may fall from hope in Christ."[84] It is also known that toward the end of the Council of Chalcedon Theodoret subscribed to the statement that Mary was θεοτόκος, though he doubtless explained the term, not in the sense that she bore God, but only in the sense that God the Word dwelt within her child. But his acceptance, nevertheless, reveals that he could look beyond disputed terminology, provided that both factions were in substantial agreement regarding the underlying reality. This is evident in a letter he wrote in 449: "our Lord Jesus Christ is no other person of the Trinity than the Son."[85] He was also doubtless impelled to this when he recognized the need to join forces with those opposing the ever rising tide of Eutychian Monophysitism among the Syrians. What

82. Theodoret, NPNF 3:195. See also 233–34.

83. Ibid., 3:255–56. See, too, Theodoret's letter to Nestorius in Martin Parmentier, "A Letter from Theodoret of Cyrus to the Exiled Nestorius (CPG, 6270) in a Syriac Version," *Bijdragen, tijdscrift voor filosofie en theologie* 51 (1990): 234–45.

84. Theodoret, NPNF 3:280.

85. Theodoret, PG 83:1393.

became more important for him was the content, not the packaging.

As one would expect, Theodoret appealed to Scripture for his proof that Christ "is not only man but eternal God."[86] He saw that Christ had to be one with the rest of humanity and with the Word, if he was to function as a true mediator between both: "He is called a mediator because He does not exist as God alone; for how, if He had had nothing of our nature, could He have mediated between us and God?"[87] In addition to being a mediator, Theodoret realized too that Christ fulfills a revelatory function in his role as the image of God's power. One can know the invisible God by the manner Christ has exercised His power: "It is therefore plain that the divine nature is invisible, but the flesh visible, and that through the visible the invisible was seen, by its means working wonders and unveiling its own power."[88] Theodoret, however, was careful to note that "the image has not all the qualities of the archetype."[89] For nothing created can fully reveal God as He is.

While Theodoret spends considerable time and effort proving from Scripture both the union and the integrity of the divine and the human natures, he discussed what he meant by the union itself only in passing in the works that are presently at hand. He maintained that "the word 'incarnation' shows the taking of the flesh, while the word 'union' indicates the combination of distinct things."[90] He regarded the title "Christ" as the term that "sums up," as it were, the union: "for this name includes alike all that is proper to the Godhead and to the manhood."[91] He also held "that the union . . . took place at the conception."[92] But realizing that this union of Christ's natures is mysterious, he confessed what Scripture has revealed: "that the manner of the union cannot be comprehended. But I have at all events been instructed by the divine Scripture that each nature remains unimpaired after the union."[93]

Theodoret becomes more explicit about his understanding of the kind of union that exists between Christ's natures when he explains how the union between Isaac and the lamb sacrificed in his place cannot be applied to Christ's natures. The lamb serves as a suitable image of Isaac, "but as touching the separation of their divided ὑπόστασεις they do so no

---

86. Theodoret, NPNF 3:228.
88. Ibid., 3:166.
90. Ibid., 3:192.
92. Ibid., 3:246.

87. Ibid., 3:187.
89. Ibid., 3:189.
91. Ibid., 3:234.
93. Ibid., 3:192.

longer,"[94] for they are two separate individuals. So likewise when this analogy is applied to Christ, it fails because: "We preach so close an union of Godhead and of manhood as to understand one person (πρόσωπον) undivided, and to acknowledge the same to be both God and man, visible and unvisible, circumscribed and uncircumscribed, and we apply to one of the *prosōpa* all the attributes which are indicative alike of Godhead and manhood."[95] The point here is that the union between Isaac and the lamb is an extrinsic, typical kind of relationship between two individuals while the union of Christ's divine and the human natures is an intrinsic union that takes place within one πρόσωπον—a term Theodoret rarely employed in his extant works.[96]

Perhaps Theodoret's best illustration[97] of how Christ's natures can be united in an unconfounded state is his example of a flaming piece of iron within a superheated forge. This suggests to him how there can exist a union beyond one fashioned by nature in which two substances can be acknowledged as being united without either one of them having necessarily to be absorbed into the other.

The nature of the iron was not damaged by contact with the fire. If then, in natural bodies, examples may be found of an unconfounded mixture, it is sheer folly, in the case of a nature which knows neither corruption nor change, to entertain the idea of confusion and destruction of the assumed nature and all the more so when this nature was assumed in order to bring blessings on the [human] race.[98]

While this analogy limps, it is interesting, for it suggests that Theodoret could conceive of the natures of iron and fire being indeed substantially united as one without either nature being changed, as in the case—

94. Ibid., 3:225.
95. Ibid.
96. This is a remarkable difference between Theodoret and Nestorius who kept referring to one πρόσωπον over and over again. Theodoret seems to appeal to the term simply as a descriptive way to sum up how the natures function together in a visible way. He does not seem to have used it in any technical sense. We can only speculate here as to what may have been the reason for this; e.g. it may simply have been the "politically correct" way for him to act after the condemnation of Nestorius at Nicea and after the later statement of reconciliation upon which Cyril and John of Antioch agreed in 433.
97. Origen has earlier used this analogy in his work *On the First Principles* to explain how Christ's rational soul could be united to the Word. See Norris, *The Christological Controversy*, 78–79.
98. Theodoret, NPNF 3:197. See also 25–26 and 229.

which he rejects—of the union of the soul and body: "for here the union is a natural union of parts that are coaeval, created, and fellow slaves, but in the case of the Lord Christ all is of good will, of love to man, and of grace."[99] But when he proceeded with the analogy, Theodoret did see some application in the way that it helps to understand how the Word can energize the humanity in that: "The soul does not crave for food. How could it when it is immortal? But the body which derives its vital force from the soul, feels its need, and desires to receive what is lacking."[100] This corroborates how Narsai and most likely Theodore interpreted their analogies of the body-soul relationship as on a par with that between the natures in Christ. The analogy was meant to illustrate how the Word can act on Christ's humanity by supplying the power it needs to act without either being altered in the process.

While one may question whether or not a prosopic union does adequately explain the union, Theodoret's insistence upon as close a union as a flaming piece of iron when taken together with his view that the Word supplies the energy that Christ's humanity needs to freely act and his willingness to accept Chalcedon's formulation of faith indicates that he understood Christ's prosopic union of natures to be a substantial one but not in the Eutychian sense that the natures have become in one way or another a single nature. It is acknowledging that ὑπόστασις should be equated with πρόσωπον as it was affirmed at Constantinople I rather than with οὐσία as was done at Nicea.

Conclusion

As long as the Antiochenes remained, as Chrysostom did, close to the concrete way that the New Testament has expressed Jesus as the Christ, they avoided a firestorm of criticism. But a dynamic was at work. After having successfully established against the Arians that the Word and Christ were divine and against the Apollinarians that Christ was truly and fully human, the Antiochenes had to confront the next logical step: how can Christ be both human and divine. The fact that Diodore was castigated as a predecessor of Nestorius and that almost his whole corpus was destroyed because of this suggests he was the first among the Antiochene

99. Ibid., 3:194.
100. Ibid., 3:194.

Fathers to have explored how one could begin from a "low" Christology and then unite Jesus' full humanity with the Word's divinity. Theodore would have certainly carried on his investigations because of the highly inquiring and systematizing bent of his mind. He would want to make sense of how one could unite the Word's transcendent divine nature with Jesus' fully integral human nature. He would also have been drawn into this if he was to prove that the Arians and Apollinarians were wrong in their dogmatic assertions about Christ.

What complicated the controversy were three factors. First, the Antiochene commitment to a literal, historical, and rational method of exegesis constrained them to adhere as closely as possible to the way that the New Testament presented Jesus as truly both human and divine. Second, while they sought to employ scripturally-based rather than metaphysical terms to express the union, they had to employ the basic cultural terms of φύσις, οὐσία, ὑπόστασις, and πρόσωπον to speak about human nature. Because of the fluidity of the language at that time, it appears that they understood these words in a way significantly different than did Cyril and the other Alexandrians. Finally—and not the least of all—the Antiochenes were influenced in their outlook by their undeviating belief that God's transcendent nature precluded any substantial union with all created natures, as well as humanity having any kind of mystical sharing in God's nature. While they held this to be a truth confirmed in the sacred Scriptures, it is fundamentally a metaphysical principle. This is highly ironic, for despite their eschewing of insights coming from pagan Greek philosophy, they had assimilated a viewpoint, albeit from Jewish understanding of God's transcendence, that affected their whole theological approach to the union of Christ's two natures.

Theodore, Nestorius, and Theodoret summed up the union of the divine and the human natures in Christ as a unity in one πρόσωπον. While they used this to denote how Christ had appeared to others as acting in human and divine ways, it does suggest that his external appearance as a living being has a metaphysical relationship to his inner natures. Because of their opinions on God's transcendence and the meaning of a hypostatic union, they rejected a substantial kind of union. But when they came to explain in a positive way what they held, they affirmed a unique graced union that takes place on two levels and at two different "moments." The first occurred at Jesus' conception when the Word dwelt within his human nature and assumed it in such way that the two have become one Son and

Lord of the universe. The second one was a continuous union of their wills whereby they both freely agreed, in a completely harmonious way, how to fulfill their Father's will.

While Nestorius was pushed to defend a prosopic union so that its underlying metaphysical meaning not only made coherent sense but also agreed with what the Scriptures and Christian tradition had affirmed about the personal unity of natures in Christ, Diodore and Theodore had established the way for him to discuss how the Word and Christ's human nature (which was carefully affirmed to be the "assumed one") could act together without compromising the Word's divine transcendency. Theodore proposed that the Word as a spiritual "entity" provided the energy or power for the humanity to act. For Theodore, such an explanation preserved unaltered both the Word's transcendent nature's and Christ's human freedom of action. But it is describing how the two natures of Christ function together, not how they are essentially or metaphysically united. As such, Theodore can be thought to be affirming what the Gospels have done—that those encountering the visible nature of Christ are also coming into direct contact with the Word. By being both God and man, Christ can truly be said to be the Son of God and the Lord of the universe who serves as the image whereby the rest of creation can know and worship God through his visible humanity.

Despite their objections to the contrary, the Antiochenes do seem to have held the same underlying reality as Cyril regarding the kind of union existing between Christ's natures. This becomes evident in their repudiations of the viewpoints taken by Paul of Samosata, the Arians, and Apollinarians, and from their oft repeated protestations that they believed that Christ was in fact both human and divine and one person. One may find fault with, and even reject as being ultimately untenable, Nestorius's metaphysical defense of how each of Christ's two natures possessed its own πρόσωπον and how both shared a common πρόσωπον. One can also label as heretical the excerpts culled out of context from Theodore's works because they can be interpreted as false in light of his opponents' metaphysical understanding of the words that he used and the kind of union that had to exist between the natures. But it seems that neither Nestorius nor Theodore, and certainly none of the other Antiochenes, can be declared stereotypical "Nestorians" who regarded Christ as merely a uniquely graced human being united in some sort of a voluntary union with the Word. This may be logically inferred from what Nestorius and

Theodore have affirmed about a prosopic kind of unity. But as Theodo-ret later admitted by his willingness to accept the term θεοτόκος, what is crucially important is not how one verbally expresses the union but whether those disputing the issue are actually in agreement as to its underlying content.

With this background established, one is in a better position to judge Theodore's view on how Christ fulfills his unitive role as God's primary image. As these last few chapters have indicated, it is exceedingly difficult to express, let alone understand, what kind of union he had been propos-ing. Theodore had no problem in asserting that Christ's human nature was consubstantial with all other creatures—humans, angels, and mate-rial beings. But since he believed that the humanity of Christ cannot be consubstantial with the Word's divine nature and that salvation cannot be a participation in God's nature, he followed a way that Paul affirmed by re-garding salvation as a transformation from a mortal to an immortal body and from a mutable to an immutable soul. So while others are able to speak of how a believer can mystically experience God in one's *nous* and grow ontologically in a spiritual life of holiness that reflects a growth in one's sharing in divine life through grace, Theodore had to consider com-munion with God as achievable only in and through Christ's humanity. Since all humans share the same general nature, Theodore turned to the idea of a union of wills united to God's will. His emphasis was upon a vol-untary and moral union rather than upon any sort of ontological union. He suggested the latter, however, when he maintained that the divine and human natures were united from the first moment of conception.

When he discussed the effects baptism and the eucharist can have upon their recipients, Theodore clearly expressed the kind of communion that he held to exist between a believer and God. Besides supplying the graces that people need to be faithful to their commitment to live out their lives according to God's will, these sacraments reinforce the solid, in fact unshakeable, assurance that recipients possess that God is going to bestow on them a future immortal life. Theodore looked upon these two sacraments as types foreshadowing a future immortality and immutabil-ity that is assured. Yet since all those receiving the sacraments are still liv-ing in a mortal state, they possess the future life only potentially. They have, as it were, a guarantee in hand that they will attain what has been promised, but this present potential state needs to be nurtured again and again until God will intervene in a future life to activate it.

When Theodore sought to illustrate how Christ can fulfill the unitive function of his role as God's image, he had to confront a fundamental question: What kind of communion with God does Christ provide? He could not comprehend how there could be a communion in the order of nature or of a present "super-natural" participation in God's divine life. He proposed instead a loving communion of wills and of activity. If Theodore's views about the union are judged in light of the theological differences existing between an incarnational and an eschatological approach, or one between a contemplative prayer form that may bring one into immediate experiential contact with God's power and an active life where a person believes that he or she is united with God in one's well-intentioned actions, or between a "sanctifying" kind of grace that raises human nature to a supernatural order and an actual grace that assists a person to act freely in a right way, Theodore's viewpoint is centered upon the second emphases. His outlook combines an eschatological outlook with the need to live at the present moment an upright life in accordance with God's will and the actual graces that one has received through the mediation of Christ. For those upholding a Chalcedonian understanding of how a believer can be united with God, Theodore's major weakness is that he is unable to account for the occasions when God can be experienced in a direct, immediate, mystical way in the present life because of a special nature-elevating grace. Perhaps this difference in outlook may be due to his inability to see the presence of a mystical, non-historical, and supra-rational dimension in Scripture because of his basic emphases upon a literal, historical, and rational method of exegesis.

What stands out as the most important result flowing from the present study into Theodore's Christology is how his understanding of πρόσωπον can be related to the functional roles that he has attributed to Christ as God's primary image within creation. A transcendent God needs a visible, symbolic image that can manifest His presence to His creatures. God has chosen to make Christ this image. But by adding to this image the notion that humans are also the bond of the universe, Theodore has also broadened his outlook on the roles that Christ plays within creation. He is not only the mediator of graces that humans need to enter into full communion with God but also the one who will recapitulate all of creation and reunite it to the Father by means of his union with the Word. The threefold roles that Christ plays as the image of God bolster the view that Theodore's Christology is primarily functional in its orientation.

6

ARE WOMEN IMAGES OF GOD?

I N OUR INVESTIGATION of "image," the Antiochenes were found to have divided into two camps on how to interpret the scriptural statement about "man" having been created in God's image and likeness. Diodore, Chrysostom, and Theodoret looked upon image as applying to men *qua* males. They believed that God has entrusted males with total power to rule over the material universe as God's viceroys. While women share in this power, they were regarded as subordinate to men. Diodore, Chrysostom, and Theodoret frequently liked to cite Paul's statement that man *qua* male "is the image and glory of God but woman is the glory of man" (1 Cor. 11:7). The most they would affirm is that women are "images of the image." Yet while following the same literal, rational hermeneutical principles of exegesis, Theodore, and perhaps Nestorius, understood image as referring to how human nature—in a general sense—plays a unitive, revelatory, and cultic role within creation. It is not clear, however, what they thought about women as images of God and, if so, how they regarded women as functioning as such.

In the present chapter, the intent is to fill in more details about the Antiochene views regarding image, by delving more deeply into their opinions on how women fit in with these views.[1] The purpose is to flesh

---

1. For meaningful studies undertaken by feminist theologians regarding the image of God, see Kari Elizabeth Børresen, ed., *Image of God and Gender Models in Judaeo-Christian Tradition* (Oslo: Solum Forlag, 1991). The few references to the Antiochenes are brief

out their treatments of image by examining and critiquing the reasons that the Antiochenes propose to support their viewpoints and to explore how these opinions provide insight into their understanding of the relationship that ought to exist between men and women. Since the matter is of contemporary interest because of concerns about sexual equality and the active roles that women are able to exercise in church ministry, Chrysostom's and Theodore's nuanced views can be interesting and valuable for the historical information they provide about the patristic period and for their answers to the question of what should be the proper kind of relationship between men and women.

In her collection of patristic texts about the status and role of women in the early church, Elizabeth Clark believes: "The most fitting word with which to describe the Church Fathers' attitude toward women is ambivalence."[2] This certainly aptly describes the various positions taken by the leading Antiochene theologians in regard to women. Since Diodore makes mention of women in only two passages and Nestorius not at all, the focus here will be upon the writings of Chrysostom and Theodore, with a few brief comments about Theodoret's views. These provide a

---

and restricted to Diodore's and Chrysostom's view of image as being associated with dominion.

2. Elizabeth A. Clark, *Women in the Early Church*, Message of the Fathers of the Church 13 (Wilmington, Del.: Glazier, 1983), 15. I am indebted in this chapter to the following for both the research results and the bibliographies they have provided about women in the early church: Elizabeth A. Clark, *Jerome, Chrysostom, and Friends: Essays and Translations*, Studies in Women and Religion 2 (New York: Mellen, 1979); George H. Tavard, *Women in the Christian Tradition* (Notre Dame: U of Notre Dame P, 1973); Rosemary Radford Ruether, ed., *Religion and Sexism: Images of Women in the Jewish and Christian Traditions* (New York: Simon and Schuster, 1974); Sarah B. Pomeroy, *Goddesses, Whores, Wives, and Slaves: Women in Classical Antiquity* (New York: Schocken, 1975); Roger Gryson, *The Ministry of Women in the Early Church*, trans. J. Laporte and M. L. Hall (Collegeville: Liturgical, 1976); Averil Cameron and Amélie Kuhrt, ed., *Images of Women in Antiquity* (Detroit: Wayne State UP, 1983); Elizabeth Schüssler Fiorenza, *In Memory of Her: A Feminist Reconstruction of Christian Origins* (New York: Crossroads, 1983); Sebastian P. Brock and Susan Ashbrook Harvey, *Holy Women of the Syrian Orient* (Berkeley: U of California P, 1987); Susanne Heine, *Women and Early Christianity. Are the Feminist Scholars Right?*, trans. John Bowden (Minneapolis: Augsburg, 1988); Ross S. Kraemer, *Her Share of the Blessings: Women's Religions among Pagans, Jews, and Christians in the Greco-Roman World* (New York: Oxford UP, 1992); and the articles on "Woman" by M. G. Mara in EEC 2:881–82 and by John L. McKenzie for the Old and New Testament times in his *Dictionary of the Bible* (London: Chapman, 1965), 935–37.

generally detailed picture of what they believed ought to be a woman's role in their society and the church of their day—but with some interesting variations.

Our treatment begins with an overview of both the societal and cultural attitudes that conditioned the thinking of Late Antiquity toward women. Afterwards there will be an examination of Chrysostom's and Theodore's arguments regarding the role and status of women and the reasons they propose to justify their positions. The main point here is to determine to what extent their understanding of society as a vital organic whole has influenced their interpretations of those scriptural passages treating a woman's relationship to a man and of her public role in society and the church.[3] This will be helpful for clarifying even further Theodore's view concerning the unitive role that he believed humans as God's image have been called to exercise within salvation history.

The Cultural Attitude Toward Women at Antioch

The past twenty years has witnessed a considerable amount of detailed scholarly re-examination of both New Testament and early patristic documents in order to try to uncover what may have been the actual ministerial role of women in the first two centuries of church life. It is difficult to assess their conclusions and speculations because the evidence is so meager and the possible interpretations so wide. Since our present focus is upon the cultural attitude toward women at Antioch from the middle of the fourth to the middle of the fifth centuries, we are concerned not with what titles and offices women may have had in apostolic times but with what appears to have been the way they were regarded within church circles during that period at Antioch. The Antiochene patriarchical attitude expressed toward women may be judged to be reprehensible. But it is indicative not merely of the cultural setting and of an evolving ecclesiastical tradition at Antioch but, even much more for our purposes, of its confirmation of what we have earlier concluded to concerning the Antiochene method of exegeting scriptural passages from a very literal, historical, and rational approach.

The most striking and disturbing feature of the fourth and fifth century attitudes toward women—and one that speaks volumes about how

3. These are Gen. 1:26–28; 2:18, 21–24; and 3:16; 1 Cor. 11:3–12 and 14:34–35; Gal. 3:26–29; Eph. 5:21–33; Col. 3:18–19; and 1 Tim. 2:11–15.

little value was placed on their roles in society and the church—is the almost total lack of any works composed by women or written about women, especially poor women. When the Fathers did mention women, they usually restricted themselves to their glowing paens of praise for the virgin Mary's total dedication to the will of God and contrasted this with Eve's tragic failure. They also waxed eloquently about the exploits of the exceptional women who had personally touched their lives, especially their mothers and sisters, or those who had sacrificed their lives in martyrdom for the faith, or those virgins who had excelled as ascetics.[4] They were also particularly grateful for those wealthy women who had enriched the church with their generous benefactions and for those powerful empresses, above all Helena, Eudoxia, Pulcheria, and Eudocia, who exercised dominion within the Eastern empire.[5] While the lives of these women are illuminating for the information they provide about the influential roles women played in the third, fourth, and fifth centuries, they, however, stand out as exceptions to the iron rule of almost complete silence about women throughout this period.

If one is willing to accept Epiphanius's assertions[6] about the Cataphrygians—a point disputed[7]—a number of minor heretical sects may not only have treated women as equals but even have consecrated a few bishops and ordained others as priests. But as will be soon seen, the Fathers, while affirming some true equality between men and women, were—

4. For a study of aristocratic women who possessed power but, when restricted in their use of it, turned to asceticism, see Rosemary Radford Ruether, "Mothers of the Church: Ascetic Women in the Late Patristic Age," *Women of Spirit: Female Leadership in the Jewish and Christian Traditions*, ed. Rosemary Radford Ruether and Eleanor McLaughlin (New York: Simon, 1979), 71–98.

5. For a richly detailed study of these empresses and the influence they wielded within the Eastern Empire, see Kenneth G. Holum, *Theodosian Empresses: Women and Imperial Dominion in Late Antiquity* (Berkeley: U of California P, 1982).

6. See *The Panarion of St. Epiphanius, Bishop of Salamis*, trans. Philip R. Amidon (New York: Oxford, 1990). When writing about the tenets of the Quintillians and Priscillians, Montanist sects, Epiphanius observed that: "They have women bishops, women presbyters, and everything else, all of which they say is in accord with: 'in Christ Jesus there is neither male nor female'" (173–74).

7. See Kraemer, 157–73, 177–78, and 183–87. Kraemer observes (162) that Eusebius, Hippolytus, and Tertullian make no mention of women serving as bishops and priests within the Montanist movement. In fact Tertullian was adamantly opposed to women even baptizing, let alone teaching. Kraemer also considers what may be other possible indications of women performing priestly functions in 84–85.

without exception—opposed to women exercising any public role in the church, other than serving as deaconesses. They allowed the latter practice since it was sanctioned in the Pauline epistles,[8] but as the following limiting canon from the *Apostolic Constitutions* (a fourth century collection of canons and liturgical prayers) states, the deaconesses were all severely restricted as to what they could and could not do. They were instructed that they were "not [to] bless, nor perform anything belonging to the office of presbyters or deacons, but [were] only to keep the doors, and to minister to the presbyters in the baptism of women, on account of decency."[9]

A broader picture of ecclesial attitudes towards women can be obtained from a section heading in the *Didascalia Apostolorum* (a church document that was most likely written at Antioch before the middle of the fourth century) that elaborates on how a Christian woman was expected to act. It instructs women

that they should please and honor their husbands alone, caring assiduously and wisely for the work of their houses with diligence; and that they should not bathe with men and that they should not adorn themselves and become a cause of stumbling to men and capture them; and that they should be chaste and gentle, and not quarrel with their husbands.[10]

While this instruction suggests a subordinate position of women in the society of the day, it is even more explicitly expressed in the guidelines as to where the bishop, priests, laymen, and women were to be seated within the church and when each of these should stand for prayer.

For the presbyters let there be separated a place on the eastern side of the house, and let the bishop's chair be among them and let the presbyters sit with him. And again, let the laymen sit in another eastern part of the house . . . and then the

---

8. To cite but a few references, see 1 Timothy 3:11, Romans 16:1, and the *Didascalia Apostolorum in Syriac*, ed. and trans. Arthur Vööbus, CSCO 401–2 / Syr. 175–76 (Louvain: CSCO, 1979), 2:26 and 3:12 and 13. For a treatment of what rank the deaconesses held within the hierarchy, see Gryson, 60–63.

9. *Constitutions of the Holy Apostles*, ed. J. Donaldson and A. Roberts, The Ante-Nicene Fathers 7 (Grand Rapids, Mich.: Eerdmanns, 1951), 494. This restriction of a woman's activity seems to be due to Saint Paul's injunction forbidding women from preaching and ruling over men. It may also indicate that the early church had incorporated the Jewish prohibition against women functioning as priests in the Temple or as elders in the synagogue.

10. *Didascalia*, 3:20.

women; so that when you stand up to pray, the leaders may stand first, and after them the laymen, and then also the women.[11]

The issue of female subordination becomes even further sharply defined in the *Didascalia's* instruction that women were not permitted to teach,[12] but when this work was incorporated into the *Apostolic Constitutions*, it was modified. Women were forbidden to teach—but only in church. The two reasons offered to explain its prohibition are very illuminating: first, that the Lord did not choose to send women to preach, although he could have done so, and second, that, in Paul's words, man is the woman's head. This latter argument is interesting for what it suggests regarding the organic roles men and women were thought to play within the body of Christ.

We do not permit our women to teach in the Church, but only to pray and hear those that teach; for our Master and Lord . . . did nowhere send out women to preach. For had it been necessary for women to teach, He Himself would have first commanded these also to instruct the people with us. For "if the head of the wife be the man," it is not reasonable that the rest of the body should govern the head.[13]

Besides being forbidden to teach publicly in church, women were also instructed by the *Apostolic Constitutions* not to attempt to baptize. Its reasons are noteworthy for illustrating how certain arguments have become commonplace among the Fathers. The appeal is once again to a scriptural justification, especially that man is to be regarded as being the "head" and therefore, in a play on words, "ahead" of women.

Now, as to women's baptizing, we let you know that there is no small peril to those that undertake it. Therefore we do not advise you to do it; for it is dangerous, or rather wicked or impious. For if the "man be the head of the woman," and he be originally ordained for the priesthood, it is not right to abrogate the order of the creation, and leave the principal part to come to the extreme part of the body. For the woman is the body of the man, taken from his side, and subject to him, from whom she has been separated for the procreation of children. For he says, "He shall rule over you." For the principal part of the woman is the man, as her head. But if the foregoing constitutions we have do not permit them to teach, how will anyone allow them, contrary to nature, to perform the office of a priest? For this is one of

11. Ibid., 130–31.
12. See ibid., 145.
13. Ibid., 427–28. Sections 1–6 of the *Apostolic Constitution* contain the same matter as the *Didascalia*, but with adaptations.

the ignorant practices of Gentile atheism, to ordain women to the female deities; [it is] not one of the constitutions of Christ. For if baptism were to be administered by women, then certainly our Lord would have been baptized by his mother.[14]

There is further evidence of the pervasive negative cultural outlook in the late fourth and early fifth centuries toward women in the writings of Cyril of Alexandria. This may strike many as contradictory, in that Cyril showed himself to be such a staunch, fervent defender of Mary's title as the Mother of God and a foe of the Antiochene teaching on Christology. His critical, negative view highlights how widespread is the cultural attitude toward women in the period being examined. Walter Burghardt sums up the viewpoint of Cyril regarding women as follows:

Cyril insists—often enough to be at once monotonous and indicative of a consistent outlook—that woman is inferior to man. Frequently he contents himself with the sheer enunciation of his thesis: man is superior, woman inferior; man holds the chief place, woman is subject and subordinate; man has the greater honor and glory, even before God, whereas woman is of less esteem. But on occasion Cyril bares a few details. The inferiority is not purely a question of physical size or physical strength. What is more momentous, woman falls short of man in "natural ability." She has not the strength to achieve the virtue of which the male is capable. She is of imperfect intelligence. Unlike her male complement, she is dull-witted, slow to learn, unprepared to grasp the difficult and the supernatural; for her mind is a soft, weak, delicate thing. Briefly, "the female sex is ever weak in mind and body."[15]

Some further inkling of how women were regarded in the first half of the fifth century can be gleaned from incidents reported in the biographies of the most renowned ascetic of the day, Simeon the Stylite. Tens of thousands of pious, and curious pilgrims, even from Britain, are said to have thronged to see him perched on the top of a sixty-foot pillar at Telneshe (about thirty miles east of Antioch). He, however, did not permit any woman, including his own mother, to come near to him.[16] While his severity towards women may simply be a sign of Simeon's understanding of what his asceticism required, it would certainly set an example for all

14. *Didascalia*, 429.

15. Walter Burghardt, *The Image of God in Man According to Cyril of Alexandria* (Washington: Catholic University of America Press, 1957), 128–29.

16. For passages substantiating this, see Simeon Stylites, *The Lives of Simeon Stylites*, trans. Robert Doran (Kalamazoo, Mich.: Cistercian Publications, 1992), 81, 92–93, 120, and 226.

the thousands who flocked to see him and reinforced their cultural attitude that women were not to be treated on the same level as men.

In summary, the cultural milieu around fifth-century Antioch indicates that a woman was thought to be inferior in a number of fundamental ways to a man, particularly in regard to the kinds of activity in which she could engage. While one can question how much this reflects actual practice, particularly in the cases of wealthy and imperial wives, it does indicate the attitude toward women that the Antiochene Fathers had to live with and respond to. With this background knowledge of the times, we are now able to probe in much greater detail what Chrysostom and Theodore thought about the roles of women in relationship to males. The intent is to see how their views reflect the culture and how their understanding of a woman's position vis-à-vis males within society has ramifications for the unitive role that Theodore has assigned to humankind as the image of God.

John Chrysostom

While Chrysostom has not discussed in any systematic way how he viewed women, his extensive writings do offer a detailed picture that mirrors what was present in the ecclesiastical texts of the day. His views on a woman's original relationship to a man at creation and whether the Fall had any major impact upon this will be first considered, followed by what Chrysostom believed to be the individual spheres of activity that nature and God have assigned to each sex and how they are to be mutually interdependent upon each other. This treatment will be concluded with some remarks concerning what Chrysostom had to say about the Virgin Mary and his friendship with the deaconess Olympias. The latter is illuminating for highlighting how he actually felt toward a woman whom he looked upon as a beloved friend.

First, regarding his view on the status of women at creation, Chrysostom maintained in his fourth homily on Genesis that there was originally an "equality of honor" between Adam and Eve. He wrote:

Before [Eve's] disobedience, she was equal in honor to the man [as male]. For when God formed her, he also used the same words in both the fashioning of man [male] and the making of the woman. For just as He said in man's regard, "Let us make man [humankind] to our image and likeness" and not "Let there be man [humankind]" so also He did not say in her regard, "Let there be a woman," but rather, "Let us make a helper for him"—not simply a helper but, "one like unto him," showing again [her] equality of honor.[17]

Judging from this passage, it would seem that Eve's "equality of honor" refers to the fact that God created Eve, like Adam, in a way different from the rest of creation. While everything else came into being when God decreed "Let it be," Adam and Eve were created at God's commands, "Let us make man to our image and likeness" and "Let us make a helper for him," which reveal God's personal concern for them. By indicating that their creation is exceptional, God called attention to the unique, special role both were to play within creation: they were given wide authority by God to rule over the earth. This is stated explicitly in the following:

Then after saying, "He made them male and female," He said, as he bestowed a blessing upon both, "And God blessed them," saying, "Increase and multiply, fill the earth and subdue it and rule over the fish of the sea." See the privilege given in the blessing. For the command, "Increase and multiply and subdue the earth," was said in relationship to both the brute beings and the reptiles. The command, "Exercise dominion and rule [over the earth]" was given to the man and the woman. See the benevolence of the Lord. Before He brought forth the woman, He made her a sharer in [Adam's] rule and deemed her worthy of a blessing.[18]

The last line in the above quotation needs clarification. One may be puzzled by Chrysostom's statement that, *before* God created Eve, He made her a sharer in man's rule over the earth. But as the next quotation makes clear, Chrysostom believed that the initial account in Genesis about the fashioning of Eve has to be understood as a foreshadowing of that later time described in the second and the third chapters of Genesis when she was actually created and then fell. He wrote:

He taught us [the meaning of] this in a cryptic manner. For since he had not yet apprised us about [their] fashioning and had not said from whence the woman came, he said: "Masculine and feminine He made them." Do you see how he has related what had not yet come to be, as though it had? Spiritual eyes can see this. Those possessing carnal eyes cannot grasp what is being seen, while those with the eyes of the Spirit can see what is invisible and immaterial.[19]

---

17. Chrysostom, PG 54:594; cf. *Homily 10 on Genesis*, PG 53:85–86 where Chrysostom speaks in amazement at how God "before He brought forth the woman made her share in [Adam's] dominion." I have translated this and the following passages from the Greek text.

18. Chrysostom, PG 53:86.   19. Ibid., 53:85–86.

Chrysostom believed, therefore, that the real creation of Adam and Eve is being recounted not in the first but in the second chapter of Genesis. It is here that Eve is depicted as having been created from Adam's rib. Though she possessed a "general shape, character, and likeness"[20] with him and shared in his authority to rule over the other creatures of the earth, Chrysostom maintained that she was made subordinate to Adam in the third chapter of Genesis,[21] for she was created after Adam, from Adam, and as a helper for Adam. From this it is evident that Chrysostom has used Genesis 3 and, as we will see, 1 Corinthians 11:7 as scriptural keys that unlock the meaning of "man" [humankind] in Genesis 1:27. This is expressed in an unambiguous way when Chrysostom insisted that God fashioned only man [as male] in His image and likeness.

For what reason, therefore, is the man [male] said to be the image of God and not also the woman? For [Genesis] is not speaking about an image [based] upon a form but an image [based] on sovereign power that only the man [male] has but not the woman. For he is subjected to no one, while she is under his control; as God has said, "Your recourse shall be to your husband, and he shall rule over you." The male, therefore, is the "image of God" because he has no one above him, just as

20. Ibid., 54:589.
21. In her article, "Male Domination of Woman in the Writings of Saint John Chrystom," *Greek Orthodox Theological Review* 36, no. 2 (1991): 134, Valerie Karras challenges Elizabeth Clark and George Tavard's interpretation of Chrysostom's understanding of image as referring to the dominion that men alone possess. She maintains that Chrysostom looked upon women as being full participants in God's image, for women share in all the traits of God's image, such as having virtue, free will, and, above all in the prelapsarian state, full dominion over the created world. The same position is taken by David C. Ford in his *Women and Men in the Early Church: The Full Views of St. John Chrysostom* (South Canaan, Penn.: St. Tikhon's Seminary P., 1996), 147, no. 28. A less definitive assessment is reached by Geoffrey V. Gillard ("God in Genesis 1:26 According to Chrysostom," *Studia Biblica* (1978): 152), who remarks in passing that "Chrysostom seems unsure whether the woman is included in the image as he contradicts himself over this." The problem that I have with these interpretations is that there are no passages, to my knowledge, where Chrysostom explicitly asserts that Eve was co-equal *in full power* with Adam before the Fall and therefore was, like him, also created in God's image. Eve may have shared in Adam's power over the rest of creation, but this does not mean that her superiority over creation precluded her being subordinate to Adam. Moreover, if the above interpretations were correct, I would expect in those passages where Chrysostom denies that Eve was in God's image, he would have pointed out that she had *lost* her dignity as God's image. Such a remark would seem to be appropriate in that context.

God has no one over Him and rules over all. The woman, however, is "the glory of man," since she is subject to her husband.[22]

Though Adam holds power over Eve because he is fashioned in the image of God, Chrysostom asserted that Adam is not immediately aware of this. He affirmed this in a passage where he is opposing those who want to prove that in the Trinity the Son is subordinate to the Father on the basis of Saint Paul's statement that "Christ is the head of every man [*qua* male] and the husband the head of his wife, and God the head of Christ (1 Cor. 11:3)." Their argument is that the Son is subordinate to his Father in the same way a woman is to a man. While denying the analogy, Chrysostom insisted that a woman is to be equally respected as a person who is free and, like Adam, specially honored by God. Chrysostom then proceeded to explain in detail why a woman has been made subject to man and when Adam became aware of this.

If Paul wanted to speak of power and subjection, as you say, he would not have introduced a woman into the midst [of this argument] but rather [spoken of] a slave and a master. For even if a women is subject to us, yet it is as a woman, and as a free person and one equal in honor . . . Among us a woman is aptly subject to man. Otherwise an equality of honor leads to strife, not only because of this [fact] but also because of the deceit perpetrated at the beginning. For when she came into being, she was not immediately a subject, not even when God brought her to the man. She did not hear of this from God. Nor did the man say anything about it. But [it came to be] when he said that she was "bone of his bones and flesh from his flesh." Yet he was not at all aware of [his] rule or control over her. When, however, she badly used her power, then she who had become his helper was found to be his ensnarer. She then lost everything.[23]

In this quotation, Chrysostom has highlighted another area where a woman is equal to man: she too is a free person. Yet as seen above where she is said to share in Adam's authority to rule but is still subject to him, the same is true here. She may be a free person who must be respected, but she still falls under man's sovereignty—a fact that Chrysostom believed is seen in Adam's statement that Eve is bone of his bones and in God's punishment of Eve because of her role in the Fall. He offered two reasons for a man's pre-eminence. These need now to be looked at in some detail.

22. Chrysostom, PG 54:589; see also 49:93.
23. Ibid., 61:214–15.

First, as the following quotation makes clear, God created a woman subject to man because, as he is convinced, partners with equal power constantly end up in bitter struggles with one another. A woman's subjection is necessary so that peace might reign in the family, just as there is a need in an organic-type society to have one person who is pre-eminent.

God made her subject [to Adam] and set him [over her] for this reason that there might be peace. For where there is an equality of honor, there will never be peace— either where a household is governed in a democratic way or where all rule. On the contrary it is necessary that there be one who is pre-eminent.[24]

If a woman is subject to man because there must be one who is pre-eminent, Chrysostom then drew the conclusion: "Man's rule [over a woman], therefore, is natural . . . For the woman is from him and for him and under him."[25] And if this is so, it follows, as seen in Chrysostom's commentary on the passage in Colossians where wives are told to be subordinate to their husbands "as is proper in the Lord (Col. 3:18)," that: "[this is] not a subjection to a despot, but rather one due not only to nature but also by reason of God."[26] This same view is also expressed in Chrysostom's explanation of why women have to cover their heads and men do not: "These [ways of acting] are imposed by law from men, even if God later confirmed them. I am speaking here of that [law imposed] by nature as to what is and is not to be covered. But when I speak of nature, I mean God. For He is the one who created nature."[27] Thus for Chrysostom, a woman's subordination to man has been instilled, as it were, into the fabric of her nature by God. God has not done this to abase and denigrate womanhood, but to ensure that there is one person who has the responsibility for making ultimate decisions. Chrysostom believed God has assigned such a role in nature to man. What appears, therefore, in his argumentation is not merely a hierarchical and patriarchical view of the family and of society but also an organic outlook where all other

24. Ibid., 62:141.

25. Ibid., 61:218–19. The ancients determined what is natural from the constant way a nature manifests itself. Their method of asserting what specifically pertained to a nature was inductive rather than deductive.

26. Ibid., 62:365.

27. Ibid., 61:216. The same idea is expressed in Homily 26 on 1 Corinthians, PG 61:219 and also in Homily 10 on Colossians 3, PG 62:365 where Chrysostom affirms that a woman's subjection flows from her nature and God's will.

members are subordinate to man's rule as the head of the family, society, and the created universe.

Chrysostom maintained, too, that Eve's fall in Eden not only has affected her but has had an impact upon all women. He has expressed this by likening the consequences of her failure to the universal effect that Adam's fall had. Once again, one can detect an organic Semitic outlook where the action of the head affects all the other members.

A woman once taught and overturned everything. For this reason, he said: "Let her not teach." What then about the women coming after her, if she incurred this? By all means [it applies to them]! For their sex is weak and given to levity. For it is said here of the whole nature. For he did not say that "Eve" was deceived, but "the woman," which is a term for her sex in general, rather than a term for her. What then? Did the whole female nature come to be in [a state of] deviation through her? For just as he said of Adam, "In the pattern of the transgression of Adam who is a type of him who is to come," so also here the female sex has transgressed, not the male's. What therefore? Does she not have salvation? Most certainly, he said. And how is that? Through that of [having] children. Thus he was not speaking [here only] of Eve.[28]

While Chrysostom's exegesis strikes us today as far-fetched and his offhanded remark that the female sex is "weak and vain" as revealing a sexually demeaning view of women, one must be careful, however, to judge it not merely as an expression of the cultural climate prevalent in his day or perhaps of his own prejudiced view of women but within the overall context of his thought and to his commitment to a literal and rational interpretation of the Genesis and Pauline passages indicating women's subjection to men. In other words, he ought to be judged on the basis of both his grounds for asserting a woman's subjection and his seemingly harsh remarks on how this subordinate relationship has to be actually carried out. First of all, Chrysostom is insistent that man and woman must both work together in an harmonious union for the well-being of each other. As the following quotation shows, God has intended that they are to strive to form together a kind of organic union that will be reciprocally beneficial for each individual and opposed to any and all claims of personal ownership or possession.

If (your) wife says "mine," say to her: "By what manner of speech do you say 'yours?' For I do not know [such a word], since I have nothing of my own. How,

28. Chrysostom, PG 62:545.

then, do you say 'mine,' since all things are yours?" Make this word acceptable to her . . . And let us also say this in the presence of the woman. For her power of understanding is more like that of a child. If she should say, "mine," tell her "All things are yours, and I am yours." . . . Teach her, therefore, never to say "mine" and "yours." And never simply speak to her, unless with mildness, with dignity, and with great love.[29]

Besides enjoying an equality of possessions with her husband because of their organic union with each other, a woman is also solidly bonded to him in a union of passionate longing. Even beyond this, she is to be cared for, as Ephesians 5:28–33 states, in love. Chrysostom was firmly convinced that by obliging a husband to love his wife, God has much more than counterbalanced her being placed in a subordinate position. He affirms it thus:

Notice God's kindness here. For lest a woman might think such mastery to be burdensome when she heard: "This one will rule over you," God makes the statement of caring first, saying: "Your recourse shall be for your husband; that is, that he will be your refuge, your haven, and your security. In all the trials assailing you, I give you this man to turn to and take refuge in." Not only did God act in this way but He bonded them solidly together by their natural needs, chaining them with a passionate longing [for each other].[30]

In the next quotation, Chrysostom insists upon love as being the motivating force that ought to guide a man in the way he is to rule over and care for a woman. In their organic union together, a woman may be required to obey, but a man has the much more onerous duty to love. Chrysostom regards these mutual obligations as having been written, as it were, in the natures of men and women and thus serving as an indisputable sign of how God wants both to integrate with each other.

It is the duty of men to love, and of women to yield. If, therefore, each makes his or her own contribution, everything will stand secure. For by being loved, the woman also becomes friendly. By her being submissive, the man becomes gentle. See that this has been provided for in this way by nature: for man to love and the woman to obey. For when he who commands loves the one who is commanded, then everything is firmly set. . . . For this reason God has made her subject to you, in order that she may be loved more. For this reason, He has made you, woman, [a person] to be loved that you may bear in a contented way that you have been made a subject. Do not fear being a subject. To be subject to one loving you entails no difficulty at all. Do not fear, O man, being a lover. For you have her yielding [to you]. Otherwise

29. Ibid., 62:148.   30. Ibid., 54:594.

there would not be a bond of union [between you]. You have accordingly a rule ne-cessitated by nature. Have a bond too that has been created out of love.[31]

Chrysostom considered a man's duty to love his wife as being neces-sary even in those situations when his wife was not obedient. For this rea-son, he believed that when a husband and wife fulfill their responsibilities toward each other, they will both savor the benefits of their mutual har-mony with each other. But it is the wife who really wins out and prospers from this arrangement, as Chrysostom has expressed in his commentary on Ephesians:

The one who loves his wife, even though she is not obedient, will nevertheless bear up with everything. [Maintaining] harmony is indeed a difficult and arduous [task], when the husband and wife are not bound by a sovereign love. Yet fear by no means sets this right. For this reason Paul spends more time on what is positive. And the woman who seems to have lost out because she was commanded to stand in fear [of her husband] wins out. For the man has been commanded in a more authorita-tive way, namely to love.[32]

A Woman's Areas of Responsibility

Yet despite the personal advantages that a woman may receive in a marriage, especially the love expressed for her, her public role is, neverthe-less, curtailed and closely circumscribed both in society and in the church. Chrysostom spelled out in great detail the works for which nature and God have best fitted her. He insists that her labors, though of a secondary order to man's, are not to be contemned, for they are necessary in order to complement those areas where a man is weak and needs assistance. He ends by stressing what is more important than fulfilling human tasks— that both men and women strive for spiritual perfection. His thought is ex-pressed in the following lengthy quotation.

There is only one task for a woman: to guard carefully what has been gathered, to watch closely the revenues, and care for [her] household. For God has given her for this reason that she is to be a helper to us in these tasks, along with all others. For since our life is customarily composed of two [activities], private and public affairs, God, being the one who has distributed both of these tasks, has assigned to a woman care of the household and to men all the affairs of the city . . . A woman

31. Ibid., 62:366.
32. Ibid., 62:140–41.

cannot introduce a motion in the council-chamber, but she can express her opinion in her home—and she has often been better able to see about the household matters than her husband. She cannot administer public affairs well, but can educate children well—which is her main occupation. . . . For this is the work of God's munificence and wisdom that the one useful in greater tasks is less [skilled] in those that are minor, [showing] that the usefulness [of both] is a necessity. For if He made man fit for both spheres, womankind would be contemned . . . God, therefore, did not entrust both tasks to one [sex], lest [the need for] the other would lessen and be thought useless. Nor did He distribute both tasks in an equal way to each singly, lest there arise some struggle and rivalry over their equality in honor, with wives clashing with their husbands by laying claim to the privilege of the front seat [in the theater]. But in order to provide for peace while at the same time maintaining a function that befits each, God, by dividing our life into these two [areas of activity], gave the more necessary and useful to man and what is less and inferior to woman. . . . Therefore, since we all know these things, let us seek only one thing: namely virtue of the soul and nobility of character, in order that we may enjoy peace, so that we may revel in oneness of mind and continuous love.[33]

Though a woman's activity is restricted to the care of her household life, Chrysostom maintained that she plays a necessary role that would be beyond the ability of men to succeed in. She is truly meant to be a helper to man and one who should not be looked upon in a condescending way as being inferior to man because her ability to function in public activity does not measure up to his. She too has a necessary role to play in life.

For from the beginning, God did not entrust everything to men. Nor did He permit the pursuits in life to depend on all of these alone. For then a woman would truly be regarded as surely contemptible, if she were contributing nothing toward our life. God, therefore, knowing this, bestowed upon her a lower destiny [in life] and made this clear from the very beginning, when He said: "Let us make him a helper." So in order that the man might not become excessively proud in regard to her, because he was made first and the woman was formed on his account, He curbed man's pride by this remark, showing that the affairs of the cosmos belong no less to a woman than a man.[34]

A Woman's Role in Church

Regarding a woman's role and activity in church, Chrysostom strongly adhered to the prohibition attributed to Saint Paul that a woman

33. Ibid., 51:230–31. See also 52:709–10.
34. Ibid., 48:615.

is not to be permitted to teach in public. In responding to what seems to have been a pressing problem in his own day, Chrysostom angrily insists against those women of his day (doubtless from the upper classes) who were seemingly aspiring to become involved in priestly activities that:

The divine law has indeed excluded women from this kind of [priestly] ministry. Yet these women continue to press to attain this; but since they are wholly unable to prevail by themselves, they act through others. And they are acquiring so much power that they can either select or expel whatever priests they want. And matters are so upside down that this adage seems to apply: "Those ruled lead their rulers." And would that it were men [who do this] and not women who have not been permitted to teach. Why do I say "teach?" For the blessed Paul does not allow them to talk in church. Yet I have heard someone say that they enjoy so much freedom of speech that they even chide church administrators and assail them more bitterly than masters do their own servants.[35]

While Chrysostom is adamant that women cannot teach in church or act in those areas restricted to priests, he totally approves of their efforts in private to advise others, especially husbands who are pagan and/or wayward. He is quick too to acknowledge that many women are more knowledgeable and more virtuous than men. Chrysostom notes how Paul in his letter to the Romans (16:3) greets Priscilla before her husband, Aquila. He reasoned that Paul would not have singled out Priscilla in this conspicuous way unless she had indeed surpassed her husband in piety. He wrote:

It is also worthwhile to pay attention to why Paul mentioned Priscilla before her husband in his greeting to them. For he did not say "Greet Aquila and Priscilla" but "Greet Priscilla and Aquila." He did not do this without reason. For he knew that she was gifted with greater piety than her husband. That this is not a conjecture on my part can be known from [what is related in] Acts.[36]

In the next quotation, Chrysostom has conceded that a woman can be a better teacher than a man. While insisting that a woman should not teach publicly because of the way that Eve had advised Adam in Paradise, he admitted that:

It was not to forbid a beneficial private conversation that he said this, but [for those times] when it is the teacher's duty to speak publicly in the assembly and also when

35. Ibid., 48:646.
36. Ibid., 51:191–92.

a husband who is a believer and well instructed can teach her. But when she is wiser, he does not forbid her from teaching and improving him.[37]

Chrysostom also readily grants that women can equal, if not surpass, men in the willingness they manifest to undergo martyrdom and in the exemplary ways they practice the ascetical life. In the following passage from Chrysostom's homily on Saint Ignatius the Martyr, he affirms this clearly. What is significant here is his citation of Galatians 3:28 as a scriptural justification of how men and women can be equal to each other. He interpreted the passage to mean that women can equal men in the totally self-giving way that they strive to live the spiritual life.

In external contests, which involve corporeal labors, only men are accepted as suitable. But as the entire contest here is one of the soul, the race-course is open to each of the sexes, and the spectators sit [in judgment] of each. But it is not only men who are to strip [for this kind of contest], lest women raise a specious argument [for not doing this] by appealing to their weakly nature. Nor do women alone show themselves as brave, lest mankind be steeped in shame. But there are many from both sides who have been proclaimed by the herald and crowned as victors, so that from their labors you may learn that "in Christ Jesus there is not male nor female." For neither nature nor bodily weakness, nor age nor anything else can incapacitate those running in the race of piety.[38]

In his commentary on Galatians, Chrysostom expanded upon what he means by Saint Paul's statement that there exists neither male nor female but all are "one in Christ." He asserted that it refers to more than the fact that men and women both possess souls. They are able to attain a more intimate unity with Christ in which all can be said to possess the same unique form as that of Christ.

"For there is neither Jew nor Greek, neither slave nor free man, neither male nor female; for you are all one in Christ." Do you see that the soul is common? For by saying that we have become sons of God through faith, he is not content with this but seeks to find something more: the ability to submit more clearly to a closer unity to Christ. And when he says, "You have been clothed with him," he is not satisfied with this statement. But in interpreting it, he moves to a closer [explanation] of such a connection. He says that "You are all one in Christ," that is, you all have the same form, a unique being, that of Christ.[39]

37. Ibid., 60:669. See also 51:192.   38. Ibid., 50:587.
39. Ibid., 61:656. What is interesting in the above passage is that Paul has used the masculine article for "one" in the quotation cited from Galatians. Its antecedent is not

This "form of Christ" is not explained. Whether intended or not, it can be interpreted to mean that women take on the masculine nature of Christ.[40] Since Chrysostom did not address this issue. I think the passage is best understood in the corporate organic way that Paul regarded Christ as the head who sums up and recapitulates all the members of the church. As Adam was responsible for breaking the union between God and human beings, Christ is the one restoring all into a true union with his Father. The phrase to be "one with Christ" also seems to imply a union beyond that of natures. It may suggest the need to live out one's life in a manner similar to the way that Christ lived out his life. This latter view may explain why Chrysostom so strongly emphasized a life of asceticism in his writings and why he looked upon an ascetical, especially a virginal, life as the way for a woman to overcome her present state of subordination to men. This outlook is expressed in Chrysostom's unyielding opposition to the practice of allowing male and female celibates to live in the same house. He urges the women celibates to recall that "God has set you free from this burden [laid upon you in Genesis] that 'your recourse is to your husband, and he will rule over you.' This has been rescinded for you because of your virginal state. Why do you again bring on servitude?"[41]

The same idea is also expressed in the following quotation, but with a distinction. Chrysostom asserted that, while the activity of a woman is defined by nature, she can achieve equality with men in the area of ascetical practices. In fact, in individual cases she can even surpass men in the courageous way that she is faithful to a virtuous life and in providing for the needs of the church.

In external affairs, these sexes are defined as well by nature as by their activity and their way of handling [something]. I am speaking [here] about a man and a woman.

"form" which is feminine, nor "a unique being" which is neuter, but "we are all one in Christ." Literally, it means that we are all "one man" in Christ.

40. This is the interpretation that Lone Fatum takes in her detailed analysis of the contrast between 1 Corinthians 11:2–16 and Galatians 3:28 in her article "Image of God and Glory of Man: Women in the Pauline Congregations," *Image of God and Gender Models*, ed. Kari E. Børresen (Oslo: Solum Forlag, 1991), 56–137.

41. Chrysostom, PG 47:530. While Chrysostom is opposed to male and female celibates living in the same house, he affirms that sexual tensions will disappear in heaven, as affirmed in the following quotation (PG 47:514): "For when bodily passions are released and tyrannical desire extinguished, there will be nothing that hinders men and women from being there together and, after all evil suspicion are put aside, to maintain the life of the angels."

For it is customary for a woman to care for the home and the man to be engaged in civic and market matters. But in divine contests and those labors which are undertaken for the sake of the church, this does not hold. But it is possible that a woman endures in a more courageous way than a man in [undertaking] these virtuous contests and labors.[42]

The example *par excellence* of a woman surpassing men in her fidelity to Christ is that of his mother Mary. In the following passage, Chrysostom has argued that, as a virgin, Mary obtained divine favors from God for all women, at least in principle. In fact, she is said to have had a some kind of causative role to exercise in the drama of salvation, perhaps in the reversal of the "penalty" imposed on women because of Eve's fault in the Garden. He wrote:

A virgin, wood, and death became symbols of our defeat. For Eve was a virgin. For she did not yet have relations with her husband, seeing that she waited for his love. The tree was wood; and death the punishment incurred on account of Adam. See how the virgin, the wood, and death became symbols of our defeat. See now how these have also become causes for our victory: Mary for Eve, the wood of the cross for the tree of the knowledge of good and evil, and the death of the Lord for the death of Adam.[43]

As must be clear from what has been seen so far, Chrysostom's attitudes toward women are highly nuanced and extremely difficult to summarize. Perhaps it is best weighed by seeing how he actually lived out his views in practice. During his years as the Patriarch of Constantinople, he formed a close friendship with the rich and influential deaconess, Olympias.[44] The following excerpt from the letter he wrote her during his exile reveals with considerable poignancy that Chysostom manifested great tenderness and affection for her as well as deep pain at being physically separated from her presence. It indicates that Chrysostom was not the cold ascetic that he is usually portrayed as but a man who was capable of passionate feelings for a close friend who is a woman. His yearning for the opportunity to meet her once again face to face is both delicately and movingly stated:

Do you see how it is the greatest ordeal to be strong enough to bear gently the absence of a loved one? . . . For it is not sufficient for those who love [one another] to

---

42. Ibid., 52:709–10. 43. Ibid., 52:768.
44. For a summary of Olympias's life and clear translations of two of its primary sources, see Elizabeth A. Clark, *Jerome, Chrysostom and Friends*, 107–57.

be joined only in a spiritual way, nor do they find sufficient comfort from this. Rather they need a physical presence. And if this is not granted, a no small amount of their good cheer has been perversely cut away.[45]

Summary

In summary of this part, we find that Chrysostom has justified his view of a woman's subordinate role in the family, society, and the church upon a very literal and rational interpretation of what Genesis and Paul have stated. He would doubtless have thought that the cultural attitudes were substantiating this and that both were simply reflecting an order that God has established in nature. But he went beyond alleging the existence of an organic, hierarchical order to affirming how men and women are to interrelate with each other. Wives are to obey their husbands, but husbands have the more arduous task of displaying a caring love for their wives as free persons who can surpass their husband in private and ascetical ways. Chrysostom urges both to be faithful to the responsibilities with which God has entrusted each, so that together they might harmonize their individual talents and activities for the mutual benefit of both.

Theodore

Though most of Theodore's theological writings have been lost, there has survived a Latin translation of his commentaries on nine of the Pauline minor epistles[46] and fragments from his commentaries on Genesis and Corinthians.[47] These provide us with a limited, yet sufficient, view of his thought on the role of women, especially when taken in tandem with

45. Chrysostom, *Lettre VIII à Olympias*, 2. The Greek text with a French translation is found in SC 13:136–37. The present passage has been translated from the Greek text.

46. In his introduction (*Theodori Episcopi Mopsuesteni in Epistolas B. Pauli Commentarii*, ed. H. B. Swete, 2 vols. [Cambridge: Cambridge UP, 1880 and 1882], 1:xxxvii) Swete offers suasive arguments that this Latin translation of Theodore's lost original is indeed reliable. He does make one caution that: "There are, however, several serious drawbacks to this general fidelity. Our translator (a) constantly uses periphrases formed with 'videor, possum. . . .'"

47. These are found in PG 66:109–13 and in the editions by Sachau, Tonneau, F. Petit, and Swete. Although the manuscripts on which these texts depend are relatively late, they are considered authentic. All the translations of these works are my own.

his view of how image is applicable to the whole of human nature as the bond linking the spiritual and the material worlds. Because Theodore's view on image has already been spelled out in abundant detail, his statements on the role of women within the church now needs to be considered. By assigning image to human nature, Theodore would seem logically to be forced to assert that it also applies to women since, like men, they possess a human soul and body.

> Thus also when dwelling upon the word of God, he interpreted "He made man" in a general sense, namely that it refers in a generic way to man and woman together. For after he said in the narrative account that "God made man in the image of God," he added that "He made them male and female," thereby [indicating] that the generic nature is being designated . . . [He said this] not rashly but because they have come to be masculine and feminine at the same time. . . Here he had to affirm that "He made them male and female." For they had come to be in separate, not the same ways. He is thus affirming that, even if their coming-to-be differs in accordance with the will of their Maker, the two of them are nonetheless one entity and one nature, even though they are masculine and feminine.[48]

Theodore is relying here upon Genesis 5:1–2: "When God created man, he made him in the likeness of God; he created them male and female. When they were created, he blessed them and named them 'man.' "

Yet a brief, one-line fragment seems to contradict this. Theodore states in commenting on how a woman is the glory of man: "[Paul] spoke of a wife as [man's] glory. He did not add image because of its being unclear, since the glory looks to responding and image to principal power."[49] Granted its authenticity, the verse can be interpreted in different ways. It may signify an understanding of image similar to the view of Diodore, Chrysostom, and Theodoret that image refers only to men *qua* males as those being entrusted with God's power over material creation and over women. If so, it may indicate that Theodore at one time held the same opinion as they did.

However in light of other, more developed passages, it may also be interpreted to mean that women are not called God's image because there

---

48. Edward Sachau, ed., *Theodori Mopsuesteni Fragmenta Syriaca* (Leipzig: G. Engelmann, 1869), 115 in the Syriac and 16 in the Latin. The Syriac text was used as the basis for this translation. The same will be true for other citations taken from Sachau.

49. *Pauluskommentare aus der Griechischen Kirche*, 2d ed., ed. Karl Staab (Münster: Aschendorff, 1933), 188.

is not enough clarity on how this can be so since women are subordinate to men. If Christ fulfills humanity's roles as God's image in the sense he is the Lord of the universe, this would seem to militate against women being called the image, especially as Paul has explicitly referred to them as the glory of man. According to this interpretation, Theodore did regard women as God's image but did not know how to explain this in a satisfactory way and still reasonably cohere with a literal exegesis of what Paul has affirmed about men as God's image and women as the glory of man. This interpretation can be confirmed by a passing comment that Išo'dad of Merv, a proponent of Theodore's teaching, makes about women. It provides reasonable grounds for presuming that this latter interpretation was Theodore's opinion.

It is man whom Scripture calls the image. [It is] not that woman is not the image; but Scripture attributes it to man, since it is to him that the good things of nature have come, seeing that he was created first. As the Apostle says, "Man must not cover his head because he is the image etc." Yet just as man and woman are one body, woman is equally [to be] included with him under this term.[50]

The sense seems to be that since Eve has been formed from Adam's body, she shares his nature and therefore must also be considered an image of God. At any rate, Theodore did assert that a woman is subordinate to man. He affirmed this when commenting upon Paul's statement about women having to cover their heads in church.

Whenever a male should cover his head, he dishonors his head, as he happens to be the head as Christ is. Whenever a woman prays with her head uncovered, she dishonors her husband, [who is] her head, by secretly taking away his honor by aiming to be the principal "head." In many charters[51] there is a prohibition against [a woman] having something on her head—which expresses her subordination to her husband.[52]

Theodore interprets Paul, therefore, as seeing a man's covering of his head and a woman's uncovering of hers as symbolic acts. For a man, his

---

50. Išo'dad of Merv, *Commentaire d'Išo'Dad de Merv sur l'Ancien Testament*, I. Genèse, trans. C. Van den Eynde, CSCO 156/Syr. 75 (Louvain: Durbecq, 1955), 155.

51. It is not clear from the fragment what Theodore was referring to here by the word ἀντιγράφοις. It literally denotes the copies of an edition or a certified official document. It may be alluding to what were accepted versions of Paul's letter to the Corinthians or to civil statutes.

52. Staab, TP, 187.

uncovered head shows that he is God's representative and, for a woman, the covering of her head signifies that she is to be subordinate to man. To act otherwise brings dishonor. When a woman does so, Theodore felt, this is an attempt on her part to usurp her husband's role as her "head" and also is the reason why there exist prohibitions against women appearing with their heads uncovered.

In another isolated one-line fragment that appears to be from his commentary on this section, Theodore remarked: "He shows this very thing to be out of place from reverence and from nature and from the [divine] economy."[53] If "this very thing" refers to a woman's uncovering of her head in church, it shows that Theodore considered a woman's subordination to a man as being established in nature by God as part of his divine plan of salvation. Yet there are other passages where Theodore seems to have softened his viewpoint or perhaps even to have changed it. For example, Theodore does seem to qualify this subordination in an excerpt that has survived from his commentary on 1 Corinthians 11:3 where Paul asserts: "I want you to know that Christ is the head of every man [male] and a husband the head of his wife, and God the head of Christ." Here the term "head" signifies the source of life.

This [verse] wishes to say that we advance from Christ to God from whom he is and from man [male] to Christ. For it is from him [we have] a second existence according to whose resurrection we will also be all incorruptible on account of [our] sharing in the grace of the Spirit [dwelling] in him. For we who are liable to change hold Adam [to be] the head from whom we have taken [our] existence. But since we have become impassible we hold Christ as [our] head from whom we have [our] existence as impassible beings. Likewise, [the verse] states, [there is] also [a similar advance] from a wife to her husband since she has her existence from him.[54]

Theodore seems to be equating a woman's dependency upon a man to our human dependency upon Christ as the source for our future new immortal and impassible existence. Since Adam was created first and Eve has been derived from him, Theodore sees Scripture as revealing the path whereby women are able to come into contact with God by being in union with the heads of their earthly and their immortal existences. The stress is upon being united with the head, not with being in a state of inferiority and subjection. Just as Christ, who signifies the union between

53. Ibid., 187.
54. Ibid., 187.

Jesus' humanity and the Word, is not inferior to the Father, so too the same can be said about the kind of relationship existing between a husband and a wife.

Furthermore, in commenting on 1 Timothy 2:11–15 where Theodore believed Paul was instructing women to be silent in church and be submissive to their husbands, Theodore asserted that a woman should do so out of consideration for the common good.

Then to interpret more clearly his [previous] statement, he adds: "I do not, however, permit a woman to teach or to have authority over her husband. Rather [she is] to be silent." It is evident that he is adding what was then being done for the common good—namely that it was not appropriate for women to teach in church. Such a prescription, however, was necessary at that time as women were then thought to have been divinely inspired prophetesses, [some] of whom seemed to have exhibited a great deal of confidence [in their right] to speak out regarding the common good. So it was that those who ought to be looking out for what was useful for others within [their] households were of necessity being instructed not to abuse [their] spiritual gift by causing a disturbance at church. Paul, however, was not at all attempting to make a statement about their household conversation. Nor was he forbidding women either to win over or teach [their] godless husbands about piety or to win over to works of virtue those pious husbands engaging in unseemly activity. For this is what he means by "For how do you know, O wife, if you will save [your] husband?" He says these things, therefore, as I have [already] said, for what will enhance the common good. For in [this] part of the epistle, he was apparently speaking at length about what was most appropriate for the common good, by stressing profusely that it is unseemly in a general gathering for women "to teach, rather than be silent."[55]

What is interesting here is the reason that Theodore gives for why women should not teach in church: for it is not fitting for the good of the community. He believed that Paul was concerned about an abuse in his day. Some prophetesses were apparently disturbing the good order that ought to be maintained in church—which indicates that women were praying and speaking openly in church. He thought that these ought to be more concerned about caring for their homes and trying to win over their pagan spouses to the faith or wayward Christian husbands to a virtuous life. He easily could have appealed to a woman's nature as being inferior and thus the reason why women should be prohibited from speaking

55. Swete, 2:93–94.

publicly in a church. Instead he affirmed that it is not "fitting," "appropriate," and "seemly" to do so, as this would be against the good order of the community. He seems here to have regarded the Pauline stress upon the need to maintain the common good as a disciplinary command.

As Theodore continued in his commentary of 1 Timothy, he noted the reasons that Paul (or more likely a Pauline disciple) is said to have given for his prohibition against women teaching in church. Theodore mentions a "proof from nature" (namely that since Adam was created first, Eve and all her descendants must regard men as their superiors) but does not elaborate upon it. Rather, he proceeded to reject at length the position of those who interpreted Eve's fall as bringing condemnation upon all women. He writes:

Paul draws his first proof from nature, adding: "For Adam was formed first, then Eve;" and his second from what took place afterwards: "And Adam was not seduced; the woman, however, was, and she acted in collusion (with the serpent)." Yet, in fact, he was also seduced. But as he was discussing this in a general way when distinguishing what were the sins committed by women and those by men, [he stated] rightly that it was not he but she who had been seduced. For the woman was seen to have been the cause of his seduction, in that she was in no way able to level a charge against him. But lest he may seem to be leveling a charge against womankind—one, as it were, of no advantage for piety—that her way of acting [in Eden] and the judgment [passed on her there] seem to pertain to all womankind, [on the grounds that, since] "she was the one seduced, justice and reason demand that the same judgment be viewed [as affecting] all women," [so he added] "yet she will be saved through the procreation of children, provided she remain in faith and love and holiness with chastity." For when he said later, "through the procreation of children," he confirmed that "the source [of women, that is Eve] is not to be rejected," thus showing to women that [their] offspring are deemed worthy of salvation through those women who have a regard for piety and remain in faith and love by living a holy life with chastity and with constancy. For when he said, "she will be saved through the generation of children," he is speaking not of Eve, but of womankind. For when he discusses womankind, he reverts to the persons of Adam and Eve, proving thereby that it is not right that women also be judged, like men, [responsible] for an act with consequences for all. And lest what was said of persons also appear to be an accusation against womankind, he rightly shows that womankind has not been cast aside. Nor are those women who are willing to be solicitous for what is right to be judged unacceptable for piety.[56]

56. Ibid., 2:94–96.

While care must be taken not to put too much store upon the fact that Theodore mentioned Paul's argument from nature without elaborating it, it seems that he either took it for granted or did not know how to respond to it. He simply mentioned it and moved on to the next argument, preferring to rebut those (including perhaps Chrystostom) who asserted that Eve's sin had consequences for all women in the same way that Adam's did for all humanity. The point to be highlighted here is his underlying view of humanity as an organic whole where an act by its head affects the entire body. Since Theodore was convinced that it did not apply to Eve, this may be another reason why he was uncertain how women could be said to be God's image together with men, for the cosmic effects of Adam's failure to obey God's will as the head of the human race is to be matched in a reverse order by Christ's total obedience as the new head. Their roles as responsible heads belong to them alone.

After this, Theodore then turned to consider the roles that men and women ought to play in the church. He stated that when Paul is speaking in a general way, he is including both men and women under his remarks. But whenever he mentions each explicitly, he refers to the ministries and tasks that each is fitted to carry out for the benefit of the whole community.

After dividing the church according to sexes, Paul mentions men and women separately [in those passages] where he is seen to be speaking by way of a general exhortation about what can be properly applied to women. He is thus embracing in his general exhortation all those who belong to the church. For when he makes mention of men and women, it is evident that he includes all within this. But afterwards, he moves on to the ways that the ministries are divided; for, as I have said, he discusses everything in light of what is beneficial for one's community and mentions the ways these ministries are to be divided, showing what tasks this and that one are fitted to do, so that nothing should seem to be left out from what ought to be done for the benefit of the community.[57]

Theodore, therefore, believed that Paul prohibits women from teaching publicly in church because this is "what is beneficial for one's community" and is based upon what each is "fitted to do." He seems to be saying, therefore, that, since nature has fitted men and women for the performance of particular tasks, the common good requires them to recognize these and not contravene the good order of the community. Because the

57. Ibid., 2:96–97.

Pauline, ecclesial, and cultural attitudes in his days were exceedingly negative toward the involvement of women in public affairs, it is easy to see why Theodore would be reluctant to concede that women could perform any public ministry within the church other than being deaconesses. His own attitude and policy are well summed up in the following where he has maintained a woman's secondary role in the church should not be so emphasized that it detracts from the equality of honor that she enjoys with men.

From this letter, we learn above all something that is both ignored and neglected by many—namely that a similar honor has been shown by Paul to both men and women in particular writings, even though in the ministering to the ecclesial community he wanted women to be in second place so that there might be due respect and a proper order [maintained]. And in addition they are not to usurp those [specific] functions which men are seen to do. Indeed he looks upon women as being individually equal to their husbands as regards honor—which [view] he seems to have stated when writing to the Corinthians about this matter, [but he did it in such a way] that they would not be seen [as equal] in regard to ministry.[58] So he added at the end: "nevertheless neither [can] a man [do] without a woman nor a woman without a man, in the Lord." Indeed in this passage who could have been better cognizant of these things, when one considers that in the preface of his letter blessed Paul mentioned Philemon's wife together with him.[59]

To Be One with Christ

Fortunately Theodore's commentary on Paul's affirmation in Galatians that there is "neither male nor female; for you are all one in Christ Jesus" has survived. He discussed this passage in light of how all humans are one with their two heads, Adam because of their mortal nature and Christ who is the source of the immortal life that awaits them at their future resurrection.

Adam is the first principle for the present life of all. For we are all one human being by reason of our nature. For each one of us belongs to this common grouping, as its members. So too is Christ the first principle for the era of the future life. All of us who share with him in his resurrection and in the subsequent immortality become as one in relationship to him, with each one of us belonging to this common grouping in the same real way a member [does within the whole

58. Swete (2:265) believes that a line has been omitted and suggests these words.
59. Ibid., 2:264–65.

body]. Then neither male nor female are to be regarded [as such]; for it is not possible to marry or to be given in marriage. Neither is there a Jew nor a Greek . . . neither a slave nor a free person. For all diversity in matters [of this sort] have been abrogated.[60]

Theodore's primary concern here is not upon the effects that Christ has had upon human differences but on the real bonding that exists between Christ and those who are joined to him as members of a body to their head. Though humans differ in many ways, Christ has brought about a unity that makes their sexual, racial, and economic differences meaningless, for they are all equally one in Christ. We see, therefore, once again another example of how Christ's unitive role as God's image functions. By being organically united to him through one's common human nature and dedicated as he was to the fulfillment of God's will, those who are members of Christ are able to share likewise in the immortal and immutable life with which God has endowed him. What the head of a living body experiences is what all the members also enjoy. So in the future life, unity with Christ will be esteemed more than one's individual sexuality, race, and societal differences. These will lose their *raison d'être* and force in light of the organically bonded relationship that Christ has now established for all creation. What will count is being one with Christ and not being male or female.

Theodore's thought can also be glimpsed in a passage from a work by Cyrus of Edessa, a sixth-century East Syrian defender of Theodore who is reputed to have been among those who translated Theodore's works from Greek into Syriac.[61] In the following, he is seeking to explain why Christ appeared first to Mary Magdalen after his resurrection.

Accordingly, on this very account (of Mary Magdalen's ardent love) and, at the same time likewise, so that the female sex might have consolation, so that they despair not over their redemption nor imagine that it was on account of their want of righteousness that they are excluded from the dispensation of the priesthood, and *not on account of ecclesiastical ordinances and canons*, it was well that it should have been to one of them whose love surpassed that of the rest that Christ our Lord first

60. Ibid., 2:57. The translation has been made from the Greek text that Swete has provided. The word for "man" is the generic word that includes men and women.

61. For an account of Cyrus' life, see William F. Macomber's introduction in his translation of Cyrus' *Six Explanations of the Liturgical Feasts* CSCO 356 / Syr. 156 (Louvain: CSCO, 1974), xi.

made the revelation of himself, in order that he might thereby teach that in his salvific Gospel, "Man is not without woman, nor woman without man in our Lord."[62]

While it is difficult to argue from the fact Cyrus is silent about a woman's nature being the reason she cannot become a priest, it is interesting to note that Cyrus excludes women from priestly ministry on the basis of what ecclesiastical ordinances and canons state. For his silence may simply be due to the fact he presumes that the cultural view is so well known and accepted that it is not necessary to state it explicitly. Nonetheless the questions can be raised as to whether this is faithfully reflecting Theodore's own position on this question and whether it is disciplinary church law and not nature and God's will that are preventing women from being ordained priests. An affirmative response to the former would imply that changed circumstances within the culture and the church's attitudes might allow for a new, changed policy regarding a woman's active participation within the church. However, it appears more likely that Theodore saw the statements of Paul and church tradition as too explicit to allow for any change.

In summary, Theodore believed that women are to be considered individually equal to men, except in their ability to function in a public manner within the church. However, it is not clear why he thought women should not be actively involved in ecclesial ministries: namely whether it was due to their nature, or, granted the prevalent attitudes, to the need to maintain a suitable order in the church and in society, or simply to his literal, historical interpretations of the Genesis and Pauline statements about women. Whatever may be the underlying reason, he urged a woman to fulfill her functional role in the church out of a concern for the common good. One detects here the same or at the least a similar general outlook on how humans are part of an organic whole. The new wrinkle, as it were, is the emphasis being placed not on accepting a secondary, subordinate role in society but on living and working for the benefit of the whole. Theodore may not have been able to explain how women could function as God's image in such a view, but his understanding of how image refers to human nature is consistent with such an outlook. Women are images of God but must function as subordinate to men as the body does to its head because they form an organic one.

62. Macomber, *Liturgical Feasts*, 103. The italics are my own.

Theodoret

As pointed out in the treatment of Theodoret's views on image, he did not consider women to be formally or strictly God's image. Though Eve shares in Adam's power over the material universe, she has been relegated to a role below him in that he is the head of society. She is, as it were, an image of man's image. Yet there are many ways whereby she is equal to a man. Though she differs bodily from him, she shares a common rational nature and is required to observe the same laws and pursue the same virtues as he. Moreover she can comprehend as well as, if not better than, a man what ought to be done in a particular situation, and she too is required to participate in the eucharist.

For this reason, God did not fashion woman from another source, but took the matter needed for her generation from a man, lest she travel a way opposed to men on the assumption that she has another nature. This is why God also prescribed the same laws for both men and women. For they differ in their bodily shape, not as regards their soul. For she, as well as he, is rational and can comprehend and be conscious of what must be done, knowing equally what to flee and what to go to. She is at times better able than he to find what is more useful and to become a good counsellor. Therefore not only men but also women must be afforded access to the holy shrines. For the law does not permit men to participate in the divine mysteries while hindering women [from doing so]. Rather it encourages women to be initiated into and celebrate the mysteries in about the same way as men. Moreover, the rewards of virtue are also set forth before women as well as men, since [the need to] struggle for virtue is a common [duty imposed on both].[63]

Regarding how Theodoret sees the role of women in church, he appears to be closer to what was ascertained to be Chrysostom's position rather than Theodore's. In his commentary on Paul's words that "Christ is the head of every man; and man is the head of the women; and God the head of Christ" (1 Cor. 11:3), he attributes the prohibition against women being official teachers to a divine command, not to ecclesial pronouncements: "[Paul used these words with the intention of] subjecting women to men and to teach that it does not belong [to them] to lay claim to [be spokespersons of] the official teaching God commanded

63. Theodoret, *The Remedies For the Greek Maladies*, ed. and trans. P. Canivet, SC 57 (Paris: Cerf, 1958), 244–45. I have translated this passage from the Greek text.

from on high to be accomplished under the authority of man [*qua* male].[64]

In Theodoret's opinion, Paul's reason for prohibiting women, even those possessing the charism of prophecy, from preaching is found in the hierarchical subordination he saw existing between Christ and man, between man and woman, and between God and Christ as stated in "The head of every man is Christ, the head of a woman is her husband, and the head of Christ is God." In his commentary on 1 Timothy 2, Theodoret regarded the prohibition against women speaking in public as being rooted in her "natural" inferiority. He cited the same two reasons for her inferiority that were noted above in our treatment of Chrysostom, namely that Eve had been created after Adam and that her transgression led to the Fall. It is interesting to note the difference here with Theodore. While Theodore states the presence of an argument from nature and then proceeds at length to reject the position of those who assert that Eve's fall affected all women, Theodoret simply paraphrases what is said in the letter: "[the author of this letter] teaches this way of behaving rightly [on the part of women] to be from nature. Verse 13, 'For Adam was formed first, then Eve.' Afterwards also from the [original] faults. Verse 14, 'Adam was not deceived. It was rather Eve who was deceived and became the transgressor.'"[65]

Conclusion

This study of Chrysostom's, Theodore's, and Theodoret's views on whether women are God's image because of their subordinate position vis-à-vis men has uncovered a fairly close agreement of opinions and arguments concerning the status and role of women within the church of the fourth and fifth centuries. Since these opinions are often nuanced, it is not easy to provide a fully coherent summary of what they held, but let us now attempt to address and critique the main arguments that have been brought forth to justify their positions.

At the outset, it needs to be emphasized that the Antiochene Fathers we have examined are all insistent that women are equal to men on several scores. When women are said to be subordinate to men, they are not considered to be unequal or subject to any patriarchal despotism. The

---

64. Theodoret, PG 82:309.
65. Ibid., 82:801.

Antiochenes were not misogynists. For instance, they asserted that men and women are equal by reason of their same general human nature. They confessed too that men and women were both singled out and honored at creation and entrusted with the authority to rule over the material world as God's envoys. They are furthermore viewed as equally called to enter into a personal relationship with God, which forms the fundament whereby they are to respect each other as being a free person. They also have a similar obligation to grow in this relationship by living a virtuous life according to the same divine laws, with the assured promise that by so doing they can attain to the same destiny of an everlasting, immortal union with God.

Although a woman is equal to a man in all the ways just noted and fashioned by God to be his closest and most intimate helper in life, Diodore, Chrysostom, and Theodoret regarded her as subordinate, like the rest of creation, to men. They justified their patriarchical outlook by appealing to their literal, historical interpretation of three scriptural passages from Genesis that they believed Paul had commented upon: 1) that only men have been created in God's image; 2) that Eve's role in the Fall is the cause why all women need the governance of men; and 3) that a woman's inferior nature has been manifested in Eve's being fashioned from Adam's side. Since these reasons have been employed to exclude completely or at least to restrict women from certain kinds of work within both society and the church, each of these needs to be appraised in light of what has been Theodore's reactions to these passages.

First, Diodore, Chrysostom, and Theodoret maintained that only males are created in God's image, in the sense that men have been entrusted by God with power to rule over creation as His viceroys. Even though women are acclaimed to be the glory of men and images reflecting man's image of God, they too fall under the authority of men. They may share in man's power over the rest of creation, but in a secondary, subordinate, and limited way. On this particular point, Chrysostom was unrelenting, for he was convinced that there is a fundamental need in families and in all other units of society to have a single head that is entrusted with final responsibility for making decisions for the good of the family, community, and nation. If not, he believed that strife and chaos will eventually reign.

Theodore looked at image in a different light. Though there is a brief comment that image is connected with power, he appears to have understood image in a much broader way than simply and solely being the dominative power that God has entrusted to men to rule over the material universe. He viewed it ultimately in terms of the unitive, revelatory, and cultic functions that Christ's humanity plays in God's universal plan for salvation. Humans image God in the sense that they serve as symbols revealing who is the God who created the universe and how all other creatures can come to know, love, worship, and serve God. But what stands out in common with Chrysostom is his view of society as an organic whole—a view that he extended also to include the universe.

Though there is no extant passage from Theodore's writings that explicitly affirms that a woman has been constituted like man in God's image, there is some justification for arguing this point. Theodore asserts that the word "man" in Genesis 1:27 is to be interpreted in a broad, generic sense as "humankind," which at the very least implies a woman has also been created in God's image. Then, too, because he attributed "image" as pertaining to the whole human composite, that is embracing the body as well as the soul, he had to understand image as applicable also to women, for they too possess a human body and soul and are to be the recipients of the special, caring concern angels and other creatures are required by God to show to humans. Finally, it seems highly likely that Išoʿdad of Merv, who declares himself an inheritor of Theodore's teaching, is expressing Theodore's thought on image when he affirmed explicitly that the term "image" applies also to women.

This difference between Diodore, Chrysostom, and Theodoret on one side and Theodore on the other regarding the meaning of image and its applicability or non-applicability to women can highlight the whole issue of a woman's status within society. One could argue, as do Diodore, Chrysostom, and Theodoret, that "image" refers to the divine dominative power that men alone share with God. This interpretation based on Genesis 1:27, where Adam and Eve are commanded to multiply and exercise dominion over all living creatures, but further refined in light of Genesis 3 and 1 Corinthians 11:7. Diodore, Chrysostom, and Theodoret believed that one must conclude from these latter passages that only men have been created as God's image. While Theodore followed the same general hermeneutical principles as his Antiochene compatriots, he came to a different understanding of how human nature, as such, functions as God's image, indicating that the interpretation restricting "image" to males is open to be questioned and seriously challenged.

The second scriptural argument brought forth to prove that a woman is subordinate to men is the charge that Eve's seduction of Adam brought down a universal punishment upon her and all women. Chrysostom granted that a woman can overcome this state, thanks to the salvation achieved by Christ, by procreating children or—and this seems to be the better path—by dedicating herself to a life of asceticism, above all of virginity. Yet while granting that a person's commitment to God is what is most important in life and that some women have been able to achieve an equality with men in the practice of asceticism and even to surpass them, Chrysostom's sincere belief that women could not engage successfully—at least in his day—in public undertakings reveals that he regarded Eve's "punishment" as still having its effect in practice upon women.

For his part, Theodore clearly rejected the view that Eve's punishment has fallen upon all subsequent women. He distinguishes in the Genesis text between the times that Eve is being mentioned as an individual and those when women are being referred to in a general way. He contends that a careful literal examination of the text does not justify the opinion that Eve's fault impacted upon all women in a way comparable to the way that Adam's affected all generations. Theodore did not discuss the point, but it is evident that he did not agree with the position championed by Chrysostom and others that women are inferior to men by reason of Eve's role in the Fall. Such an argument should be set aside, as Theodore has done, with as little comment as possible, for it presents God in his treatment of women, if not as vindictive, at the very least as arbitrary. Even more so, it runs counter to the parallelism Paul established between the effects that Adam and Christ have had upon all humanity.

The most important of the arguments raised by the Antiochenes to justify a woman's subordination to man is that she is inferior by reason of the nature that she has received from God. Chrysostom believed that this is affirmed in Genesis 2 where Adam is said to have been created first and Eve to have been fashioned from him and for him. Chrysostom interpreted this passage as a clear indication that men do have a priority over women and that women are to assist them. Chrysostom contends that Adam was not immediately aware of a woman's status in relationship to his own, but it became known to him after the Fall, when God declared to Eve: "Your recourse shall be for your husband, and he shall be your master" (Gen. 3:16). This verse strikes a deep chord within men whereby many believe that it affirms what they sense in their hearts—that they are to hold the pre-eminent positions in their families, in society, and in the church.[66]

Chrysostom concluded from this and other passages that Eve's nature contains a weakness or flaw. Since he holds that a woman is endowed with the same nature as man and can at times outdistance him in the spiritual pursuit of virtue, it would seem that a woman is inferior to a man because of something inherent within her body and her psychological makeup that renders her less capable than a man for certain public activities. If one can surmise from the fact that Chrysostom delegated to women household tasks and to men warfare, commerce, and governmental policy-making, it seems apparent that his division of works is based upon the premise that a woman's natural qualities do not prepare her to succeed as well as men in these areas. She does not possess the necessary bodily strength and psychological stamina needed to withstand the stress involved in such works. Yet her qualities do enable her to function well in private, especially in the care of her own family and its household resources. However, when one considers that women, except for those reared in wealthy families, received little education, were married to older men, and conditioned by their family and community settings to be always subordinate to men, it is easy to understand why most women, as well as men, would passively accept as a universal principle that women are to defer to men and to avoid public life.

Before passing judgment on Chrysostom's restriction on what a woman can and cannot do, one has to keep in mind that Chrysostom was convinced that the division of labor that he imposed upon the sexes is actually a benefit for both society as a whole and men and women as individuals, for he understood his divisions as enabling men and women to perform what each is best suited to do. By having each do what the other could not do as well or at all, men and women would complement and supplement each other's deficiencies. Chrysostom likens this interrelationship to the dynamic way that the head and body work together for the productive and peaceful well-being of the whole person. One may re-

66. We find a contemporary expression and defense of why men have been and will continue to be the leaders in public affairs and the final authority at home, in Steven Goldberg's, "Can Women Beat Men at their own Game?" *National Review*, December 27, 1993. Goldberg argues that men are driven by deep psychophysiological forces to achieve dominance and that: "If being 'the man of the family' means nothing special, many men will find it not worth the cost" (35).

gard the head as superior to the body, but it cannot exist separately from the body. Nor can it on its own do certain functions, such as walking. When both work together, then what is good for one is good for both. But if the head should dismiss the body as worthless, then it is in point of fact passing a similar judgment on itself as part of the whole.

Chrysostom defined the basic responsibilities of a woman and a man toward each other as the dynamic interplay between obedience and love. He maintained that a woman must take on a dutiful attitude toward her husband, but he insisted that man has been burdened with the more onerous task: he is required to love his wife in the way that Christ loves his church. This kind of love demands at the very least that a man has to treat his wife caringly with due respect as a free person. Besides helping her attain her true well-being and happiness, he must engender the attitude that enables his wife to sense that what belongs to him is also fully hers. Whatever belongs to one should not be referred to as "mine" or "yours" but only as "ours." One should judge not what each as an individual contributes but what they share together as an organic whole where the two of them are in communion with one another as one flesh.

As regards Theodore's outlook on the nature of women, there are not sufficiently numerous texts available to pass judgment. He has remarked that 1 Timothy 2:13 mentions as one of the reasons why a woman is by nature inferior to man that Eve was fashioned after Adam, but he does not state whether or not he is in agreement with this. He proceeds immediately to the second proof presented in the passage. One may be able to infer Theodore's reason for passing over the first argument by pondering the reply that he gives as to why women should keep silent in church. They are required to do so for "the common good." Whether this is the only reason why a woman ought to be quiet can be questioned. So while it is very difficult to judge an argument from silence, it does provide some grounds for speculating as to what Theodore meant when he interpreted what he took to be Paul's emphasis upon the common good. When one considers the prevailing negative cultural and ecclesial attitudes regarding women at Antioch in Late Antiquity, it is easy to see why Theodore would be opposed to women speaking out in church. It would be extremely upsetting to all those conditioned over centuries to a woman's subordinate role within both society and the church.

If Chrysostom and Theodore were willing to admit that women can grow into a complete equality with men over a period of time,[67] we would expect to find some reference to this in their exegeses of Galatians 3:28's assertion that Jesus has introduced equality into the sexual, ethnic, and socio-economic dimensions of life. However, instead of addressing this question, Chrysostom and Theodore center their remarks on the need that all have to be one with Christ. To be sure, such a spiritual union renders the distinctions between Jew and Gentile, slave and free person, male and female irrelevant. For if the one supreme standard for judging what counts in life is being one with Christ, then no group can claim that they enjoy any real preference or superiority over others because of their sex, race, or wealth. Nor do any of these prevent a person from entering into a relationship with Christ. It is possible, too, that Theodore may be understanding this oneness with Christ as expressing the way that Christ will recapitulate all beings—spiritual and material as well as male and females—within himself.

In other words, Chrysostom and Theodore interpret Galatians 3:28 as heralding the abolition of religious inequality and those kinds of "secondary" differences between individuals that can both threaten and undermine relationships. This implies that a person's race, class standing, and sex have no real bearing in themselves as to whether a person will be saved. Beyond this, Chrysostom and Theodore's responses suggest that they look upon such differences as still present but no longer causing separation. This highlights a critical point, namely that they do not consider there will ever be a total equality in either this or the next life. Individuals

67. This may have been true also for Paul. McKenzie in his entry on "Women" in his *Dictionary of the Bible* (937) believes that Paul was concerned about the growing breakdown in sexual morality in the society of his day. To counter this, Paul sought to strengthen the traditionally solid customs of Jewish family life that respected and protected women, even though they were regarded as inferior and subordinate to men. He accepted the Genesis account that attributed a woman's subjection to man as indeed a penalty for Eve's sin in the Garden. McKenzie suggests that perhaps this outlook of Paul can be interpreted as meaning that, while Christ has removed this subordination in principle, it will require time before women can regain the position which was originally theirs by nature but then lost by Eve's sin. By insisting upon the subjection of women, Paul would, therefore, seem to be saying that this was not yet the moment for women to claim their equality with men. For the cultural attitudes then prevalent regarding the status and role of women needed to be kept in force. This seems to be the position of the Antiochenes.

will always be unique and ought therefore to be judged in light of their own particular talents and not excluded arbitrarily because of racial, ethnic, socio-economic, and sexual stereotyping—such as Chrysostom appears to have fallen into when he forbade women from involvement in any and all kinds of public activity.

Contemporary Ramifications

Since the Antiochene Fathers were negative toward any public ecclesial involvement by women and, with the possible exception of Theodore, were opposed to their being regarded as God's image, it is difficult to find contemporary value in their opinions. Three points, however, merit some consideration. First, their arguments for justifying women's exclusion from all active roles in church ministry except for that of deaconesses lay bare how a strictly literal interpretation of Genesis and Pauline passages can lead one to interpret the human and cultural elements in Scripture as divine. While admitting that women are equal and at times superior to men in other areas, they were incapable of seeing how one could interpret in any other way those scriptural passages asserting that women are to be subordinate to their husbands and are not to speak in church or teach in public. They believed that nature itself and cultural attitudes about the role of women provided further proof that such a view was correct. For them, these arguments were simply too strong to think otherwise.

Secondly, it is exceedingly difficult for those immersed in contemporary personalistic values to conceive how such a learned and holy man as Chrysostom could reach the conclusion that no woman was fit for any public activity. While one must be careful to judge Chrysostom in his own historical and cultural setting, our present age is sensitive to how every person has both the right and duty to develop and exercise his or her God-given talents within society. To bar an individual solely because of his or her sex or race on the premise that there exists some sort of a lack or weakness in his or her nature is not merely to restrict God's freedom to bestow His gifts as He intends but to arbitrarily assume the role of God. As the parables of the Owner of the Vineyard and the Prodigal Son reveal so forcefully, God is free to bestow His generosity whenever and upon whomever He wants.

Thirdly, the proverbial statement that one is usually right in what one asserts in a positive way and wrong in what one denies is applicable here.

While Chrysostom is wrong in excluding women from all public tasks, there is some truth in what he teaches about the ways that male and female talents must complement one another for the benefit of both. To replace complementarity with the goal of achieving a total equality with men runs the risk of ending up in a masculinization of women and a unisex view of the world. Granted Chrysostom's basic premise regarding the need for a complementarity between the sexes, the issue then becomes what standard is to be used to judge which sex is superior. To assert that Eve is inferior to Adam because she has originated from him is a logical leap. To derive one's origin from another does not signify by itself that one is inferior or subordinate to another, for otherwise this would mean that all males from the time of Adam ought to be considered to be subservient to females because they proceed from their mothers' wombs. So too Christians recognize that in the Trinity the Word and the Holy Spirit are derived from the Father as their source but are essentially equal to Him in all regards. Such distinctions ought to make one hesitant to equate subordination to inferiority, for one can be in a lower sub-order than another but still be equal and perhaps superior to that other.

Both Chrysostom and Theodore recognized that the theological criterion for judging the value of a human being ultimately rests not on the fact that one is subordinate to another but on whether the person is one with Christ. While admitting that men and women are equal in many regards, they felt that their natures prepared them for excelling the other in certain external tasks and in the process complementing one another. These tasks, however, assigned by nature and thus by God, are not the criteria for determining whether one is actually one with Christ. They are simply the roles with which each sex has been entrusted. While it is undeniable that, generally speaking, men and women are each able to do certain tasks better than the other, this became a problem when the Antiochenes turned it into a rigid, universal principle, supposedly dictated by God and society, that allowed for no exceptions.

Finally, both Chrysostom and Theodore have judged the roles of men and women in the context of an organic body. Just as each of the bodily members has its own specific function to play for the benefit of the whole body, the same can be said about the ways that men and women are to labor for the common good. While this organic perspective has Stoic undertones, the Antiochenes doubtless derived it from Paul's comments about the members of Christ's body having different functions to play within the church. They would also be indebted to Paul's criterion that love is what determines the value of one's labors, not the fact that one is an able administrator or an authentic prophetess. But what is significant for the present study is how Chrysostom and Theodore's appeal to an organic union indicates that this was the outlook, if not at Antioch at the time, at the School of Antioch. It helps to clarify, too, why Theodore would choose to relate image to the way humans were believed to be the bond of the universe.

Perhaps the answer to the uncertainty about Theodore's opinion as to whether women have been created like men in God's image can be found in the following response. He would grant that women are God's image because they share the same general human nature that bonds the spiritual and the material worlds to human beings, to one another, and to God. But in this organically unified world, women—while equal to men in general—are subordinate to them as the body is to its head and must function in the complementary ways that the head and body do in life. It is a view that Ephesians 4:15–16 sums up in a succinct, eloquent way.

If we live by the truth and in love, we shall grow in all ways into Christ, who is the head by whom the whole body is fitted and joined together, every joint adding its own strength, for each part to work according to its function. So the body grows until it has built itself up in love.

7

CONCLUSION

TRYING TO DETERMINE the Antiochene opinions on the image of God has been like piecing together a pictorial puzzle whose plain, quaint box simply describes the panoramic scene as an ancient Roman city and notes that some of its parts are missing. The present approach started, as most would likely do, by determining the edges of the framework. We first moved to establish what the Antiochenes' training as monks had instilled within them—namely, a deep passionate love for and a mastery of the Scriptures. Together with the traditional teaching that was sanctioned by the Councils of Nicea and Constantinople I, the Scriptures were the source for both their knowledge of their faith and the meaning of life. In order to understand how they interpreted Scripture, we began by filling in the background of our picture by delving into their exegetical method, for this exercised, without doubt, the primary influence upon how all the Antiochenes determined their understanding not merely of image but of human nature, Christ, the divine economy, and women's role in the church. Even when the Antiochene Fathers split into two groups in their explanations of the *imago Dei*, each was convinced that his position was justified by a close literal interpretation of the Scriptures. Despite some major differences on specifics, they regarded their exegetical method with its hermeneutical principles as the assured way to determine what God was actually revealing about a particular topic.

The Antiochenes resolved the knotty issue of how to interpret the Scriptures in a way similar to that of the Palestinian rabbis. Whether and how much Jewish hermeneutical principles had an impact upon the second and third century Antiochene commentators is not clear, but by the fourth century, the Antiochenes were firmly dedicated to a literal exegesis as the way to determine the meaning of a Scripture passage. Like the conservative rabbis in Palestine, they unequivocally rejected the allegorical method proposed by Philo and then later approved by Origen, who considered it one method for interpreting the spiritual meaning concealed in obscure or inappropriate scriptural texts. The Antiochenes did concede one could come to a deeper or more lofty meaning from Scripture through a process they called *theoria*. They admitted this because Scripture includes prophecies that were later proven to be true, such as the Jewish prophecies concerning the restoration of Israel, as well as types whose fulfillments have been recognized as being intended by God, such as Paul's explanation of how Sarah and Hagar are in fact types of the Christian and Jewish covenants.

Diodore, Chrysostom, and Theodore sharply distinguished a type from an allegory. They insisted in their writings that an antitype or archetype must be objectively related to what is being affirmed in its type. They regarded the meaning proposed in an allegorical interpretation as subjective with no inherent connection with what a sacred writer was saying, such as those asserting that the life of Moses can be likened to growth in the spiritual life. Theodore also added another criterion: the true meaning of a type had to be substantiated by a New Testament author. Theodoret broke with the other Antiochenes regarding the inadmissibility of an allegorical interpretation. While Theodore rejected all allegories and admitted very few types, Theodoret was more willing to accept the legitimacy of an allegory, provided it was appropriate in its context. What emerges, however, above all from the Antiochene arguments against an allegorical interpretation is how strictly they sought to adhere to what was being affirmed in a scriptural text and to what could reasonably be deduced from this in light of its association with other passages in Scripture.

General Views of Image

The next remaining task in assembling our picture was to fill in the center's immediate foreground. Time was spent looking at how several contemporary scripture exegetes and leading patristic Fathers have interpreted the meaning of "image." Their explanations fell into two general camps regarding "image." The first maintained it had to be a spiritual reality, for since God is a pure Spirit, they argued that creatures can image Him only in a spiritual way. Philo first set the pattern for this approach and later Plotinus expanded upon it when he maintained the existence of two creations for human beings. In the first, they were spiritual intellects who were able to contemplate the Word in his role as the image of the One. Then after some sort of a "fall," they were placed within a body that restricted their contemplative ability. Origen and those following him appropriated this outlook by looking upon image as a spiritual character or potency residing in the *nous* (or the highest rational part of the soul) that enabled a person to enter into a union with God and to grow in this, while preserving at the same time one's own personal identity.

The second group of Scripture scholars insisted that the author or priestly redactor of Genesis was applying the term "image" to the whole human being. They point out that the ancient Hebrews did not conceive of a human being as a composite of a separate soul and body but as a psychosomatic unity. To speak of the soul was also to imply the presence of its body. As regards the intended meaning of the term "image," most contemporary scripture scholars believe that it refers to the power and dominion that God has given human beings over the created material universe. Because human beings were singled out by God at the end of the sixth day of creation, they are the "embodiment," as it were, of God and his official representative within the cosmos.

Scripture scholars have differed, too, over whether the title "image of God" was meant solely to denote a state affirming some relationship to God or whether it was also associated in some way with a dynamic quality enabling a person to grow in one's image of God (that is, into holiness), for some made a distinction between the terms "image" and "likeness." While it appears that the author of Genesis understood these as parallel synonyms for each other, a number of Fathers have identified "image" with the rational soul's natural state in relation to God and "likeness" with one's state of holiness or one's actual spiritual relationship to God. Such a distinction helped to develop an understanding of a divinizing or sanctifying kind of grace. It also presented those who espoused it with a vexing question, if not a problem: how does such an emphasis upon the spiritual role of the rational soul affect the role—if any—that

Christians believe the human body is called to play in the economy of salvation. From the surviving comments found among the Antiochenes as to how humans are "like" God, they appear to have understood "image" and "likeness" as expressing how humans can be said to be able to act in various ways analogous to God's creative activity and how the human mind, thought, and spirit can be likened to the Persons within the Trinity.

The Antiochene Understanding of Image

The Antiochenes fall within the camp of those who include the body as essential within the notion of "image." In fact, they strongly opposed the opinion of those who maintained that "image" was simply a spiritual reality, not the least reason being that it was reached through allegory. The Antiochenes argued that, if image referred only to what is spiritual, then the angels ought also be construed as images. Scripture, however, says nothing at all about this. It explicitly declared that it was "man" who has been created in God's image and likeness. From this they concluded, in light of their literal exegetical principles, that the author of Genesis had conceived of "image" as applying to man. They differed over whether it was said of man as male or in a generic sense to the whole human person. Such a holistic outlook toward image is, of course, the way human nature was portrayed throughout the Hebrew Bible. To separate the soul and body from one another was a Greek conception foreign to the Semitic mentality.

Diodore, Chrysostom, and Theodoret understood "image" as being the dominative power that Adam *qua* male received to rule in God's place over the material universe. They arrived at this because the first chapter of Genesis explicitly affirms that it was conferred upon Adam. They then connected this statement with the following verse in which God commanded Adam to exercise rule over the material world. They took this to be the literal meaning of the text. While their position on why women are excluded from a full participation in image will be discussed below, it suffices here to observe only that they sought to justify their position as being corroborated by the third chapter of Genesis and by comments attributed to Saint Paul that women are subordinated to men. For them, God appointed only men *qua* males to act as His supreme viceroys on earth.

Theodore and, insofar as one can judge from limited evidence, Nestorius looked upon image in a different way. They maintained that it pertained to the whole human composite of soul and body together, but not in the sense that the other Antiochenes thought of it as solely the power that God had entrusted to Adam to be his representative on earth. By combining image with the role that humans exercise as the bond uniting the spiritual and the material worlds within the universe, Theodore had a much broader notion of how image should be specifically applied to human beings. He perceived that image signified not only how humans have been given a power to rule but how they also play a revelatory, cultic, and unitive function within the cosmos similar to what Christ exercises as God's primary image. These purposes are only discerned when one reflects on Christ's role as the true, perfect, archetypical image of God. Because Christ's human nature is united to the Word, he is the one who manifests in a visible way who God is, what His will is and how all creation not only can be united in communion with God but can worship Him. This is the same approach that Paul took by seeking the meaning of image not from the Genesis context but from Christ's role as the perfect image of God.

Both Antiochene understandings of image are actually close to one another. This can be seen by relating their approaches to the "elements" in a faith symbol (understood in the sense Paul Tillich has explained it).[1] For the Antiochenes, "image" does not denote any kind of a photographic likeness or similarity with God. Nor can it connote a sharing in the same or a similar nature with God's because God's transcendent nature precludes both possibilities. Rather they looked upon Adam as being God's "image" in the sense that he serves in creation as a concrete, living, and visible symbol that points to the existence of God and moreover that he shares in His power. When other creatures show their care for human needs, they are also giving the glory due to God as the all-powerful Creator of the entire universe. Such a view would have been easily and readily acceptable in Antioch because of the inhabitants' experience during the tax rebellion of 387. When the emperor Theodosius learned that his images had been shattered, he construed this as a personal affront as well as a political attack against his tax policy, for his imperial image embodied his own actual presence within the city—a viewpoint reflected in the earliest literature and in Roman emperor worship.

Similar to how scripture scholars interpret the meaning of image in

---

1. Paul Tillich, *Dynamic of Faith* (New York: Harper, 1957), 41–54.

Genesis, this symbolic outlook may actually be what the author or redactor of Genesis had in mind when he declared that God had created Adam in His image. He sought to highlight how not merely the emperor or king but every human being was God's "image" and ought to be treated respectfully as a sacred representative of God. If this is the original meaning of the Genesis text on image, it coincides with Diodore, Chrysostom, and Theodoret's opinion of "image" as God's viceroy and with Theodore's comparison of God's "image" with that of an emperor situated in the center of a city. Theodore further utilized the similarity to bring out why humans must be reverenced and cared for by the angels and the rest of creation, for they are sacred beings who exist in a unique relationship to God because of the role that Christ was destined to play in salvation.

Theodore's Understanding of Image's Revelatory Function

Theodore's view of image is more illuminating and evocative in content than that of Diodore, Chrysostom, and Theodoret, for it can explain why God appointed Adam as His plenipotentiary on earth. By being a type of Christ who is God's primary and perfect image, Adam foreshadows the universal power belonging to Christ because of his union with the Word. By being one with the Word, Christ's humanity shares in the Word's Sonship and power as the Lord of the universe. Moreover, his humanity is the perfect instrument for wielding God's power because his nature and will are so perfectly joined to the Word's. When Adam is said to be God's image with plenipotentiary powers, this ought to be understood in the sense that he possessed power by extrinsic denomination. The power God bestowed on him at creation reveals that he is both the symbol and the true type anticipating the plenitude of power conferred on Christ. Adam is the one who anticipates Christ's role as the possessor of God's universal power and the "medium" through whom His power is to be dispensed.

Theodore, therefore, goes beyond what Diodore, Chrysostom, and Theodoret asserted about image. He explicitly affirms other aspects of a symbol besides that of power. He may have reasoned this by reflecting on how Christ's visible humanity, because of its union to the Word, is revealing who God is and what is His plan for universal salvation. Because His transcendent nature cannot be grasped, God needed a visible being in order to manifest Himself to creation. It is analogous to the way that a

238

spiritual love requires a body, so it can reveal its presence in symbolic ways. Theodore may also have come to this realization by connecting the revelatory function of image with the fundamental premise of Antiochene exegesis that one must seek out what God is revealing within a text through a careful examination of what is its literal or actual meaning. To sever the spiritual meaning from what the "body" of the text affirms, as the allegorists do, would in fact be equivalent in Theodore's mind to those denying the need that the soul has for its body and the Word has for the "assumed man" so as to be able to reveal themselves in a visible manner. For the "body" is in all these cases the way that God has chosen to reveal Himself to the rest of creation.

From the few isolated comments that Nestorius has made about image, he appears also to have understood image as possessing a similar revelatory function. Nestorius looked upon Christ's human activity as indicative of how a person can reach God through a voluntary commitment of oneself to His will. Theodore, however, had expanded upon this by including within the idea of "image" a cultic function. Christ serves as a means for all created beings to give glory and worship to God, for he reveals to them in a visible way where and how these are to be bestowed. Connected with this too is Theodore's view of how the unitive role that Adam's human nature plays in the universe is a foreshadowing of Christ as the Lord of the universe. It is Christ who will later recapitulate in his own being all human beings, the angelic powers, and the animate and the inanimate material worlds. He is, in Paul's word, the *plērōma* who will restore all at the end of time to God his Father and the one in whom all sexual, racial, and economic differences are subsumed and abrogated.

Theodore's Sources

Theodore's understanding of the unitive function image plays as the bond linking together all creation raises a question, first of all, as to where he has derived this idea. It appears at first glance to have been derived from both the Stoic and the Neo-Pythagorean world-views of the universe as a living organic "body" wherein all beings, rational and irrational, including God, are joined in a "sympathetic" harmony with each other. When this is present, there is a resulting growth for the individual, the state, and the universe. But whenever there is a disharmony, every being suffers a loss that affects all individually and communally. While Theodore most probably concluded his unitive function of image because of what Paul declared to be the effects that both Adam's sin and Christ's redemptive death have had on creation, and perhaps also because of Paul's teaching about the body of Christ,[2] it is still possible that Theodore may have been influenced, as certainly Nemesius was, by the Stoic and Neo-Pythagorean world-views present in the cultural outlook of his own day.

To sharpen even more our understanding of Theodore's outlook on Christ's unitive role as image, it was set against the backdrop of his thought regarding the union of the natures in Christ. For Christ's role as the "image" who reveals God, unites all creation to its Creator and can receive worship is founded on his indissoluble union with the Word. The reason Theodore had to turn to his notions of "image" was likely due to his view about God's transcendence, for he believed that God's nature is so totally invisible to all created beings that even His existence cannot be known. Thus, a concrete image that manifests Him and His will is required. God chose to create Christ as His "image" par excellence and human beings as types foreshadowing the time when God would later reveal Himself in, through, and with Christ's visible humanity.

To understand how Christ fulfills his unitive function as the true "image of God," our attention was next directed to how Theodore, Nestorius, and Theodoret understood the kind of union that exists between Christ's human and divine natures. Because the issues are complex, the question was approached in three stages. We first considered what was most likely the metaphysical outlook present at Antioch in the late fourth and early fifth centuries by analyses of the creedal statements of Nicea and Constantinople I and Nemesius's work *On Human Nature*. Through a comparison with basic Antiochene viewpoints it was concluded that the Antiochenes likely drew their metaphysical terms and ideas from Scripture and from the cultural outlook of the day. What seems fairly clear is that the Antiochenes did not try, as some Alexandrians did, to ferret out deeper theological truths by seeking to apply Greek philosophical insights, especially as regards personal divinization. They did, however, employ Greek thought and terms whenever doing so was useful for articulating positions that they had already first attained from their literal, rational exegesis of Scripture. So except for Nestorius and Theodoret, who were drawn into metaphysical arguments about the kind of union existing

---

2. This is not meant to exclude the possibility of Stoic influences upon Paul.

between the two natures in Christ, the three earlier Antiochenes showed slight interest in using philosophical insights as a tool for further deeper theological reflection. Interpreting Scripture in a literal, historical, and rationally critical way was their primary method for proceeding.

Fundamental Principles

To assess accurately the Antiochene christological thought, it is important to keep in mind three fundamental principles that have predetermined to what the Antiochene Fathers could readily assent and not assent. First, they had a viewpoint on God's transcendence that precluded the acceptance of any substantial union between God and a creature, including Christ's humanity. They reasoned: if such a union did happen, it would also mean that the infinite, eternal Word would be limited to that finite space where He was at that moment said to be present. Such a point of view—which may be mainly due to a Semitic understanding of God's unique nature rather than to any philosophical school—ruled out the possibility that the natures in Christ could be united in a "hypostatic" kind of union. They were convinced that those who spoke of Christ as one ὑπόστασις had changed his two natures into one φύσις. It rendered, too, every affirmation about human divinization totally incomprehensible. For Theodore, to be united with God and to share His everlasting life meant to be transformed from a mortal to an immortal state either in potency or actuality.

The second principle is a cultural world-view that may have been influenced by the Stoic and Neoplatonic understanding of the cosmos as a living organic body whose members are sympathetically linked to each other. This cosmological view would have appealed to the Antiochenes because it coincided with the Pauline outlooks on the body of Christ, the cosmic damage caused by Adam's sin and its restoration by Christ's redemption, and the role of Christ as the one who will recapitulate the whole universe. While the source of Theodore's association of *imago Dei* with humans as the bond of the universe may be debated, the linking of the two was at the heart of Theodore's outlook on image. It may be detected too as present in Chrysostom's view concerning the subordinate role that women should play in the organic unity of a family. They both may have welcomed the Stoic teaching about a universal organic unity as an instance of how the "science" of their own time corroborated the natural order God has proclaimed to be a fact through Scripture.

The third principle concerns who or what is the subject of an action: the person or one's nature. Because of their understanding of a φύσις as a concrete existing reality, the Antiochenes looked upon human nature as the subject responsible for personal actions. From where they derived this existentialist, rather than essentialist, view of nature is clouded in obscurity. It may reflect the cultural viewpoint at that time at Antioch, or be due to their oral Semitic background, or flowed as a consequence of their literal reading of the Gospels where Jesus is portrayed as acting in human ways and would thus fit in well with their efforts to defend Christ's human nature against suggestions that Christ's human actions were simply those of the Word. Theodore, however, did distinguish here between the source of Christ's human activity and the agent responsible for an action. He willingly granted that the Word provided the energy Christ's assumed human nature needed to act. But the responsibility for Christ's human actions resided solely in his humanity's free will whereby he chose to be totally faithful to whatever God has manifested as His will.

One other point connected with the last principle needs to be mentioned. It was something discussed when Nemesius and Narsai were used to clarify Theodore's oblique, passing reference to the union of natures in Christ as analogous to the soul-body union. Nestorius rejected this outright on the grounds that it implied a substantial union between Christ's natures—a principle with which Theodore totally agreed. It was concluded that Theodore must not have been linking the *kind* of union existing between the soul and body with that between the divine and human natures in Christ. Rather he was noting how a spiritual entity can provide the energy source for its bodily co-partner without its spiritual nature being altered in any way. Such an interpretation coincides with the point that Theodore is making when he compared the union of Christ's natures to the ways that God is said to be present in the Jewish Temple and a husband and wife to be in one flesh. In other words, the sole point being stressed there was how a spiritual and a corporeal nature can exist together and function with one another within a true union where both can be said to be one, yet with each retaining its own natural integrity.

Theodore's Understanding of the Union

To understand Theodore's teaching on how the natures in Christ are united and thus his view on how Christ as image unites the rest of creation to God, it was necessary to establish the parameters of Theodore's christological thought. This was accomplished by noting what he had repudiated and thus obtaining in a converse way what he positively held. Like the other Antiochenes, he utterly opposed the positions held by Paul of Samosata, the Arians, and Apollinaris. By his outright condemnation of Paul, he demonstrated that He regarded Christ as being more than merely human. His unbending opposition to the Arians confirms that he believed Christ as well as the Word to be truly divine. And his rejection of Apollinaris further confirms his unshakeable belief in Christ's integral humanity. In brief, he believed that Christ (a term used to affirm the union between the divine and the human natures) is a complete human being who is also in some unique sense truly divine.

When Theodore came to explain how he conceived of the union between Christ's natures, he excluded both a substantial and an accidental union. He sought a middle (or higher?) ground which he affirmed to be "a union of good pleasure in one πρόσωπον." He decribed this as a unique, graced union that began at the moment Jesus was conceived and continued throughout his mortal life as a union of his will in perfect unison with the Word's. This union of natures and wills was so complete and permanent that Christ's humanity could be called, together with the Word, God's Son in name, honor, and power. While this description of the union does verbally support his belief in Christ as truly human and divine, it has appeared to many as making Jesus and the Word into two separate individuals united in a graced moral union. It has also perplexed philosophers and theologians as to what sort of metaphysical union Theodore was actually proposing that was neither a substantial nor an accidental union.

If the interpretation taken here is correct, Theodore was not trying to offer a metaphysical explanation of the union of natures in Christ but employing "a prosopic union of good pleasure" as a phrase meant to sum up in a descriptive way how the evangelists and Saint Paul portrayed Christ as being overshadowed by the Spirit at his conception and as acting throughout his life in both human and divine ways. While there is certainly a metaphysical basis to this, Theodore appears to have wanted to express the union of the natures in Christ in this scriptural way, so as to maintain the integrity of Christ's human nature in its union with the Word. Since he had to exclude a hypostatic (in the sense of a "substantial") union because of his outlook about divine transcendence, while preserving, as he knew he must, a unity of natures that was personal, he turned to a way that characterizes how the Word and Christ's assumed humanity could act together. If he had then merely stated he was relying on the scriptural terms of "inhabitation," "good pleasure," and "image" to safeguard the integrity and freedom of both natures, it would be evident that he was prescinding from a metaphysical explanation of this union. This is, in fact, what Chrysostom did by leaving it to God. If Theodore had asserted that he was employing πρόσωπον in the sense that the ancient Hebrews and Paul had understood a "person," he could have escaped having others pushing his ambiguous expression to its logical conclusion. His vagueness, however, allowed both those who affirm and those who deny his orthodoxy ample reasons to justify their opinions on the basis of what he wrote.

When Nestorius was pressed afterwards by Cyril to explain how Theodore's and his understanding of πρόσωπον could be harmonized with creedal statements about the Word becoming man, suffering and dying on the cross and about traditional belief about Mary's title as "Mother of God," Nestorius fell into a metaphysical maze that had no exit. Because of the twin Antiochene premises that the Word cannot be substantially united with Jesus' assumed nature and that their union was a wholly graced and unique one that fell between a substantial and accidental unity, he was caught in a no-man's land. While πρόσωπον can be justified as a functional term describing how Christ appeared and acted in the Gospels with some vague assertion of a true underlying unity between a divine and an assumed human nature, it became "non-sense," however, when its meaning was pushed to a metaphysical level. What complicated this question were two other factors: the Antiochenes understood the term ὑπόστασις in a different way than Cyril and his supporters and the dispute quickly became embroiled and entangled in quarrels between commanding personalities, national and city self-interests, and ecclesial power politics. These combined to magnify a basically semantic and ultimately metaphysical question into a divisive and embittered theological battle over what words can most accurately define how Christ is and acts as one in divine and human ways. The Council of Chalcedon tried to resolve the impasse by affirming what it thought to be true in both Nestorius' defense of Christ's integral humanity and Cyril's assertion that Christ's human nature was hypostatically united to the Word's divine nature in such a way that the Word is the subject to whom all divine and human attributes and actions are applied.

Because of his view on God's transcendent nature, Theodore had to explain πρόσωπον in a functional way. He may have reasoned that just as the spiritual soul can truly function in an organic union with a material body without its nature being compromised and just as the spiritual and material worlds can be bonded in true kinship with human beings, something similar can be said about the union between the divine and human natures in Christ. Theodore insisted over and over that the latter union could only be a uniquely graced union that had commenced at the assumed man's conception and that was voluntarily and lovingly maintained by his human free-will throughout his life. It may appear similar to other voluntary kinds of union but, in the mind of Theodore, it was a radically different kind of union.

The Nature of the Communion Between God and His Creatures

While one can argue that the Word's assumption of Jesus' human nature implies some sort of substantial union (in the sense that this is the way the creeds and traditional Christian language speak of the Word as the subject of human attributions), Theodore did interpret the Scripture and the creeds differently. He expressed the Word's assumption of Christ's humanity as a unique union that was effected by grace, enabling Christ to image God to creation and to act as the Spirit's "instrument" for transmitting graces to other humans. If human beings responded in a positive way to these graces, they could actually enter into communion with the humanity of Christ and share potentially in the heavenly state of immortality and immutability that Christ now enjoys.

Theodore's commentary on Paul's statement in Galatians 3:28 that there no longer exists either male or female but all are "one in Christ" provides additional insight into what this communion and future everlasting life will be like. Theodore asserts that Paul is expressing something much more than the fact that men and women possess a human nature similar to Christ's. There exists an organic unity wherein all humans are united to their two heads, Adam and Christ. Following Paul, Theodore insisted that just as all human beings are one by reason of the nature that each has received from Adam, so too all can become one with Christ, which will enable them to share in his present resurrected state. However, simply having a human nature does not by itself insure that a person will share an immortal life with Christ in the age to come. Something more is required.

In the Galatian passage, Paul professes that sexual, social, and economic roles have no real bearing *in se* as to whether or not a person will be saved and also will be meaningless in the next life. As to how one can become one with Christ, the answer has to be sought in Theodore's opinion that God created all humans with a mortal body for a pedagogical purpose. God intended this life to be a period of learning and moral testing where each person must live out, as fully as one can, a life similar to Christ's fidelity to the graces that he received. The importance of living a morally virtuous life explains why Theodore placed so much stress upon why Christ had to exercise a human free will and why he needed graces beyond that enabling his human nature to be united to the Word's nature. Theodore considered such voluntary co-operation on the part of Christ's free human will a constitutive element within Christ's functionary role as the perfect image and "instrument" for mediating God's graces to all others. Just as Christ became one with God's will, so must others do the same with the aid of His mediating graces, especially those coming through baptism and the eucharist. By becoming one with him in this way, they can also enter into communion with God as Christ did.

The same viewpoint is also reflected in the way Theodore has conceived of what happens in the reception of the sacraments. For him, the sacraments function as types of the eschatological life awaiting those in communion with Christ. He likened their effects to seeds that he believed require God's intervention before they can produce a new life. They provide the graces one's free-will needs so that one can live uprightly in this present life. Only after a person has been tested and has had an opportunity to learn about oneself and the meaning of life does God intervene and judge each according to his or her actions. God then fulfills His promise to grant a new life of immortality and immutability to those who have lived according to the graces imparted to them through Christ.

What happens when one does not live according to God's image is highlighted by what occurred when Adam and Eve failed to obey God's commandment and ate of the fruit from the tree of knowledge. Theodore (and also Nestorius) held that Adam's act distorted and corrupted his roles as the "image of God" and the bond of the universe. He corrupted his "image," turning it into a sign of inner contradiction. He now imaged a disordered will in full rebellion—not harmony—with God's will. He also sundered the bond uniting his human nature with the rest of creation by having introduced death into the world. Not only did he cease to disclose how to serve God but he broke the link enabling all other creatures to enter into their communion with God. He was, of course, unable to obliterate fully his role as image because it referred primarily to the future union of Christ's human and divine natures in one πρόσωπον. By voluntarily uniting his will in every act with God's will, Christ radically altered the effects of the cosmic disaster that Adam had inflicted upon himself and all those united by nature to him. What all this insinuates is that the role of "image" is a gift that entails an obligation to live responsibly according to God's will.

By applying Theodore's outlook on how Christ's human nature is energized by the Word while still remaining the free psychological subject of his own human actions, one can also presume a parallel with the way other humans are to commit themselves voluntarily to God's will. The energy that they receive would be the graces coming to them through Christ, who mediates all needed graces by means of his prosopic union with the Word and his own human nature's victory over sin and death. But these graces can be rejected, for all human beings have the freedom to spurn as well as to accept them. It is helpful here to attend to a distinction the Scholastics proposed between an actual grace that enables one to act in a free, virtuous way and a "sanctifying" grace that transforms and divinizes one's nature. Theodore could not admit the latter kind of grace because it affirms that a person can be raised in a "super-natural" way to become, in reality, a child of God who shares in God's divine nature. For Theodore, to share in God's life meant that one's mortal nature would become immortal.

Nestorius expressed the same viewpoint. First, in general, he argued that Christ had to be consubstantial with all other humans. Otherwise, this would render meaningless the church's solid belief that those receiving the eucharist worthily are sharing in Christ's victory over death. If he were to exist in a consubstantial union with the Word, he would be, in Nestorius's way of conceiving it, so completely assimilated into the divine nature he could no longer be the link uniting those bonded to him with God. This means that all other human beings could not participate in a bodily resurrection. Also, the eucharist would not be a true type assuring its recipients that they will likewise be raised as Christ has been to an immortal life. From this, Nestorius concluded that Christ's human nature has to remain human in its union with the Word, for it is the essential link enabling Christ to serve as the true mediator between God and all creation.

Such an outlook clearly indicates Nestorius believed a *hypostatic* union of Christ's natures meant that the human nature of Christ was absorbed into the divine.

Nestorius specified more clearly the critical role he believed the human will plays in the attainment of salvation by the numerous times that he stressed Christ's voluntary union with the Word. He repeated this so frequently that he gave the impression that he held this was the only kind of union between Christ's two natures. His intent, however, becomes evident when one realizes how he was contrasting a "voluntary" union with a "necessary" one in which Christ's human will would be necessitated to act as God wanted. If it were necessary, then Jesus would be, as it were, a mere puppet in God's hands. Nestorius sought to counteract this by insisting on Christ's human ability to act in a truly free way, for if he were not free, he could not have fulfilled his human role in what God requires for the achievement of salvation. Nor would he be able to serve as an image-exemplar pointing out how others were to follow his path and become more one with his humanity and assured of a future life where they too will become immortal and immutable.

Such an outlook explains why the Antiochenes as a group were so concerned about the importance of living a moral and virtuous life within the sacramental life of the Church. Furthermore, it illuminates the underlying reason Chrysostom asserted that an ascetical, especially a virginal, life can wholly transform a woman's present state of subordination to men. Since he mentions this when commenting on how there will be neither male nor female in the next life because all will be one in Christ, he appears to equate an ascetical state with the means whereby a person can become one with Christ in this life. The implication is that the quality of one's life is what truly counts. The more one lives an upright, virtuous, and ascetical life, the more one will grow in communion with Christ. Throughout the succeeding centuries, it will be a viewpoint that Benedict, Francis of Assisi, and later Ignatius of Loyola will share that counteracts the prevalent view that a virtuous life disposes one for a contemplative life where God can be experienced. The Antiochenes insisted that one can be united with God in one's everyday virtuous activity.

One final observation about Christ's mediating role deserves some comment. In the future age of immortality and immutability, the cultic aspect of Christ's mediatorship becomes evident. Since no creature can see or enter into an immediate relationship with God's transcendent nature, one can contemplate God only through Christ's visible human nature, with the confident assurance of being truly in contact and communion with the Divinity. This sense of a direct but a mediate union with God differs from the kind of union espoused by the Alexandrian mystics who believed the highest reaches (or inner depths) of the human mind can be united directly, immediately, and experientially to God. But as Augustine and such renowned mystics as Teresa of Avila and John of Cross have often cautioned, one must allow a mediating role for Christ even within the highest reaches of a mystical experience. The Antiochenes were especially sensitive to this, but while this is a praiseworthy point in their overall synthesis, they nevertheless excluded any direct, immediate mystical experience even through the mediatorship of Christ. One could be mystically united to his humanity but only in a moral sense with God.

Are Women Created in God's Image?

To complete our picture of the Antiochene views on image, the question was then raised as to whether women have also been created as "images of God." The cultural attitudes in the early church toward women were first discussed. These were found to be indicative of a pervasive and deeply-rooted patriarchical stance toward women. With this as a backdrop, an in-depth examination was undertaken into the reasons that the Antiochenes alleged to defend their interpretation and then into the ramifications that this might have had upon their understanding of "image." Diodore, Chrysostom, and Theodoret sought to justify their opinions by a literal, rational interpretation of those passages in Genesis where God tells Eve after the Fall that she must seek her recourse from her husband and of the Pauline corpus where a woman was to have her head covered and be silent in church. Their outlook here reflects what is contained in canonical collections emanating from fourth-century Antioch that laid down firm instructions on how a Christian woman ought to behave.

Diodore, Chrysostom, and Theodoret taught that women were not created as God's "image," at least in the same sense Adam is said to have been. Theodoret granted that Eve shared in Adam's power to rule over the material universe but maintained that she too had to comply with his decisions. Since the cultural outlook presented men as having the responsibility for making the final decision in both the family and society, their exegesis of the scriptural passages that dealt with the role of women vis-à-vis men made perfect sense to them. Everything seemed to point in one direction—that God had not created women as "wholly" equal with men, even though they too had received the same human nature. The question was: whether this inequality was due to a weakness of a woman's nature, a punishment, a culturally imposed attitude, or simply God's will.

While not denying these Fathers' patriarchical opinions, above all those expressed by Chrysostom, one must judge them within their proper context. While they insisted that women were subordinate to men, who alone share fully in God's dominative power as His images, they recognized that women are equal to men in several other areas. They possess the same human nature and authority to rule with men over the material universe. They too have been equally called to enter into a graced relationship with Christ, with the assurance that they, too, can attain an immortal communion with God in a state where present sexual and social differences will be irrelevant. The Antiochenes even admitted that women are indeed superior to men in the ways that they care for children and manage a household. They can surpass men, too, in virtue, intelligence, wisdom, counseling in private, and courage. The general area, however, from which they believed a woman was wholly restricted was that of public careers as soldiers, elected officials, and priests.

Judging from the few fragments that have come down of Theodore's and Nestorius's writings, one can only speculate about their views regarding women. While we have sufficient material to assess what Theodore thought, absolutely nothing was affirmed about women in Nestorius's *Bazaar*. From Theodore's passing remarks on how a wife dishonors her husband when she appears in public view with her head uncovered and how women ought to be quiet in church out of respect for the common good, it is evident that he, too, held that women are subordinate to men within society and the church. But judging from the several texts available to us, it is not clear whether Theodore thought out fully the ramifications that his outlook on "image" could have regarding how men and women ought to relate to one another. Perhaps the one fragment attributed to him stating that there is a lack of clarity in this matter indicates that he was never able to resolve this issue or that he never considered it important enough to settle. Or, if he did, his view was lost with most of his works.

When we consider how Theodore has associated "image" with human nature as the bond of the universe, it would seem that he also had to admit—at least logically—that women were created in God's image, for they possess the same human nature composed of a soul that is akin to that of the angels and a body that is related to that of corporeal beings. To justify a woman's subordination to men, Theodore would have to have anticipated those who argue today that Adam *qua* male can alone serve as a symbol and a type of Christ, for he had based his understanding of "image," so it seems, on his understanding of Christ as God's primary and perfect image. There is, however, no text supporting such an emphasis upon Christ's maleness as being a critical element in Theodore's understanding of image.

Perhaps the answer is best sought in what appears to have been Theodore's world-view of the universe as an organic whole. With an outlook such as this, he could easily have thought of women having a different position within the family and society than men. But such a belief has to be understood correctly. One should be careful not to equate an organic society with a hierarchical one. To be in a subordinate role does not necessarily connote inferiority, for as Christians realized as a consequence of the Arian controversy, the Son and the Spirit are derived from and thus "subordinate" to the Father as their source but nevertheless essentially equal to Him in all regards. Such a distinction ought to make one reserved about making a universal judgment as to who is superior and inferior in an organic unity where the two partners complement one another in a relationship described by Paul as being "in one flesh."

When Theodore stressed in his commentaries that women should keep quiet in church for the common good, it is best understood in an organic framework. Like Chrysostom, he was concerned that the "body"—that the members of the church—function together for the productive and peaceful well-being of the whole congregation. While one may regard the head as superior to its body, it cannot exist separately from its body. Nor can the head alone perform the functions belonging to other bodily members, such as eating and walking. It has need of other bodily members working cooperatively with it. When this happens, then what is good for one is also good for all and what is a successful operation for one entails success for the entire organism. If, however, one member dismisses another as inferior and thus worthless, then it is, in point of fact, passing a similar judgment on itself as part of the whole. So for Theodore, women may have a subordinate but not necessarily inferior role in their relationship with men. Both require each other for the well-being of their efforts together.

Another interpretation can be drawn from Theodore's view of image with an interesting application for how a man and a woman ought to relate to one another. Since men and women alike share the same general human nature composed of body and soul, his thought can be also construed to mean that image encompasses both masculine and feminine qualities. In the same way that the body and soul and the human natures in Christ must function together in a harmonious union with each other, the sexes, too, should relate to each other in a union where there exists a unity of mutual purpose. Since each person is endowed with masculine and feminine qualities that need to be psychologically integrated with each other, Theodore's view of image can be interpreted in a way that suggests men and women must function harmoniously together, if each is to become fully human and thus able to enter into a truly personal relationship with God. This interpretation, however, intriguing though it may be, does not square with the fact that Adam as a male is affirmed in Genesis 5:3 to be God's image. Theodore would have taken this verse into account when he examined—as his hermeneutical method required—all the passages dealing with the "image of God."

Relevance for Today

The Antiochene, especially Theodore's, full understanding of "image" offers a number of important points relevant to our concerns today. First, it provides a viewpoint that neatly and sharply sets off the Alexandrian and Augustinian opinion of "image" as a spiritual reality and, in so doing, highlights some of the primary differences between the Antiochene and Alexandrian "schools of theology" regarding such topics as "image" and Christ's christological, soteriological, and eschatological roles. Excluding the times "image" is interpreted as indicating the ways that a person can act similarly to God, it can also be understood as affirming a person's unique relationship to God. As such, the term "image" is expressing the fundamental faith relationship that ought to exist between God and human beings and can thus serve as a means for exploring how one's understanding of *imago Dei* can have much wider ramifications for different fields of theology, especially in systematics.

By situating the Antiochene and Alexandrian views against the backdrop of the "elements" in a faith act, one can catch a glimpse of the strengths and weaknesses present in both approaches. In addition to being a free, personal, self-giving act of the whole person that unites one in a moral and sometimes a mystical way to God, a faith act also contains communal, moral, and eschatological dimensions. Taking Theodore's synthesis as expressing the fullest expression of the Antiochene theological approach about "image," one can see that he has included the body not only as being integral to a person's total commitment to God but also as playing an essential role in God's redemptive plan for universal salvation. It highlights how Christ acts as the true mediator who unites all in the universe to God through his human nature because of his union with the Word. By his death and resurrection, he has opened the way for all who will follow his lead to enter into an immortal and an immutable state where one can know and worship the transcendent God through Christ's πρόσωπον or the visible "aspect" of his humanity that manifests the divine. It is a viewpoint that brings out not only the communal but also the cosmic implications of a faith relationship that are so central to Paul's theological teaching.

The Alexandrians and Augustine are far superior in the ways they illuminate the inner spiritual dynamics at work in a faith act. They realized how image is involved with the need in a faith act that requires a believer be raised ontologically—however one may want to depict this—to a divinized or supernatural state. They interpreted the New Testament's affirmations about becoming a true child of God as requiring this. Such an outlook is totally at odds with the core belief of the Antiochenes that no created being, even Christ's human nature, can be so united in a mystical relationship with God that it becomes divine. As a result, they cannot affirm a true "substantial" union between the divine and the human natures in Christ. Nor can they admit the possibility of any mystical kind of prayer experience that unites one directly and immediately with God.

While one can judge the lack of a mystical element in faith as a serious lack in the Antiochene theological outlook, they do have aspects of faith that the Alexandrians passed over or minimized in their theological syntheses. The Alexandrians have so emphasized the inner, individual, and spiritual elements in their theological explorations that they say relatively little about the role of body in salvation, about the necessity of a free, total commitment of oneself in a faith surrender, and about the communal and cosmic dimensions to faith. Being staunch believers, they certainly would not have denied that the body is good and that it will be resurrected in the next life, just as they did not deny the true and complete humanity of Christ, for all these points are affirmed for them in Scripture and the Church Councils. So the central question that Theodore's theological synthesis raises for those who adhere to the Alexandrian and Augustinian emphases is: How do you incorporate the free, moral, communal, and cosmic elements of faith in your own theological understanding of image insofar as it can be understood as expressing one's most fundamental faith relationship to God?

What emerges from all this is how these two theological views complement, much more than oppose, each other. Each side tends to be right in what it affirms positively and more likely wrong or deficient in what it denies or omits; this suggests that both sides must be harmonized with each other. The functional, communal, cosmic, and eschatological aspects of faith also need to be assimilated with those that are individual, ontological, and mystical. The same can be said about the two different christological approaches that have characterized the schools of Alexandria and Antioch. The unity of Christ's natures must be expressed in a way that preserves the integrity of his human nature and his free will. The Alexandrians affirm better the substantial unity, and the Antiochenes the true separateness of the natures and the ability of Christ's humanity to function fully and freely. A blending of these two emphases was what the Council of Chalcedon attempted to do.

Since we live today in a theological age when the emphasis is upon a "low" Christology similar to that which preoccupied all the Antiochenes, many, if not most, believers are more sympathetic to what they attempted to do. The contemporary preference is to begin the christological question from Christ's human perspective and try to explain how he can be like other humans except for sin. If one starts with the conviction that Christ's humanity was united to the Word from the moment of his conception, it is necessary to affirm as Theodore did that, although the assumed man was always conscious of being truly one with the Word, it required time before he could articulate and understand what this meant for him and his mission. This approach also permits one to stress Christ's human freedom and his human growth in physical, intellectual, and psychological ways.

Those espousing a "low" Christology must face, and hopefully learn from, the difficulties and possible weaknesses that beset the Antiochene approach. Since no one approach can explain and fully encapsulate the fulness of the mysterious paradox of how two integral natures can both function as one and be one subject, it is difficult to integrate Christ's divine nature and his ontological personhood when one begins with his humanity. The same, of course, can be said of the Alexandrian approach which has so emphasized the divine personhood of Christ as the agent of his human actions that his freedom and responsibility may easily be lost in the process. So what is gained by one approach can result in the loss in another area. It is like pushing in one side of a balloon and discovering it bulges on the other side.

For those interested, too, in a functional christological type of approach, the Antiochenes offer an early historical example for examination. Remaining close to what the Scriptures have revealed, especially the way that the evangelists portray Jesus, all of the Antiochenes have adopted a Christology that is heavily functional in its orientation. In fact, their approach may date back to the Semitic, oral tradition that can be detected in the Gospels, above all in the evangelists. But whatever may have been its origins, they remained steadfast to a functional Christology and resisted the efforts of those who sought to introduce into Christian theology Neoplatonic insights that could help to explain such basic truths of faith as how Christ's divine and human natures could be personally united as one and how human beings could be divinized with God. The Antiochenes, however, missed the significance of something that those who were responsible for the establishment of the canon realized: that the functional emphases of the evangelists needed to be harmonized also with the spiritual but basically metaphysical reflections of John. They were also unable to accept at face value, as Cyril did, the creedal statement that the "one Lord Jesus Christ, the Son of God" is the subject who "became human, suffered and rose up on the third day."[3]

The Antiochenes, especially Theodore, have raised two other issues that are of contemporary concern: what is the role of the body in God's salvific plan and does theology have something to say about humans' responsibility for their material environment. First, Theodore's understanding of "image" shows that the body is not to be regarded simply as an ad-

3. Norman P. Tonner, ed., *Decrees of the Ecumenical Councils*, vol. 1 (Washington: Georgetown UP, 1990), 5.

junct or appendage to the soul but a constitutive and essential element in God's plan for a universal redemption. For God has determined that it is through the medium of Christ's human body that one can come in real contact with His transcendent nature and truly worship God in the way He intends.

So understood, Theodore's viewpoint regarding the body's role in the economy of salvation helps to correct an overemphasis that the Alexandrians and Augustinians place upon an inner search for a mystical union with God. This emphasis has led some to extol a mystical and contemplative approach as the supreme way to discover God and to regard the body and an active life as of secondary importance, if not as major impediments, to one's spiritual well-being and growth in prayer. It is a view, too, that tended to associate the body so closely to concupiscence that it was something to be feared more than reverenced as sacred. Yet, the body is the way that God has imaged His love and the way that humans are to express their self-giving love symbolically to others. Such love, whether it is given or received, manifests God's love.

Secondly, Theodore's understanding of "image" as the bond that links the spiritual and material worlds within human nature also permits us to elaborate on how theology can speak to contemporary ecological concerns regarding our material environment, for he conceived of the universe as an organic "body" where all created beings are related to each other. They are united first under Adam and suffer because of his sin, for when he died, his nature could no longer fulfill the revelatory, unitive, and cultic functions in the universe that God wanted His image to exercise. These functions were then restored by Christ, who enables all creation the possibility of entering into communion with God. Because all humans are created in Christ as God's primary "image," the spiritual and material worlds are called to care for their human needs. Though Theodore does not state any reciprocal duty for human beings to care for the material world, it would seem to be inherent in the responsibilities humans have as God's "image" to lead, in creative and loving ways, the non-human worlds to their fulfillment, for these worlds are organically united to humans. While it is true that the spiritual and material worlds have not been created as "images of God" and therefore their beings are not sacred as such, humans can no more abuse them than the head can mistreat the other parts of its body without suffering harm to itself.

Theodore's viewpoint, therefore, brings out in a striking way how God has established a real symbiotic relationship between human beings and the material world. It also makes one sensitive to the fact that the human body is meant to be the medium par excellence for relationship and dialogue—not merely with other human beings but with nature itself. Such a perspective provides a Christian theological basis for accepting the Native American and Oriental religions' insistence upon the need for humans to exist in harmony with nature. This bond with the physical world is very difficult to grasp, let alone experience, for those conditioned by the western, technological attitude that regards the corporeal world as simply something to be used, and even abused, as an object. Yet, an understanding of this view gives additional meaning to what Saint Paul asserts so movingly in Romans 8:18–23 about creation's eagerness to share in the redemption of our bodies. Also the relationship of kinship between the human body and the material universe widens the root theological meaning of the word "atonement," indicating that humans are called to be "at-one-with" not merely God, oneself, and other human beings, but also all the rest of creation.

Finally, the Antiochene perspective on the role Christ's body plays in reconciling all to God can afford some insight into the meaning of the Pauline and Irenaean statements on how all creation, spiritual and material, will be recapitulated in the God-man, Jesus Christ. It is a topic rarely treated today, other than perhaps in an occasional reference to Teilhard de Chardin,[4] even though we now live in an age sympathetic, if not committed, to ecological issues and to a general evolutionary outlook toward life. The value, therefore, in reflecting upon the Theodorean synthesis is that it instills within us a critical awareness of a cosmic dimension to life. For Christ is the one who unites in his human nature the corporeal as well as the spiritual worlds and will restore all as a unified whole to his Father, and, in fact, we can apply this also to all religions as being included within Christ's recapitulation. Since no one has expressed this in a more eloquent way than Saint Paul, there is no better and more fitting conclusion to this

4. For example, see Christopher Mooney, *Theology and Scientific Knowledge. Changing Models of God's Presence in the World* (Notre Dame: U of Notre Dame P, 1996), and Arthur Peacocke, *Theology for a Scientific Age. Being and Becoming—Natural, Divine, and Human* (Minneapolis: Fortress, 1993). Both theologians insist that their own positions are not the same as de Chardin's vitalistic immanentism (Mooney, 159–60 and Peacocke, 185–87).

study into the Antiochene outlook on how humans have been created "in the image and likeness of God" than to repeat his deeply stirring and personally uplifting words from Colossians (1:15–18, 19–20):

He [the Christ] is the image of the invisible God, the firstborn of all creation. For in him were created all things in heaven and earth, the visible and the invisible. . . . He is before all things, and in him all things hold together. . . . For in him all the fullness was pleased to dwell, and through him to reconcile all things for him, making peace by the blood of the cross, whether those on earth and those in heaven.

BIBLIOGRAPHY

Primary Sources

Abramowski, Luise, and Alan E. Goodman, ed. *A Nestorian Collection of Christological Texts.* 2 vols. Cambridge: Cambridge UP, 1972.

Abramowski, Luise. See also Theodore of Mopsuestia.

Aristotle. *Nicomachean Ethics.* Trans. H. Rackham. Loeb Classical Library. Cambridge: Harvard UP, 1962.

Augustine. *Commentary on Genesis.* PL 34:245–486.

———. *De Trinitate.* Trans. Stephen McKenna. The Fathers of the Church. Washington: Catholic University of America Press, 1963.

Basil of Caesaria. *Sur l'origine de l'homme* (Hom. X et XI de l'Hexaéméron). Ed. and trans. Alexis Smets and Michel van Esbroeck. SC 160. Paris: Cerf, 1970.

Codex Theodosianus. Ed. Charles Henry Coster. The Medieval Academy 10. Cambridge, Mass.: Medieval Academy of America, 1935.

Constitutions of the Holy Apostles. Ed. A. Roberts and J. Donaldson. Ante-Nicene Fathers 7. Grand Rapids, Mich.: Eerdmanns, 1951.

Cosmas Indicopleustès Topographie Chrétienne. Ed. and trans. Wanda Wolska-Conus. SC 141, 159, 197. Paris: Cerf, 1968–73.

Cyprian. "De Bono Patientiae." PL 4:622–38.

Cyril of Alexandria. *Commentary on Matthew.* PG 72:365–474.

Cyrus of Edessa. *Six Explanations of the Liturgical Feasts.* Trans. William F. Macomber. CSCO 356/Syr. 156. Louvain: CSCO, 1974.

Decrees of the Ecumenical Councils. Ed. Norman P. Tonner. Vol. 1. Washington: Georgetown UP, 1990.

The Didascalia Apostolorum in Syriac. Ed. and trans. Arthur Vööbus. CSCO 401–2/Syr. 175–76. Louvain: CSCO, 1979.

Diodore. "Der Theologische Nachlass des Diodor von Tarsus." Ed. Rudolf Abramowski. *Zeitscrift für die neutestamentliche Wissenschaft* 42 (1949): 19–69.

———. *Fragmenta Ex Catenis in Genesim.* PG 33:1562–1579.

———. *Diodori Tarsensis Commentarii in Psalmos.* Ed. Jean-Marie Olivier. CCSG 6. Turnhout: Brepols, 1980.

Ephrem. *Sancti Ephaem Syri in Genesim et in Exodum Commentarii.* Ed. and intro. R. M. Tonneau. CSCO 152–53/Syr. 71–72. Louvain: CSCO, 1955.

Epiphanius of Salamis. *The Panarion of St. Epiphanius, Bishop of Salamis*. Trans. Philip R. Amidon. New York: Oxford UP, 1990.

Eusebius of Caesarea. *The History of the Church from Christ to Constantinople*. Trans. G. A. Williamson. New York: Dorset, 1965.

Evagrius Scholasticus. *The Ecclesiastical History of Evagrius with the Scholia*. Ed. J. Bidez and L. Parmentier. London: Mehuen, 1898.

Irenaeus. *Contre les Hérésies*. Ed. Adelin Rousseau and Louis Doutreleau. Book 4, SC 100.1 and 100.2; Book 5, SC 152–53; Book 3, SC 210–11; Book 1, SC 263–64; Book 2, SC 293–94. Paris: Cerf, 1965, 1969, 1974, 1979, and 1982.

———. "Irenaeus Against Heresies." Ed. A. Roberts and J. Donaldson, 309–567. *Ante-Nicene Fathers*. Vol. 1. 1885. Reprint, Peabody, Mass.: Hendrickson, 1994.

Išo'Dad of Merv. *Commentaire d'Išo'Dad de Merv sur l'Ancien Testament*. I. Genèse. Trans. C. Van den Eynde. CSCO 156/Syr. 75. Louvain: Durbecq, 1955.

Jerome. *The Lives of Illustrious Men*. Ed. and trans. Ernest Cushing Richardson. NPNF, Second Series. Vol. 3. Ed. Philip Schaff and Henry Wace. 1892. Peabody, Mass.: Hendrickson, 1994.

John Chrysostom. *Opera Omnia*. PG 47–64.

———. *Against Those Who Introduce Virgins into Their Homes*. PG 47:495–514.

———. *Women Religious Ought Not to Dwell in the Same House as Men*. PG 47:514–30.

———. *Homily on Not Remarrying*. PG 48:609–20.

———. *On the Priesthood*. PG 48:623–92.

———. *Eight Homilies against the Jews*. PG 48:839–942.

———. *Homily 7 to the People of Antioch*. PG 49:93.

———. *Homily on Saint Ignatius the Martyr*. PG 50:587–96.

———. *Homily 1 on Salute to Priscilla and Aquila*. PG 51:187–208.

———. *On Which Women Ought to Be Taken as Wives*. PG 51:225–42.

———. *Epistle 170*. PG 52:709–10.

———. *Homily 6 on The Holy Pasch*. PG 52:765–72.

———. *Homily 4 on Genesis*. PG 53:39–48.

———. *Homily 8 on Genesis*. PG 53:70–76.

———. *Homily 9 on Genesis*. PG 53:76–81.

———. *Homily 10 on Genesis*. PG 53:81–90.

———. *Sermon 2 on Genesis*. PG 54:586–90.

———. *Sermon 3 on Genesis*. PG 54:590–94.

———. *Prologue to the Psalms*. PG 55:531–32.

———. *Homily 66 on Matthew*. PG 58:625–32.

———. *Homily 31 on Romans*. PG 60:667–76.

———. *Homily 26 on 1 Corinthians*. PG 61:211–24.

———. *Homily 8 on 2 Corinthians*. PG 61:454–60.

———. *Commentary on Galatians*. PG 61:611–82.

———. *Homily 20 on Ephesians*. PG 62:135–50.

———. *Homily 3 on Colossians*. PG 62:317–24.

———. *Homily 10 on Colossians*. PG 62:365–74.

———. *Homily 9 on 1 Timothy*. PG 62:543–48.

———. *Homily 4 on 1 Corinthians 1:18–20*. NPNF, First Series. Vol. 9. Ed. Philip Schaff and Henry Wace. 1889. Reprint, Peabody, Mass.: Hendrickson, 1994.

———. "Two Letters." NPNF, First Series. Vol. 9. Ed. Philip Schaff and Henry Wace, 85–116. Grand Rapids, Mich.: Eerdmans, 1956.

———. *Lettre VIII à Olympias*. Ed. and trans. Anne-Marie Malingrey. SC 13. Paris: Cerf, 1964.

———. *On the Statues*. Trans. W. R. Stephens. NPNF, First Series. Vol. 9. Ed. Philip Schaff and Henry Wace. 1889. Reprint, Peabody, Mass.: Hendrickson, 1994.

———. *Sur Virginité*. Ed. Herbert Musurillo. SC 125. Paris: Cerf, 1966.

Lactantius. *Divinae Institutiones*. Corpus Scriptorum Ecclesiasticorum Latinorum. Lipsiae: G. Freytag, 1890.

Libanius. *Autobiography and Selected Letters*. Ed. and trans. A. F. Norman. Cambridge: Harvard UP, 1992.

———. *Libanii opera*. 12 vols. Ed. R. Forster. Leipzig: Teubner, 1903–27.

Loofs, Friedrich. "Theodor von Mopsuestia," *Realencykopädie für protestanische Theologie und Kirche* Band 19:598–605.

Malalas, John. *The Chronicle of John Malalas*. Ed. Elizabeth and Michael Jeffreys, Roger Scott, et al. Melbourne: Australian Association for Byzantine Studies, 1986.

———. *The Chronicle of John Malalas, Books 8–18*. Trans. M. Spinka with Glanville Downey. Chicago: U of Chicago P, 1940.

Narsai. *Homélies de Narsai sur la Création*. Ed. and trans. Philippe Gignoux. PO 34, Fasc. 3–4. Turnhout: Brepols, 1968.

———. "Homélie de Narses sur les trois Docteurs nestoriens." Ed. F. Martin. *Journal Asiatique* 14 (1899): 446–62; 15 (1900): 469–525.

———. *Narsai doctoris syri homiliae et carmina*. 2 vols. Ed. A. Mingana. Mosul, Iraq, 1905.

———. *Narsai's Metrical Homilies on the Nativity, Epiphany, Passion, Resurrection and Ascension*. Ed. and trans. Frederick G. McLeod. PO 40, Fasc. 1. Turnhout: Brepols, 1979.

Nemesius of Emesa. *Cyril of Jerusalem and Nemesius of Emesa*. Ed. and trans. William Telfer. Library of Christian Classics 4. Philadelphia: Westminster, 1955.

Nestorius. *The Bazaar of Heracleides*. Ed. Godfrey R. Driver, trans. Leonard Hodgson. Oxford: Clarendon, 1925.

———. *Nestoriana: Die Fragmente des Nestorius*. Ed. Friedrich Loofs, with S. A. Cook and G. Kampffmeyer. Halle: Neimeyer, 1905.

Origen. *The Commentary of Origen on S. John's Gospel*. 2 vols. Ed. A. E. Brooke. Cambridge: Cambridge UP, 1896.

———. *Contra Celsum*. Trans. H. Chadwick. Cambridge: Cambridge UP, 1953.

———. *Homélies sur la Genèse*. Trans. Louis Doutreleau. SC 7. Paris: Cerf, 1976.

———. *On First Principles*. Trans. G. W. Butterworth. New York: Harper, 1966.

———. *Origen: Spirit and Fire*. Ed. Hans Urs von Balthasar, trans. Robert J. Daly. Washington: Catholic University of America Press, 1984.

Palladius. *Dialogue sur la vie de Jean Chrysostom*. Ed. and trans. Anne-Marie Malingrey with Phillippe Leclercq. SC 341–42. Paris: Cerf, 1988.

Petit, Françoise, ed. *Catenae Graecae in Genesim et in Exodum*. II Collectio Coisliniana in Genesim. CCSG 15. Turnhout: Brepols, 1986.

———. See also Theodore of Mopsuestia.

Philo. *Opera Omnia*. Trans. F. H. Coulson and G. H. Whitaker. Loeb Classical Library. 11 vols. Cambridge: Harvard UP, 1949.

———. *Philo of Alexandria: The Contemplative Life, the Giants and Selections*. Trans. David Winston. Classics of Western Spirituality. New York: Paulist, 1981.

Plotinus. *Enneads: A New Definitive Edition*. Burdett, N.Y.: Paul Brunton Philosophical Foundation, 1992.

Procopius. *Commentary on Genesis*. PG 87:122–512.

The Seven Ecumenical Councils. Ed. H. R. Percival. NPNF, Second Series. Vol. 14. 1900. Reprint, Peabody, Mass.: Henrickson, 1994.

Simeon Stylites. *The Lives of Simeon Stylites*. Trans. Robert Doran. Cistercian Studies Series 112. Kalamazoo: Cistercian, 1992.

Socrates. *Historia ecclesiastica*. Trans. A. C. Zenos. NPNF, Second Series. Vol. 2. Ed. Philip Schaff and Henry Wace. 1890. Reprint, Peabody, Mass: Hendrickson, 1994.

Sozomen. *Historia ecclesiastica*. Trans. Chester D. Hartranft. NPNF, Second Series. Vol. 2. Ed. Philip Schaff and Henry Wace. 1890. Reprint, Peabody, Mass.: Hendrickson, 1994.

Theodore of Mopsuestia. *Opera Omnia*. PG 66:10–1020.

———. *Commentary on Obadiah*. PG 66:303–18.

———. *Commentary on Haggai*. PG 66:474–494.

———. *Commentary on Genesis*. PG 66:633–46.

———. *Commentary on the Epistle to the Romans*. PG 66:787–876.

———. *Commentary on the Incarnation*. PG 66:971–94.

———. *Fragment of a Work against Apollinaris*. PG 66:1001–1004.

———. *Epistle to Domnus*. PG 66:1011–14.

———. *Commentaire sur les Psaumes I–LXXX*. Ed. Robert Devreese. Studi et Testi, 93. Vatican City: Vaticana, 1939.

———. *Commentary of Theodore of Mopsuestia on the Nicene Creed*. Ed. and trans. A. Mingana. WS 5. Cambridge: Heffer, 1932.

———. *Commentary of Theodore of Mopsuestia on the Lord's Prayer and on the Sacraments of Baptism and the Eucharist*. Ed. and trans. A. Mingana. WS 6. Cambridge: Heffer, 1933.

———. "Ein unbekanntes Zitat aus *Contra Eunomium* des Theodore von Mopsuestia." Ed. Luise Abramowski. *Le Muséon* 71 (1958): 97–104.

———. *Expositio in Psalmos*. Ed. Lucas de Coninck. Turnhout: Brepols, 1977.

———. *Fragments syriaques du commentaire de Psaumes (Psaume 118 et Psaumes 138–148)*. Ed. and trans. Lucas van Rompay. Louvain: Petters, 1982.

———. *Les Homélies Catéchétiques de Théodore de Mopsueste*. Trans. Raymond Tonneau with Robert Devreese. Vatican City: Vaticana, 1949.

———. "L'homme créé 'à l'image' de Dieu quelques fragments grecs inédits de Théodore de Mopsueste." Ed. and trans. Françoise Petit. *Le Muséon* 100 (1987): 269–77.

———. *Pauluskommentare aus der Griechischen Kirche*. 2d ed. Ed. Karl Staab, 113–212. Münster: Aschendorff, 1984.

———. "Théodore de Mopsueste, Interprétation (du livre) de la Genèse (Vat. Syr. 120, ff. I–V)." *Le Muséon* 66 (1953): 45–64.

———. *Theodori Episcopi Mopsuesteni in Epistolas B. Pauli Commentarii*. Ed. H. B. Swete. 2 vols. Cambridge: Cambridge UP, 1880 and 1882.

———. *Theodori Mopsuesteni Commentarius in Evangelium Joannis Apostoli*. Ed. J.-M. Vosté. CSCO 115–116 / Syr. 62–63. Louvain: Officina Orientali, 1940.

———. *Theodori Mopsuesteni Fragmenta Syriaca*. Ed. E. Sachau. Leipzig: G. Engelmann, 1869.

Theodoret of Cyrrhus. *Opera Omnia*. PG 80–84.

———. *Questions on Genesis*. PG 80:75–226.

———. *Epistle to the Romans*. PG 82:43–226.

———. *Commentary on 1 Corinthians*. PG 82:225–376.

———. *Commentary on 1 Timothy*. PG 82:787–830.

———. *Compendium of the Heretics' Fables*. PG 83:335–555.

———. *Ecclesiastical History*. NPNF, Second Series. Vol. 3. 1892. Reprint, Peabody, Mass.: Hendrickson, 1994.

———. *Eranistes*. Trans. Gerald H. Ettlinger. New York: Oxford UP, 1975.

———. *Letters*. NPNF, Second Series. Vol. 3. 1892. Reprint, Peabody, Mass.: Hendrickson, 1994.

————. *Theodoret of Cyrrhus, A History of the Monks of Syria.* Kalamazoo: Cistercian, 1985.

————. *Thérapeutique des Maladies Helléniques.* Ed. and trans. P. Canivet. SC 57. Paris, Cerf, 1958.

Theophilus of Antioch. *Ad Autolycum.* Ed. and trans. Robert M. Grant. Oxford: Clarendon, 1970.

Secondary Sources

Abramowski, Luise. "Zur Theologie Theodors von Mopsuestia." *Zeitschrift für Kirchengeschichte* 72 (1961): 263–93.

————. See also Theodore of Mopsuestia.

Abramowski, Rudolf. See Diodore.

Adam, A. K. M. *What is Postmodern Biblical Criticism?* Minneapolis: Fortress, 1995.

Allen, Pauline. *Evagrius Scholasticus, the Church Historian.* Leuven: Spicilegium Sacrum Lovaniense, 1981.

Amann, E. "Théodore de Mopsueste." *Dictionnaire de Théologie Catholique* 15: col. 258–80.

Amidon, Philip R. See Ephiphanius.

The Anchor Bible Dictionary. Gen. ed. David Noel Freedman. New York: Doubleday, 1992.

'Arbaia, Barhadbshabba. *Cause de la Fondation des Écoles.* Trans. A. Scher. PO 4. Turnhout: Brepols, 1908.

Arnou, R. "Nestorianisme et Neoplatonisme: L'unité du Christ et l'union des 'Intelligibles.'" *Gregorianum* 17 (1936): 116–31.

Atiya, Aziz S. *A History of Eastern Christianity.* London: Methuen, 1968.

Badger, G. P. *The Nestorians and Their Rituals.* London: Joseph Masters, 1852.

Bardy, G. *Recherches sur S. Lucien d'Antioche et son école.* Paris: Beauchesne, 1936.

Baur, Chrysostomus. *John Chrysostom and His Time.* 2 vols. Trans. M. Gonzaga. Westminster, Md.: Newman, 1959–60.

Bergjan, Silke-Petra. "Die dogmatische Funktionalisierung der Exegese nach Theodoret von Cyrus." *Christliche Exegese.* Ed. J. Oort and U. Wickert. Kampen: Kok Pharos, 1992.

Børresen, Kari Elizabeth, ed. *Image of God and Gender Models.* Oslo: Solum Forlag, 1991.

————. *The Image of God: Gender Models in Judaeo-Christian Tradition.* Minneapolis: Fortress, 1995.

Brock, Sebastian. "Early Syrian Asceticism." *Numen* 20 (1973): 1–19.

Brock, Sebastian P., and Susan Ashbrook Harvey. *Holy Women of the Syrian Orient.* Berkeley: U of California P, 1987.

Brooke, A. E., ed. *The Commentary of Origen on S. John's Gospel.* 2 vols. Cambridge: Cambridge UP, 1896.

Brown, Hunter, et al., ed. *Images of the Human: The Philosophy of the Human Person in a Religious Context.* Chicago: Loyola UP, 1995.

Brown, Peter. *The Body and Society: Men, Women and Sexual Renunciation in Early Christianity.* New York: Columbia UP, 1988.

Brown, Raymond E., and John P. Meier. *Antioch and Rome.* New York: Paulist, 1983.

Bultmann, Rudolf. *Die Exegese des Theodore von Mopsuestia.* Posthum ed. Helmut Feld and Karl Hermann Schelke. Stuttgart: W. Kohlhammer, 1984.

Burghardt, Walter J. *The Image of God in Man According to Cyril of Alexandria.* Washington: Catholic University of America Press, 1957.

————. "The Image of God in Man." *Catholic Theological Society of America Proceedings* 16 (1962): 147–60.

————. "Free Life of God: Recapturing an Ancient Anthropology." *Theology Digest* 26 (1978): 343–64.

Cairns, David. *The Image of God in Man.* London: Collins, 1973.

Cameron, Averil, and Amélie Kuhrt, eds. *Images of Women in Antiquity.* Detroit: Wayne State UP, 1983.

Capper, LeRoy S. "'The *Imago Dei* and Its Implications for Order in the Church," *Presbutérion* 11, No. 1 (Spring 1985): 21–33.

Cavalcanti, E. "Theodoret of Cyrrhus." EEC 2:827–28.

Cavalera, F. *Le schisme d'Antioche.* Paris: Picard, 1905.

Chadwick, H. "Eucharist and Christology in the Nestorian Controversy." *Journal of Theological Studies,* New Series 2 (1951): 145–64.

Clark, Elizabeth A. *Jerome, Chrysostom, and Friends: Essays and Translations.* Studies in Women and Religion 2. New York: Mellen, 1979.

———. *The Origenist Controversy.* Princeton: Princeton UP, 1992.

———. *Women in the Early Church.* Message of the Fathers of the Church 13. Wilmington, Del.: Glazier, 1983.

Clifford, R., and Roland Murphy. *New Jerome Biblical Commentary.* Ed. Raymond Brown, et al. Englewood Cliffs, NJ: Prentice, 1990: 11–13.

Clines, J. A. "The Image of God in Man." *Tyndale Bulletin* 19 (1968): 52–103.

Cousin, Ewert. "The Humanity and the Passion of Christ." *Christian Spirituality: High Middle Ages and Reformation.* Vol. 2. Ed. Jill Raitt, 375–91. (New York: Crossroad, 1987).

Crouzel, Henri. *Théologie de l'image de Dieu chez Origène.* Théologie 34. Paris: Aubier, 1957.

———. "Image." EEC 1:405–7.

———. "Philo." EEC 2:682–83.

Curtis, Edward. "Image of God." *The Anchor Bible Dictionary.* Ed. David Noel Freedman, 3:389–91. New York: Doubleday, 1992.

Daly, Anthony. "Nestorius in the *Bazaar of Heracleides*: A Christology Compatible with the Third Letter and Anathemas of Cyril of Alexandria." Ph.D. diss., University of Southern California, 1983.

Daube, D. "Rabbinic Methods of Interpretation and Hellenistic Rhetoric." *Hebrew Union College Annual* (Cincinnati) 22 (1949): 239–64.

Devreese, Robert. "La méthode exégétique de Théodore de Mopsueste," *Revue Biblique,* April 1946: 207–41.

———. *Essai sur Théodore de Mopsueste.* Studi e Testi 141. Vatican City: Biblioteca Apostolica Vaticana, 1948.

———. *Le Patriarcat d'Antioche: depuis la paix de l'église jusq'à la conquête arabe.* Paris: Gabalda, 1945.

———. "Le commentaire de Théodore de Mopsueste sur les psaumes," *Revue Biblique,* July 1928: 340–60; Jan. 1929: 35–62.

de Vries, Wilhelm. "Der 'Nestorianismus' Theodor von Mopsuestia in seiner Sakramentenlehre." *Orientalia Christiana Periodica* 7 (1941): 91–148.

Dewart, Joanne McWilliam. *The Theology of Grace of Theodore of Mopsuestia.* Catholic University of America Studies in Christian Antiquity 16. Washington: Catholic University of America Press, 1971.

———. "The Notion of 'Person' Underlying the Christology of Theodore of Mopsuestia." *Studia Patristica* 12 (1975): 199–207.

Donaldson, James. See *Constitutions of the Holy Apostles.*

Downey, Glanville. *A History of Antioch in Syria From Seleucus to the Arab Conquest.* Princeton: Princeton UP, 1961.

———. "Antioch." In the *New Catholic Encyclopedia.* New York: McGraw Hill, 1967.

Drewery, Benjamin. "Antioch." *Theologische Realenzyklopädie*. Ed. F. Schumann and M. Wolter, 2:99–113. Berlin: de Gruyter, 1990.

el-Khoury, Nabil. "Der Mensch als Gleichnis Gottes: Eine Untersuchung zur Anthropologie des Theodor von Mopsuestia." *Oriens Christianus* 74 (1990): 62–71.

———. "Gen. 1,26 dans l'interprétation de Saint Éphrem ou la relation de l'homme à Dieu." *Symposium Syriacum 1976. Orientalia Christiana Analecta* 205: 199–205.

Encyclopedia of the Early Church. Ed. Angelo Di Berardino, trans. Adrian Walford. 2 vols. New York: Oxford UP, 1992.

Fantino, Jacques. *L'homme image de Dieu chez saint Irénée de Lyon*. Paris: Cerf, 1986.

Fatum, Lone. "Image of God and Glory of Man." In *Image of God and Gender Models*. Ed. Kari Elizabeth Børresen, 56–137. Oslo: Solum Forlag, 1991.

Ferguson, Everett. *Backgrounds of Early Christianity*. 2d ed. Grand Rapids: Eerdmans, 1993.

Festugière, A. J. *Antioche païenne et chrétienne: Libanius, Chrysostome et les moines de Syrie*. Paris: De Boccard, 1959.

Fiorenza, Elizabeth Schüssler. *In Memory of Her: A Feminist Reconstruction of Christian Origins*. New York: Crossroads, 1983.

Ford, David C. *Women and Men in the Early Church: The Full Views of St. John Chrysostom*. South Canaan, Penn.: St. Tikhon's Seminary P, 1996.

Friedrich, Gerhard, ed. *Theological Dictionary of the New Testament*. Trans. Geoffrey W. Bromiley. Grand Rapids, Mich.: Eerdmans, 1968.

Froehlich, Karlfried, trans. and ed. *Biblical Interpretation in the Early Church*. Sources of Early Christian Thought. Philadelphia: Fortress, 1984.

Fuller, Reginald. "Image of God." *A New Catholic Commentary on Holy Scripture*. New York: Nelson, 1969.

Galtier, P. "Théodore de Mopsueste: sa vraie pensée sur l'incarnation." *Recherches de Science Religieuse* 45 (1957): 161–86, 338–60.

Gillard, Geoffrey V. "God in Gen 1:26 according to Chrysostom." *Studia Biblica* 1 (1978): 149–56.

Goldberg, Steven. "Can Women Beat Men at Their Own Game?" *National Review*, Dec. 27, 1993: 30–36.

Gorday, Peter. *Principles of Patristic Exegesis: Romans 9–11 in Origen, John Chrysostom, and Augustine*. Studies in the Bible and Early Christianity. New York: Mellen, 1983.

Gounelle, André. "L'homme image de Dieu." *Foi & Vie*, Dec. 1988: 27–40.

Grant, Robert M. *The Letter and the Spirit*. New York: MacMillan, 1957.

———. *Gods and the One God*. Library of Early Christianity. Philadelphia: Westminster, 1986.

Grant, Robert M., and David Tracy. *A Short History of the Interpretation of the Bible*. 2d ed. Philadelphia: Fortress, 1984.

Greer, Rowan A. "Antiochene Christology of Diodore of Tarsus." *Journal of Theological Studies* 17 (1966): 327–41.

———. *The Captain of Our Salvation: A Study in the Patristic Exegesis of Hebrews*. Tübingen: Mohr, 1973.

———. "Image of God and the Prosopic Union in Nestorius' *Bazaar of Heracleides*." *Lux in Lumine: Essays for W. N. Pittenger*. Ed. Richard A. Norris, Jr., 46–59. New York: Seabury, 1966.

———. *Theodore of Mopsuestia: Exegete and Theologian*. Westminster: Faith, 1961.

Grillmeier, Aloys. *Christ in Christian Tradition: From the Apostolic Age to Chalcedon (451)*. Vol. 1. 2d rev. ed. Atlanta: John Knox, 1975.

Gross, Jules. *La divinisation de chrétien d'apres les pères grecs*. Paris: Gabalda, 1938.

Gryson, Roger. *The Ministry of Women in the Early Church*. Trans. J. Laporte and M. L. Hall. Collegeville: Liturgical, 1976.

Guillet, J. "Les exégèses d'Alexandrie et d'Antioche. Conflit ou malentendue?" *Recherches de Science Religieuse*, April 1947: 257–303.

Hadot, Ilsetraut. *Arts libéraux et philosophie dans la pensée antique.* Paris: Études Augustiniennes, 1984.

Hall, Douglas John. *Imaging God: Dominion as Stewardship.* Grand Rapids, Mich.: Eerdmans, 1986.

Halleux, Andre de. "Nestorius: Histoire et Doctrine." 2 parts. *Irenikon* 66 (1993): 38–52, 163–78.

Hamman, A.-G. *L'homme, image de Dieu.* Paris: Desclée, 1987.

Harrent, A. *Les Écoles d'Antioche: essai sur le savoir IVe siècle apres J-C.* Paris, 1898.

Hatch, Edwin. *The Influence of Greek Ideas and Usages upon the Christian Church.* Ed. A. M. Fairbairn. 5th ed. 1895. Reprint, Peabody, Mass.: Hendrickson, 1995.

Hay, C. "St. John Chrysostom and the Integrity of the Human Nature of Christ." *Franciscan Studies* 19 (1959): 298–317.

Heine, Susanne. *Women and Early Christianity. Are the Feminist Scholars Right?* Trans. John Bowden. Minneapolis: Augsburg, 1988.

Hendricks, O. "La vie quotidienne du moine syrien oriental." *L'Orient Syrien* 5 (1960): 293–330, 401–31.

Hitchcock, R. F. M. "Loofs' Theory of Theophilus of Antioch as a Source of Irenaeus." *Journal of Theological Studies* 38 (1937): 130–39, 255–65.

Hobbel, Arne J. "The *Imago Dei* in the Writings of Origen." *Studia Patristica* 21:301–7.

Hodgson, Leonard. See Nestorius, *The Bazaar of Heracleides.*

Hoekema, Anthony A. *Created In God's Image.* Grand Rapids, Mich.: Eerdmans, 1986.

Holum, Kenneth G. *Theodosian Empresses: Women and Imperial Dominion in Late Antiquity.* Berkeley: U of California P, 1982.

Horowitz, Maryanne Cline. "The Image of God in Man—Is Woman Included?" *Harvard Theological Review* 72 (July 1979): 175–206.

The International Standard Bible Encyclopedia. Gen. ed. George Bromiley. Grand Rapids, Mich.: Eerdmans, 1970.

The Interpreter's Dictionary of the Bible. Gen. ed. George A. Buttrick. New York: Abingdon, 1962.

Jarrett, James. *The Educational Theories of the Sophists.* New York: Teachers College P, 1969.

Jewett, Paul K. *Man as Male and Female.* Grand Rapids, Mich.: Eerdmans, 1975.

The Jewish Encyclopedia. 12 vols. Gen. ed. Isidore Singer. New York: Ktav, 1964.

Jónsson, Gunnlaugur A. *The Image of God: Genesis 1:26–28 in a Century of Old Testament Research.* Trans. Lorraine Svendsen. Lund: Almqvist, 1988.

Jourjon, Maurice. "L'homme image de Dieu selon Irénée de Lyon." *Christus* 31 (Oct. 1984): 501–8.

Karras, Valerie. "Male Domination of Woman in the Writings of Saint John Chrysostom." *Greek Orthodox Theological Review* 36, no. 2 (1991): 131–39.

Kelly, B. "Divine Quasi-Formal Causality: Divinization by Grace: Inhabitation of the Trinity." *Irish Theological Quarterly* 28 (1961): 16–28.

Kelly, J. N. D. *Early Christian Creeds.* 3d ed. San Francisco: Harper, 1978.

———. *Golden Mouth: The Story of John Chrysostom—Ascetic, Preacher, Bishop.* London: Duckworth, 1995.

Kennedy, George. *Classical Rhetoric and Its Christian and Secular Tradition.* Chapel Hill: U of North Carolina, 1980.

Kepple, Robert J. "Analysis of Antiochene Exegesis of Galatians 4:24–26." *Westminster Theological Journal* 39 (1977): 239–49.

Kittel, Gerhard and Gerhard Friedrich, eds. *Theological Dictionary of the New Testament*. Trans. G. Bromiley. Grand Rapids, Mich.: Eerdmans, 1968.

Kollwitz, J. "Antiochia am Orontes." *Reallexicon für Antike und Christentum*. Band 1: 462–69.

Köster, Helmut. *Theological Dictionary of the New Testament*. Ed. Gerhard Friedrich, trans. Geoffrey Bromiley. Grand Rapids, Mich.: Eerdmans, 1968.

Kraemer, Ross S. *Her Share of the Blessings: Women's Religions among Pagans, Jews, and Christians in the Greco-Roman World*. New York: Oxford UP, 1992.

Lampe, G. W. H., ed. *A Patristic Greek Lexicon*. Oxford: Clarendon, 1961.

Lavenant, R. "Edessa." EEC 1:263.

Lazenby, Henry F. "'The Image of God: Masculine, Feminine, or Neuter?" *Journal of the Evangelical Theological Society* 30, no. 1 (March 1987): 63–70.

Leconte, R. "L'Asceterium de Diodore." *Melanges bibliques rediges en l'honneur d'Andre Robert*. Paris: Bloud, 1957.

Leroux, Jean-Marie. "Joanis Chrysostom." *Theologische Realenzyklopädie*. Ed. G. Krause and G. Müller, 17:118–27. Berlin: de Gruyter, 1981.

Letham, Robert. "The Man-Woman Debate: Theological Comment." *Westminster Theological Journal* 52 (Spring 1990): 65–78.

Leys, R. *L'image de Dieu chez Grégorie de Nysse: Esquisse d'une doctrine*. Paris: Desclée, 1951.

Liddell, H. G., and R. Scott, eds. *A Greek-English Lexicon*. Oxford: Clarendon, 1961.

Liebeschuetz, J. H. W. G. *Antioch: City and Imperial Administration in the Later Roman Empire*. Oxford: Clarendon, 1972.

Lilla, S. "Aristotelianism." EEC 1:73–76.

———. "Neoplatonism." EEC 2:585–93.

Long, Anthony A. *Hellenistic Philosophy: Stoics, Epicureans, Sceptics*. 2d ed. 1974. Berkeley: U California P, 1986.

Loofs, Friedrich. *Theophilus von Antiochien Adversus Marcionem und die anderen theologischen Quellen bei Irenaeus*. Texte und Untersuchungen 46. Leipzig: J. C. Hinrichs, 1930.

Lossky, Vladimir. *In the Image and Likeness of God*. New York: Vladimir's, 1974.

Macomber, William. "Newly Discovered Fragments of the Gospel Commentaries of Theodore of Mopsuestia." *Le Muséon* 81 (1968): 441–47.

———. See also Cyril of Edessa.

Maertens, Guido. "Augustine's Image of Man." In *Images of Man in Ancient and Medieval Thought*. Ed. F. Bossier, 175–98. Leuven: Leuven UP, 1976.

Malé, J. "La Sanctification d'aprés saint Cyrille de Alexandrie." *Revue d'histoire ecclesiastique* 10 (1909): 30–40, 469–92.

Malina, Bruce J., and Jerome H. Neyrey. *Portraits of Paul: An Archeology of Ancient Personality*. Louisville: Knox, 1996.

Maloney, George. *Man: The Divine Icon: The Patristic Doctrine of Man Made According to the Image of God*. Pecos, N.M.: Dove, 1973.

———. *The Cosmic Christ, From Paul to Teilhard*. New York: Alba, 1983.

Mara, M. G. "Woman." EEC 2:881–82.

Marrou, Henri I. *A History of Education in Antiquity*. Trans. George Lamb. New York: Sheed, 1956.

McCool, G. "Ambrosian Origin of St. Augustine's Theology of the Image of God in Man." *Theological Studies* 20 (1959): 62–81.

McCormick, Amy Smyth. "Example of Antiochene Exegetical Tradition: John Chrysostom's Homily #50." *Patristic and Byzantine Review* 12 (1993): 65–82.

McCracken-Flesher, Paul V. "The Targumim in the Context of Rabbinic Literature." In *Introduction to Rabbinic Literature*. Ed. Jacob Neusner. New York: Doubleday, 1994.

McGinn, Bernard. *The Foundations of Mysticism* I. New York: Crossroad, 1992.

———. "The Human Person as Image of God: Western Christianity." *Christian Spirituality: Origins to the Twelfth Century*. Vol. 1. Ed. Bernard McGinn and John Meyendorff, 312–30. New York: Crossroad, 1985.

McGuckin, John. "Did Augustine's Christology depend on Theodore of Mopsuestia?" *Heythrop Journal* 31 (1990): 39–52.

McKenzie, John L. *Dictionary of the Bible*. London: Chapman, 1965.

———. "A New Study of Theodore of Mopsuestia." *Theological Studies* Sept. 1949: 394–408.

———. "The Commentary of Theodore of Mopsuestia on John 1:46–51." *Theological Studies*, March 1953: 73–84.

———. Rev. of *The Christology of Theodore of Mopsuestia*, by Francis A. Sullivan. *Theological Studies* 19 (1958): 345–73.

McLeod, Frederick G. *The Soteriology of Narsai*. Rome: Pontificium Institutum Orientalium Studiorum, 1973.

———. "The Antiochene Tradition Regarding the Role of the Body within the 'Image of God.'" *Broken and Whole: Essays on Religion and the Body*. Ed. Maureen A. Tilley and Susan A. Ross, 23–53. The Annual Publication of the College Theology Society 1993. Lanham: UP of America, 1995.

———. "Man as the Image of God: its Meaning and Theological Significance in Narsai." *Theological Studies* 42 (Sept. 1981): 458–68.

McNamara, Kevin. "Theodore of Mopsuestia and the Nestorian Heresy." *The Irish Theological Quarterly*, July 1952: 254–78; April 1953: 172–91.

McVey, Kathleen E. "The Use of Stoic Cosmogony in Theophilus of Antioch's *Hexaemeron*." *Biblical Hermeneutics in Historical Perspective: Studies in Honor of Karlfried Froehlich on His Sixtieth Birthday*. Ed. M. S. Burrows and P. Rorem, 32–58. Grand Rapids, Mich.: Eerdmans, 1991.

———. "Biblical Theology in the Patristic Period: the Logos Doctrine." *Biblical Theology: Problems and Perspectives*. Ed. S. Kraftchick, et al., 15–27. Nashville: Abingdon, 1995.

Meeks, Wayne A., and Robert L. Wilken. *Jews and Christians in the First Four Centuries of the Common Era*. Missoula: Scholars, 1978.

Merki, H. *Von der platonischen Angleichung an Gott zur Gottähnlichkeit bei Gregor von Nyssa*. Paradosis 7. Freiburg: Paulusverlag, 1952.

Middleton, J. Richard. "The Liberating Image? Interpreting the *Imago Dei* in Context." *Christian Scholar's Review* 24 (Sept. 1994): 8–25.

Mingana, A. See Narsai and Theodore of Mopsuestia.

Montmasson, E. "L'Homme créé à l'image de Dieu d'après Théodoret de Cyrrhus et Procope de Gaza." *Échos d'Orient* 15 (1912): 154–62.

Mooney, Christopher. *Theology and Scientific Knowledge. Changing Models of God's Presence in the World*. Notre Dame: U of Notre Dame P, 1996.

Nash, H. S. "The Exegesis of the School of Antioch. A Criticism of the Hypothesis that Aristotelianism was the Main Cause of its Genesis." *Journal of Biblical Literature* 11 (1892): 22–37.

Nash, Ronald H. *Christianity and the Hellenistic World*. Grand Rapids, Mich.: Zondervan, 1984.

Nellas, Panayiotis. *Deification in Christ: Orthodox Perspectives on the Nature of the Human Person*. Trans. Norman Russell. Contemporary Greek Theologians 5. Crestwood, N.Y.: St. Vladimir's, 1987.

Neusner, Jacob, ed. *Introduction to Rabbinic Literature*. Anchor Bible Reference Library. New York: Doubleday, 1994.

The New Catholic Encyclopedia. 15 vols. New York: McGraw-Hill, 1967.

New Encyclopedia Britannica. 15th ed. Ed. Robert McHenry. Chicago: U. of Chicago, 1993.

The New Jerome Biblical Commentary. Ed. Raymond Brown, et al. Englewood Cliffs, N.J.: Prentice, 1990.

Nielson, J. T. *Adam and Christ in the Theology of Irenaeus of Lyons.* Berlin: Assen, 1968.

Norris Jr., Richard A., trans. and ed. *The Christological Controversy.* Sources of Christian Thought. Philadelphia: Fortress, 1980.

———. "Antiochene Interpretation." *A Dictionary of Biblical Interpretation.* Ed. R. J. Coggins and J. L. Houlden. Philadelphia: Trinity, 1990.

———. *Manhood and Christ.* Oxford: Clarendon, 1963.

———. "Toward a Contemporary Interpretation of the Chalcedonian Definition." *Lux in Lumine: Essays for W. N. Pittenger.* Ed. Richard A. Norris, Jr., 62–79. New York: Seabury, 1966.

Olivier, Jean-Marie. See Diodore.

O'Meara, Dominic, ed. *Neoplatonism and Christian Thought.* Albany: State U of New York P, 1982.

Parmentier, Martin. "A Letter from Theodoret of Cyrrus to the Exiled Nestorius (CPG, 6270) in a Syriac Version." *Bijdragen, tijdscrift voor filosofie en theologie* 51 (1990): 234–45.

Pasquato, O. "Antioch." EEC 1:47–48.

Patterson, Leonard. *Theodore of Mopsuestia and Modern Thought.* London: Society for Promoting Christian Knowledge, 1926.

Peacocke, Arthur. *Theology for a Scientific Age. Being and Becoming—Natural, Divine, and Human.* Minneapolis: Fortress, 1993.

Pépin, Jean. *Mythe et Allégorie: Les origines grecques et les contestations judéo-chrétiennes.* 2d ed. Paris: Études Augustiniennes, 1976.

Petit, Paul. *Les étudiants de Libanius.* Paris: Nouvelles Éditions latines, 1957.

Pirot, D. Louis. *L'Oeuvre exégétique de Théodore de Mopsueste.* Rome: Instituti Biblici, 1913.

Pomeroy, Sarah B. *Goddesses, Whores, Wives, and Slaves: Women in Classical Antiquity.* New York: Schocken, 1975.

Porteous, N. W. "Image, Imagery." *The Interpreter's Dictionary of the Bible.* Gen. ed. George A. Buttrick, 3:681–85. Nashville: Abingdon, 1962.

Prestige, G. L. *God in Patristic Thought.* London: Society for Promoting Christian Knowledge, 1964.

Purves, James G. M. "The Spirit and the *Imago Dei*: Reviewing the Anthropology of Irenaeus of Lyons." *The Evangelical Quarterly* 68.2 (1996): 99–120.

Quasten, Johannes. *Patrology.* 4 vols. Westminster, Md.: Christian Classics, 1986.

Reallexicon für Antike und Christentum. Herausgegeben von Theodor Klauser. Stuttgart: Hiersemann, 1950.

Richard, M. "La tradition des fragments du Traité Περι ἐνανθρωπῆσεως de Théodore de Mopsueste." *Le Muséon* 46 (1943): 55–75.

Ruether, Rosemary Radford, ed. *Religion and Sexism: Images of Women in the Jewish and Christian Traditions.* New York: Simon and Schuster, 1974.

———. "Mothers of the Church: Ascetic Women in the Late Patristic Age." In *Women of Spirit: Female Leadership in the Jewish and Christian Traditions,* ed. Rosemary Radford Ruether and Eleanor McLaughlin, 71–98. New York: Simon, 1979.

Ruether, Rosemary Radford, and Eleanor McLaughlin, eds. *Women of Spirit: Female Leadership in the Jewish and Christian Traditions.* New York: Simon, 1979.

Schäublin, Christoph. "Diodor." *Theologische Realenzyklopädie.* Ed. F. Schumann and M. Wolter. Berlin: de Gruyter, 1990.

Sachau, Edward. See Theodore of Mopsuestia.

Scipioni, L. I. *Ricerche sulla cristologia del 'Libro di Eraclide' di Nestorio. La formulazione teologica e il suo contesto filosofico.* Paradiso 11. Freiburg: Universitarie, 1956.

Segal, Alan F. *Rebecca's Children: Judaism and Christianity in the Roman World.* Cambridge: Harvard UP, 1986.

Segal, J. B. *Edessa 'The Blessed City'.* Oxford: Clarendon, 1970.

Sellers, R. V. *Two Ancient Christologies.* London: Society for Promoting Christian Knowledge, 1954.

Sherwin, Byron L. "The Human Body and the Image of God." *A Traditional Quest.* Sheffield, England: Sheffield Academic, 1991: 75–85.

Simon, Marcel. *Versus Israel: A Study of the Relations between Christians and Jews in the Roman Empire.* Ed. H. McKeating. 1948. Reprint, Oxford: Oxford UP, 1986.

Simonetti, Manlio. *Biblical Interpretations in the Early Church: An Historical Introduction to Patristic Exegesis.* Trans. John A. Hughes. Ed. A. Burgquist and M. Bockmuehl. Edinburgh: T&T Clark, 1994.

———. "Antioch II. Councils and Schisms." EEC 1:48–50.

———. "Diodore of Tarsus." EEC 1:236–37.

———. "Eusebius of Emesa." EEC 1:301.

———. "Exegesis, Patristic." EEC 1:309–11

———. "Lucian of Antioch." EEC 1:507.

———. "Meletius." EEC 1:550.

———. "Nestorius." EEC 2:594.

———. "Theodore of Mopsuestia." EEC 2:824–25.

Solignac, A. "Philon d'Alexandrie II. Influences sur les pères de l'église," *Dictionnaire de spiritualité ascétique et mystique, doctrine et histoire* 12a. Paris: Beauchesne, 1983.

Spanneut, M. *Le Stoïcisme des Pères de l'église.* Paris: du Seuil, 1957.

Stramara, Daniel. *Unmasking the Meaning of* ΠΡΟΣΩΠΟΝ: *PROSOPON as Person* in the Works of Gregory of Nyssa. Ph. D., diss. Saint Louis U, 1996.

Sullivan, Francis A. *The Christology of Theodore of Mopsuestia.* Analecta Gregoriana 82. Rome: U Gregorianae, 1956.

Sullivan, John E. *The Image of God: The Doctrine of St. Augustine and Its Influence.* Dubuque: Priory, 1963.

Sutcliffe, E. F. *A Catholic Commentary on Holy Scripture.* Ed. B. Orchard, et al. New York: Nelson, 1953.

Staab, Karl. See Theodore of Mopsuestia, *Pauluskommentare aus der Griechischen Kirche.*

Swete, H. B. See Theodore of Mopsuestia, *Theodori Episcopi Mopsuesteni in Epistolas B. Pauli.*

Tavard, George H. *Women in the Christian Tradition.* Notre Dame: U of Notre Dame P, 1973.

Taylor, Lily Ross. *The Divinity of the Roman Emperor.* Middleton, Conn.: American Philological Assoc., 1931.

Telfer, William. See Nemesius of Emesa.

Theologische Realenzyklopädie. Ed. G. Krause and G. Müller. Berlin: de Gruyter, 1981.

Thunberg, Lars. "The Human Person as Image of God." *Christian Spirituality: Origins to the Twelfth Century.* Vol. 1. Ed. B. McGinn and J. Meyendorff, 291–312. New York: Crossroad, 1985.

———. *Microcosm and Mediator: The Theological Anthropology of Maximus the Confessor.* 2d ed. Chicago: Open Court, 1995.

Tibiletti, C. "Stoicism and the Fathers." EEC 2:795–97.

Tillich, Paul. *Dynamic of Faith.* New York: Harper, 1957.

Tonneau, R.-M. "Théodore de Mopsueste, Interprétation (du Livre) de la Genèse (Vat. Syr. 120, ff. I-V)." *Le Muséon* 66 (1953): 45–64.

———. See also Theodore of Mopsuestia.

Tonner, Norman P. See *Decrees of the Ecumenical Councils*.

Trakatellis, Demetrios. "Being Transformed: Chrysostom's Exegesis of the Epistle to the Romans." *Greek Orthodox Theological Review* 36.3–4 (1991): 211–29.

Turcescu, Lucian. "*Prosôpon* and *Hypostasis* in Basil of Caesarea's *Against Eunomius* and the Epistles." *Vigiliae Christianae* 51 (1997): 374–95.

Vawter, Bruce. "Genesis." In *A New Catholic Commentary on Holy Scripture*. Gen. ed. Reginald C. Fuller. New York: Nelson, 1969.

Vogels, Walter. "The Human Person in the Image of God (Gn 1,26)." *Science et Esprit*, May-Sept. 1994: 189–202.

Vööbus, Arthur. *A History of Asceticism in the Syrian Orient*. 2 vols. CSCO 184 and 197. Louvain: CSCO, 1958–1960.

———. *History of the School of Nisibis*. CSCO 266/Subs. 26. Louvain: CSCO, 1965.

———. "Regarding the Theological Anthropology of Theodore of Mopsuestia." *Church History*, June 1964: 115–24.

Vosté, J.-M. "La chronologie de l'activité litteraire de Théodore de Mopsueste." *Revue Biblique* 34 (Jan. 1925): 54–81.

———. "L'oeuvre exégétique de Théodore de Mopsueste au II Councile de Constantinople." *Revue Biblique* 38 (July 1929): 382–95; (Oct. 1929): 542–54.

———. See also Theodore of Mopsuestia.

Walden, John W. H. *The Universities of Ancient Greece*. New York: Scribner's, 1912.

Wallace-Hadrill, D. S. *Christian Antioch: A Study of Early Christian Thought in the East*. Cambridge: Cambridge UP, 1982.

Walsh, Brian J., and J. Richard Middleton. *The Transforming Vision: Shaping a Christian World View*. Downers Grove, Ill.: Intervarsity, 1984.

Warne, Graham J. *Hebrew Perspectives on the Human Person in the Hellenistic Era: Philo and Paul*. Lewiston, N.Y.: Mellen, 1995.

Wickert, Ulrich. *Studien zu den Pauluskommentaren Theodors von Mopsuestia: Als Beitrag zum Verständnis der Antiochenischen Theologie*. Berlin: Töpelmann, 1962.

Wiles, Maurice. *The Christian Fathers*. 2d ed. New York: Oxford UP, 1982.

Wilken, Robert L. "The Image of God: A Neglected Doctrine." *Dialog* 28 (1989): 292–96.

———. *John Chrysostom and the Jews: Rhetoric and Reality in the Late Fourth Century*. Berkeley: U of California P, 1983.

———. "Judaism in Roman and Christian Society." *Journal of Religion* 47 (1967): 313–30.

Wilson, R. "The Early History of the Exegesis of Genesis 1:26." *Studia Patristica* 1. Berlin: Akademie, 1957: 420–37.

Wolfson, Harry A. *The Philosophy of the Church Fathers*. Vol. 1: *Faith, Trinity, Incarnation*. Cambridge: Harvard UP, 1964.

Young, Frances M. *From Nicea to Chalcedon*. Philadelphia: Fortress, 1983.

———. "The Rhetorical Schools and Their Influence on Patristic Exegesis." In *The Making of Orthodoxy: Essays in Honour of Henry Chadwick*. Ed. Rowan Williams. Cambridge: Cambridge UP, 1989.

Zaharopoulos, Dimitri Z. *Theodore of Mopsuestia on the Bible: A Study of His Old Testament Exegesis*. New York: Paulist, 1989.

INDEX

Accommodated sense, 20–21, 30, 79

Allegory, 13–14, 16–22, 25–26, 29, 34–35, 39–41, 53n28, 125n27, 233, 235, 238

Anagōgē. See Diodore: exegetical terms

Andragathias, 117–18, 121

Apollinaris, 99, 108n51, 109, 113, 121–23, 128n35, 129n42, 141, 157, 181, 186–88, 242

Apostolic Constitutions, 195–96

Aristotle and Aristotelianism, 17, 22, 93, 97, 100, 106–10, 121, 130–31, 139–40, 142, 151n112

Arius and Arianism, 94, 119, 139, 141, 174, 188, 242, 250

Arnou, R., 135n62

Augustine, 25n44, 43, 50n25–26, 57, 70, 74n118, 80, 248, 252

Baur, Chrysostomus, 24–25, 117n3, 118

Bavli, 14n11

Bergian, Silke-Petra, 182n80

Body, Role of, 64–65, 68, 72–73, 81–83, 254–56

Børresen, Kari E., 191n1

Bromiley, Geoffrey W., 44

Brown, Peter, 80n137

Bultmann, Rudolf, 17

Burghardt, Walter J., 51n28, 81n138

Cataphrygians, 194

Chadwick, H., 173n52

Chalcedon, Council of (451), 96, 103, 134–35n59, 143, 155, 182–83, 186, 190, 243, 253

Christology: functional, 33, 82, 86, 124, 135–37, 163–66, 179–80, 188, 190, 241–44; "low" vs "high," 33, 187, 253–54. *See also* the individual Antiochene Fathers

Clark, Elizabeth A., 192n2, 200n21

Constantinople I, Council of (381), 34, 58, 87, 93–95, 113, 119, 132, 136n67, 139, 186, 232, 239

Constantinople II, Council of (553), 29, 62, 96–97, 156

Constantinople VI, Council of (681), 147n102

Cousin, Ewert, 9n5

Curtis, Edward, 46n8, 45–47, 66

Cyril of Alexandria, 39–40, 50n25, 59, 90, 119n14, 185n96; union of Christ's natures, 95–96, 130, 140–44, 162, 173n52, 174, 176, 180–81, 187–88, 243, 254; view toward women, 197

Cyrus of Edessa, 219–20

Daly, Anthony, 141n79, 142–44, 146, 179–80

Devreese, Robert, 27

Dewart, Joanne McWilliam, 167n36

Didascalia Apostolorum, 195–96

Diodore: christological thought, 117n2, 154n1, 186–88; exegetical terms, 21–22; exegesis, 20–24, 141; life and works, 16–17, 58–60; School of, 88–89, 113, 139; understanding of image, 59, 82; view toward women,59, 192, 223

Dioscorus, Patriarch, 183

Divinization, 50, 56–57, 81, 84, 125n27, 129, 134, 139, 169n43, 234, 239–40, 246, 252, 254

Doxographies, 40, 108, 114, 118

Driver, G.G. *See* Hodgson, Leonard

Edessa, 70, 71n108

el-Koury, Nabil, 63n86, 122n21

Ephrem, 71n107

The Image of God in the Antiochene Tradition was composed in Monotype Dante by Generic Composi-
tors, Stamford, New York; printed on 60-pound Glatfelter Natural Smooth and bound by Braun-
Brumfield, Inc., Ann Arbor, Michigan; and designed by Kachergis Book Design, Pittsboro, North
Carolina.